SUB ROSA
THE CIA AND THE USES OF INTELLIGENCE

SUB ROSA
THE CIA AND THE USES OF INTELLIGENCE

Peer de Silva

NYT Times BOOKS

Copyright © 1978 by Peer de Silva.

All rights reserved, including the right to reproduce this book or portions thereof in any form. For information, address: Times Books, a division of Quadrangle/The New York Times Book Co., Inc., Three Park Avenue, New York, N.Y. 10016. Manufactured in the United States of America. Published simultaneously in Canada by Fitzhenry & Whiteside, Ltd., Toronto.

Library of Congress Cataloging in Publication Data

De Silva, Peer.
  Sub rosa.

  Includes index.
  1. United States. Central Intelligence Agency.
I. Title.
JK468.I6D47 1978   327'.12'06173   77-87821
ISBN 0-8129-0745-0

TO

Marilyn
Perry, Paul, and Cabbie
for whom these things were done

Contents

	Introduction	ix
I	Prelude to CIA	3
II	Assignment: Moscow	15
III	Cold War Russia	23
IV	The Gehlen Organization	37
V	The "Count"	42
VI	Headquarters	53
VII	The Soviet Agent	62
VIII	No One Is Immune	71
IX	CIA Civilian	75
X	Vienna: The Occupation Ends	84
XI	A Cautionary Tale	104
XII	Bugs and Radios	112
XIII	Hungary, 1956	118
XIV	The Refugees	127
XV	Transition	139
XVI	Korea	151
XVII	Coup d'Etat	172
XVIII	Hong Kong—R and R	190
XIX	Into War	203
XX	The Vietcong Challenge	214
XXI	The Key to Counterinsurgency	234
XXII	Vietcong Terror	247
XXIII	Vietnam Turning Point	277
XXIV	Plowing Back	286
	Epilogue	294
	Glossary	296
	Index	299

Introduction

I retired from the Central Intelligence Agency in January 1973, having served that agency or its predecessors since 1945. If one adds to that nine years of prior service as an officer, as a cadet at the United States Military Academy, and as a soldier, it is clear that I can be termed a card-carrying bureaucrat, and the book that follows should be read in that light. My retirement was voluntary and entirely my own idea, not part of the bloodletting that began in February 1973 under the new director of the CIA, James Schlesinger. I hasten to add that while the Schlesinger purge took a little of the muscle away along with the fat, the action was long overdue and one I applauded.

But I have been dismayed by a much more irrational threat to the CIA. Since early 1973, up to the present and presumably into the future, the American public has been witness to a crucifixion of intelligence work in general and certainly the crucifixion of the CIA itself. As a professional in the field of espionage and counterespionage, I can only say that the flood of written and spoken material about the CIA is characterized by distortion, inaccuracy, and plain ignorance.

While I am neither a court-appointed or self-appointed defender of the CIA, I regret little of my service during the years of my involvement, almost always years which were served abroad and almost always as the CIA chief-of-station in the country of my assignment. There is a need for a correct and honest picture of how the CIA does in fact work and operate abroad and at home.

Let me tick off a few points which seem to arouse and confuse the critics: outside of a wartime situation, such as Vietnam, there are no killings; yes, there are agents who are paid; yes, we do indulge in king-making when we are told that this activity is in the national interest; yes, there is secrecy; yes, there is no freewheeling and I have the scars to prove that; yes, there is responsibility; and yes, there is great discipline. Also, there is honesty, no graft, no misappropriation of funds; yes, there are wire taps, bugs, radios, and mail coverage, abroad.

CIA work abroad is indeed very often petty, humdrum, and dull. There is also excitement, some danger, some death. There are terrible failures and magnificent successes. Many Americans, conditioned by the media, view intelligence work as some arcane endeavor, probably not needed, involving fools who have nothing better to do. The facts are otherwise. The work of the CIA is aimed at the furthering of U.S. national interests, as these interests are defined by the President and the National Security Council. These expressed interests are relayed to the CIA through the State Department, the Defense Department, and of course by the director of Central Intelligence. There is no idiocy in this line of command, or if there is, it was brought in by the Administration, which in turn was voted in by the electorate.

In an agency of over fifteen thousand people, operating at home and abroad, the factors of morality and integrity at once are to be examined. Is there dedication to the United States? Is there a fundamental honesty on which our policymakers can depend? On these counts, I am proud to have served in the CIA and I believe most officers, junior and senior, have a reason to share this pride. The need for intelligence? Anyone seriously concerned about this matter need only read Soviet speeches and observe Soviet performance since 1945; for that matter since 1917.

The harshest critics of the CIA seem to be in academe and the media. I can find only two factors that seem to link these two disparate elements: they both consider themselves to be intellectually objective, and neither has any responsibility for dealing with the problems faced by the CIA. Both exhibit a lack of concern with facts; one need only note the way the odious cloak of Watergate was slipped over the shoulders of the CIA without fairly assessing the truly minuscule role played by a few CIA personnel in the entire aberration that came to be known as the Watergate affair. The nation is indeed badly served by this irresponsible equating of the work of a serious governmental agency, unable really to defend itself, with a sleazy crew determined to push the guilt of wrongdoing away from themselves. All this at a time when the CIA is caught up in a deadly struggle with its natural enemy, the KGB (the Soviet CIA), an aggressive, amoral, and implacable foe of the American government and the American people.

I served with the Manhattan Engineer District (the atom-bomb project) during World War II and saw at first hand the terrible destruction in Hiroshima and Nagasaki. Those bombs are now referred to as the Model Ts of their time. If our social structure and our people and our way of life are worth defending at all, we must realize there can be no defense without adequate intelligence information available to our government. There are tigers roaming the world, and we must recognize this or perish.

SUB ROSA: THE CIA AND THE USES OF INTELLIGENCE

1 Prelude to CIA

World War II was just over and I was on the island of Tinian in the western Pacific, to which I had carried the plutonium sphere which had obliterated Nagasaki. As an Army lieutenant colonel, I was in charge of a small group of scientists and technicians whom I had brought out from the laboratories at Los Alamos, New Mexico. On Tinian, the civilian scientists had assembled both bombs, the first one that had flattened Hiroshima and then the Nagasaki bomb. After the Japanese surrender I had taken the scientific team to Tokyo, where we based ourselves during survey trips to Hiroshima and Nagasaki to make preliminary assessments of the terrible damage in those cities. A much larger group of scientists arrived in October 1945 to begin a massive survey of the effects of the atomic bombs, a survey that was to last almost two years. Upon their arrival, I sent the Los Alamos group back to New Mexico and I returned to Washington, D.C.

In Washington I reported to the headquarters of the Manhattan Engineer District, to General Leslie Groves's office. There I learned that the Manhattan District, a United States Army entity, would be closing shop within a few weeks and the entire atomic-bomb project would be returned to civilian control. Military personnel were to be assigned to new duties by the War Department. After attending a number of ceremonies connected with the closing down of the Manhattan Engineer District, including collecting my own Legion of Merit, I began answering messages that I had found waiting for me. Many of these were from old friends who had spent the war with the Office of Strategic Services (OSS), either at home or abroad. The OSS itself had been abolished the previous September, but had been replaced by a new military office, the Strategic Services Unit (SSU), which was then a part of the War Department. These friends and I brought each other up-to-date on the wartime years, and it emerged that SSU was in reality an administrative holding unit for intelligence officers, and that shortly a Presidential directive would bring into being the Central Intelligence Group. Further, legislation was already being framed in Congress to create a Central Intelligence Agency, which would be the first organization in American history in which one could make a career in intelligence. Many of us had during the war come to the conviction that just such a civilian agency, separate from the armed services and State Department intelligence offices, would be needed in the postwar world; that such a body was being legislated seemed almost too good to be true. The SSU officers urged that I join them, and I went to General Groves to ask for his assistance in being transferred to that organization, inasmuch as the Manhattan Engineer District was going out of existence and its military personnel were being reassigned. Because of the successful atomic-bomb project, General Groves was indeed a VIP in Washington; a telephone call from him was all that was needed to take care of my transfer to SSU, to which I reported for duty a few days later.

This gave me time to find a place to live, and I rented a small house in Arlington, across the Potomac from my new offices. I then flew to New York where my wife, Jayne, and two daughters, Robin and Sharon, were living with her parents, bought a car which had been a wartime taxi and sounded like it, and we all drove back to Washington, settling in the house in Virginia.

I first reported to Brigadier General John Magruder, the chief of SSU, who had decided that my first assignment should be in the counterespionage section of SSU, referred to as X-2. I was sent around to see the chief of X-2, James Murphy, who was before the war (and since) a well-known and influential Washington lawyer.

We talked about my duties with the wartime Manhattan Engineer District and I told him in some detail of the massive Soviet espionage attack on the bomb project. All of this was new to Murphy. He listened closely as I described Soviet successes in this regard. He quizzed me on the security measures and techniques we had employed on the bomb project, which had successfully maintained its wartime secrecy from the American people (but not from the Soviets). After several hours, Murphy leaned back in his chair and told me what my assignment in X-2 should be. From what I had told him, he said, it was clear that certain various specific types of scientists and technicians were essential to successful atom-bomb research and development—experimental and theoretical physicists, explosives experts, certain kinds of inorganic chemists, radiologists, and other specialists. It was already known that the Soviets were rounding up East German and Austrian scientists, and shipping them to undisclosed destinations in the USSR. Murphy's plan was to run intelligence-collection operations into the Soviet zones of Germany and Austria, there to determine the presence or absence of prominent scientists in these critical categories. The great German universities at Leipzig, Jena, and Dresden and the laboratories of the Kaiser Wilhelm Institute, on the outskirts of Berlin, were to be among our first targets. It was to be our assumption, later proved correct, that the Russians would need German and Austrian help, certainly at the outset of their own research. Carrying on this kind of intelligence work in East Germany and Austria was more feasible than trying to carry on similar work within the USSR itself. Thus, my first intelligence assignment in SSU was in effect an extension of my earlier duties for General Groves.

During the months spent in framing these intelligence requirements I learned that the United States had no intelligence structure of any kind at work within the USSR. There was, of course, the American Embassy in Moscow; it had never had any serious intelligence responsibilities and as a result was not organized or staffed to carry out such work. Besides, its activities were severely restricted and isolated by the Soviets and its personnel did very little more than read and translate Soviet newspapers and whatever technical books they could get their hands on.

One day in the early summer of 1946, while having lunch with a West Point classmate in the Pentagon, we sat at a table with some other officers. One of them was apparently responsible for selecting field-grade army officers for a three-year tour of duty, during which the officers would study the Russian language and be given extensive instruction in such matters as Communist ideology, Russian history, Soviet economics, and Soviet literature. He was having trouble, he said in a voice loud enough to be heard at my end of the table, finding a full quota of ten officers for the next course which would be given at Columbia University in New York. After lunch I introduced myself and asked him some questions about the course and was told that it would include one year at Columbia, followed by two years in the American Zone of Germany, continuing these studies at a small school the Army had set up for that purpose. Typical of the unrealistic postwar optimism of the U.S. government at the time, the study program even included a fourth year during which the student officers would go to Moscow and there attend Moscow University. This never came to pass. I told him where I was assigned at the moment and further added that I would be very much interested in the training he spoke of. He was delighted at the prospect of getting one more officer for his quota of ten and asked me if I would find out if I could be released from my current assignment. If so, I could be attached to the group starting study at Columbia that coming September.

Later that day I spoke with General Magruder and Jimmie Murphy; I told them I wanted to take this Russian training and in three years return to the CIA, equipped with the Russian language and possibly with experience within the USSR itself.

They were enthusiastic about this prospect and said that they would approve a request for my transfer from SSU to the Army program. I phoned the Pentagon and told my newfound friend that I was available for the Russian course. He said that transfer orders would be cut within the next few weeks and that I and my family would be sent to New York for the beginning of the course.

General Magruder then detached me from the office of X-2 and named me the director of security. My duties were to organize this new office, to set security standards and requirements, and to prepare the office for inclusion in the CIG (Central Intelligence Group) which was just then being brought into existence by Presidential order. This work occupied the summer of 1946. The orders, naming me as a student officer in the Russian program, arrived on schedule and I began study at the Russian Institute at Columbia with nineteen other officers in September of 1946.

Nothing remarkable happened during the twelve months at the Russian Institute; it was simply a long and hard academic grind. The only really notable event during my time at Columbia was the visit of Jan Masaryk, who was to become the foreign minister of Czechoslovakia. Masaryk was an elegant, urbane, and intelligent man of considerable personal charm. He was visiting Columbia for two reasons: giving lectures and holding seminars on political matters concerning the Soviet Union and Central European states. Naturally, he gravitated to the Russian Institute. A few of us were lucky enough to dine with him on several occasions and to spend evenings exchanging political views in the paneled rooms of the University Faculty Club. He spent much time explaining what he thought Czechoslovakia's role should be in the postwar years in Central Europe; a bridge between the USSR and the Soviet-dominated states and the free world in the West. He expressed apprehension at Soviet intentions in Central Europe. An unassuming man, Masaryk was proud of the reputation of his father, Thomas Masaryk, as the "Father of Czechoslovakia."

I especially remembered these evenings of conversation later in 1948. I was then in Germany; the news broke to announce that a Communist government had taken over in Prague and that Soviet troops had already entered the city. In the general confusion Jan Masaryk had died. The Soviets announced that he had fallen or more likely leaped from a window in the Foreign Ministry to the courtyard below. It was not until later, when I spoke with Soviet defectors, that I learned Masaryk had been thrown from his office window by Soviet secret-police agents and had died on the pavement below.

In August 1947 our training came to an end and the ten officers in my group, with their families, were shipped to Germany. We were each assigned a requisitioned home in Garmisch-Partenkirchen, while our school was established in an old German army barracks in Oberammergau, to which we drove every day to classes. The commandant of the school was an American colonel, assisted by a staff sergeant handling administrative affairs. This colonel had preceded the students to Germany in time to organize the school itself, establish a curriculum, and locate instructors for the various courses to be given. These instructors were all Displaced Persons of Russian background; all instruction was given in the Russian language. Needless to say, they were all strongly anti-Soviet; each had refused to return to the USSR after World War II. They had fled to western Germany, following the Wehrmacht, as the German Army was pushed back by the Soviets. There were altogether about ten of them, all intelligent and of different cultural or social origins.

I had one particularly interesting duty assignment during 1948 which provided a welcome break from the daily classroom routine. There were at the time about 500,000 DPs remaining in temporary camps in the American Zone of Austria even after many thousands had been forcibly "repatriated." These people, who led disrupted and aimless lives while they waited for opportunities to emigrate to other countries in the West, were a mixture of Russians, Ukranians, and persons from the three Baltic states of Latvia, Lithuania, and Estonia. They had all fled to the West, many of them in family groups, before the advancing Soviet Army and had refused to return to the USSR when hostilities came to an end. In the immediate post-World War II years, the American military government in Austria had acceded to the Soviet demand that these DPs be forcibly returned to the Soviet Union. This shameful program of repatriation continued over two years, and thousands of unwilling Soviet POWs or DPs, even entire families from Eastern Europe or from Russia itself, were forced by U.S. bayonets into boxcars for transport to the USSR. The British followed the same policy in their zone of Austria. This degrading policy was finally rejected and in its place Americans allowed the Soviets to send into the American Zone of Austria and Germany so-called repatriation teams. These Soviet teams were authorized entry into the DP camps, there to speak to the camp inmates and attempt to persuade them to return to the "motherland." In addition to this mission, the Soviet teams were to carry on a program of registering the location of graves of Soviet soldiers who had been killed in what later became the American Zone of Austria and Germany.

The commandant told me that the Graves Registration and Repatriation Team had been approved by the American authorities in Austria and that a group of Soviet officers and enlisted men was being formed for this purpose. This team needed the services of an American liaison officer, able to communicate with the team members in Russian and able to serve as their escort while the team was in the American Zone. He had arranged that this liaison officer be selected from the officers in the Russian school. Each liaison officer would serve three months with the Soviet team and then be replaced by a succeeding fellow officer. I was the first to be selected for this duty and, he said, I was to go to Vienna and there report to the senior American general on the Allied Control Commission.

The Orient Express drew slowly into the cavernous interior of the Munich main railway station amid a squeal of breaks and the clank of couplings. Finally at rest, the engine of this great train panted. This would be my first visit to Vienna and my first ride, but certainly not the last, on the Orient Express. The sleeping car, reserved for U.S. Army personnel, provided me with a single compartment. By the time the train drew out of the station for the overnight run to Vienna, the first sitting for the dining car was announced. Well fed and full of wine, I went back to my compartment to find my berth turned down; I slept like a log. The next morning after breakfast, the train clattered down the tracks along the Danube and drew to a halt at the Franz Josefsbahnhof, in the northern section of Vienna in the American Sector. Grabbing a cab, I headed for the Hotel Bristol on the Ringstrasse, across the Kaerntnerstrasse from the bombed-out State opera house. The Bristol was reserved for U.S. Army officers of field grade or higher and there I had laid on a single room and bath. I was due to meet the senior American general, Lieutenant General Keyes, at two o'clock, which gave me the rest of the morning to stroll around in the First Bezirk of Vienna, known in those days as the International District. The city of Vienna was divided into four sectors, one for each of the occupying powers. The First District comprised the center of the city, bounded by the arcing Ringstrasse and the Vienna Canal. This Bezirk was supervised by one of the four occupying powers, one month at a time, on a rotational basis, as was the chairmanship of the Allied Control Commission. Whoever was in the chair also supervised the administration of the First Bezirk, which in practice meant that country provided the military police patrols and settled whatever disputes might arise among the four powers and Viennese officials. During the morning, I walked down the Kaerntnerstrasse to the Graben to have a look at St. Stephen's Cathedral and got back to the Bristol in time for lunch. The baroque splendor of the Bristol dining room, glowing with polished paneling, was more than a match for the cuisine, which was strictly U.S. Army. For some reason the Austrian headwaiter served me personally. This person, attired in a frockcoat and a stiff shirt, introduced himself to me as Pold. He was a short man of perhaps sixty years. Pold had pure white hair and a very stylishly cut white mustache. In later years, when I moved to Vienna to live, we frequently asked Pold (who moonlighted as a waiter) to take charge of parties we would have at our own home.

He was a delightful person and an excellent linguist. While the food at the Bristol was straight out of the Army cookbook, the service was not—it was Viennese, and that means elegant. Pold himself pushed the serving cart to my table, drew back the silver dome over the main course, and expertly sliced two pieces from the loaf of spam. From another covered dish, he served some Brussels sprouts and boiled potatoes and then retired at a discreet distance to make sure I enjoyed my lunch. All this for twenty-five cents a meal—breakfast, dinner, and supper. Some seven years later, I was to live with my family in the Hotel Bristol; the prices were slightly higher and the food infinitely better, but the same impeccable Viennese courtesy and service were there. And so was Pold.

At two o'clock I presented myself to General Keyes's aide in the Allied Control Commission Building on the Schwarzenburgplatz and was ushered into his presence. General Keyes had been in Vienna about a year and a half as the Allied Control commissioner on the U.S. side, and was by that time an old hand in dealing with his Soviet opposite numbers. Our meeting was rather brief. He sat me down and asked about my military background and as to the purposes and conduct of the Russian-language program at Oberammergau. He wound up by saying that his aide would arrange for me to be introduced to the Soviet colonel who would head the repatriation team. As General Keyes walked me to the door of his office, he emphasized one point: "Above all, colonel, I don't want any trouble with this Soviet team. While they're in our zone make sure that nothing unfavorable is drawn to my attention, here in Vienna." With these words he smiled threateningly at me and closed the door. His aide was waiting and at once took me to the office of a colonel next on my schedule. The colonel gave me a rundown on the rules that had been agreed upon in the negotiations between the Soviets and Americans concerning the conduct of the Russian team while in the American Zone. No visitors to our quarters, which were to be in Salzburg, no team activity of any kind unless I were present, and no threats direct or implied while the team members were appealing to DP audiences to return to the USSR.

The selected chief of the Soviet repatriation team, Colonel Kireyev, was due to meet with us shortly. Kireyev and I were to agree upon a time when I would greet him at the border between the American Zone and Soviet Zone of Austria, which lay somewhat to the east of Linz, along the Danube. Once I had met them and brought them into the American Zone, the colonel emphasized, "They're all yours, and for your own good, don't let them make any problems that will wind up on the old man's desk."

The colonel and I chatted on about a variety of things, until a noncommissioned officer entered and said that Colonel Kireyev had arrived. The colonel asked him to come in and I then faced the Soviet officer with whom I would have some unusual experiences over the next three months.

Colonel Kireyev was, typically for a Russian, of about middle height and somewhat corpulent. He had a pink complexion, short hair, a Slavic slant to the eyes, and a turned-up pointed snub nose. He spoke no English, so our subsequent Russian conversation left the American colonel uninformed. We sat around a coffee table in the colonel's office and came to an agreement on the date and hour when we would meet at the border of our respective zones. The Soviet party would consist of two Red Army soldiers who would cook and double as housekeepers, two Red Army drivers who would also be record keepers and note takers, and five other officers who would assist Colonel Kireyev in handling the overall repatriation chore. Kireyev himself came over to me somewhat on the stiff and formal side; in the subsequent months he didn't bend away from this posture very much. Several of his officers turned out to be friendly sorts, but Kireyev maintained a demeanor that could only be defined as correct. Our arrangements made, we said our good-byes and Kireyev left. I returned to General Keyes's office and informed him of the plans. He looked at me and said only, "No waves."

After a couple of days back at home in Regensburg—the school had moved there from Oberammergau—I took the train to Salzburg to get things underway per schedule. The local Army commandant in Salzburg had been instructed by Vienna to supply me with a military sedan and driver and I cashed this check on arrival. After a visit with the commandant, a lieutenant escorted me out to the south edge of Salzburg to the hotel set aside for the repatriation team and for me. The Kasererhof had been an Army officers' billet, but had been vacated for the use of the Soviets. It was a large unprepossessing building done in the style we used to call "Nazi modern." There were two floors and a basement; the basement was largely underground but did have windows high up along the walls. In this basement floor were the kitchen, pantry, service rooms, and a large lounge room with a fireplace, pool table, and some easy chairs. It was in this room that we spent most of our informal evenings and the Soviets showed a movie there almost every night. The main floor had a formal living room and a dining room, which was located above the kitchen, connected with it by a dumbwaiter. The top floor consisted of bedrooms. Colonel Kireyev and I, as the official liaison officer, each had a private room and bath. The other officers doubled up and shared baths.

For three months, I spent all of my time with this team, eating with them, drinking with them and taking them to the DP camps. To say that the inmates of these camps loathed the Communist system and the Russians would be to understate the situation. They were there because they had refused to return to Russia; they were in no mood to be threatened or cajoled by a Soviet officer into going back. As a result, with the attitudes and atmosphere in these camps so poisonously hostile to the Soviets, I found it necessary, before they were to speak, to promise the camp committee that no one would be forcibly repatriated. I asked them to insure that a certain number of inmates would turn out for the harangue to show that the Americans were doing their best to give the Soviets a fair try. Invariably they would cooperate, although there was open derision and dislike of the Soviets.

These meetings were held in an auditorium or common room, where Colonel Kireyev would speak to the group before him. During my duty with the team, not one person elected to go back.

We visited scores of DP camps, sometimes driving for hours to get to them. The purported Soviet objective of reporting the location of graves held no real interest; they openly used this excuse to go to remote villages, where they had heard a Soviet was buried, to photograph roadways, railways, tunnels, and power lines. The purpose was actually a combination of propaganda and low-level collection of intelligence. They constantly complained about the food, their billets in the hotel, and their reception at the camps. The hostility and unfriendliness were blamed on me.

When not traveling we stayed in the hotel. One evening before dinner Colonel Kireyev invited me to his room to have a drink with some of his officers. On arrival I found he had set up a table with plates of herring, caviar, pickles, and stuffed eggs. There were several two-ounce shot glasses and several bottles of vodka, which I had never tasted. The colonel pointed proudly to the label on the bottles, Stolichnaya vodka, the strongest and the best. Anyone who had dealt with Russians knows that sooner or later he will be put to the ordeal of endless vodka toasts. This was obviously to be my time of testing and we drank much before dinner, much during the meal, and for those still present, much during the movies that followed. It was a very long evening. Some officers dozed during the film, some danced together and some with enough strength did the *kazatska*, breaking lamps and knocking over furniture in the process. At about eleven o'clock we said good night and collapsed in our rooms.

Nursing a monumental hangover the next day, I felt some pleasure in planning how I might return that kind of hospitality. At about three in the afternoon I went to the Army liquor store and bought some I.W. Harper bourbon, which in those days was one-hundred proof. I went to Colonel Kireyev's room, where he was "napping," and asked if he and a few officers could join me for a drink at about six. He could only accept; they arrived on time. I had also set up a table with cheese, salami, crackers, and peanuts; the bottles of bourbon were lined up along with some water tumblers.

There was no ice but I explained what an American highball was, pouring in about one inch of bourbon, and filled my glass with water. I sipped my drink. The Soviets watched and then smiled; one didn't add water to a drink—vodka was drunk neat. Whereupon they filled their tumblers to the brim with bourbon and proceeded to gulp down the whiskey. Over their high military collars their faces gradually became pink, or even purple. After the first tumbler had been downed I informed them "a bird cannot fly on one wing only," and refilled their tumblers. Grimly, they turned to the duty of putting away the straight bourbon. They did it, but on the way to dinner several of them excused themselves and were seen no more that night.

I learned a lot of Russian and a lot about Russians, especially the Soviet variety, during these three months. When they were being Russian, they were thoroughly enjoyable; as Soviets, they were insufferable.

One memorable incident took place toward the close of my three-month tour. There was a DP camp at Aspen, just east of Linz. This camp held only people whose homes had been in the three Baltic states. These countries had been overrun and absorbed by the Soviet Union in 1940, during the period of the alliance between the USSR and Nazi Germany; thus Baltic DPs had a special hatred for the Soviets. I made my usual preliminary visit and asked the camp chairman to try to control the members of the camp population, numbering about four thousand. He told me, in good English, that the Balts had a bitter, murderous sentiment toward anything Russian, let alone Soviet, but that he would do the best he could. I told him that we, the Americans, would be grateful.

The next day I made the usual introductions and the camp committee led us with impassive faces to the auditorium, where there were about four hundred people. Following the customary twenty-minute appeal, there was not a sound to be heard. Every face was stony and set. To a man, they filed out the front door without a word. Kireyev at once accused me of setting the committee and inmates against the repatriation team. I shrugged; we went to our cars for the drive back to Salzburg. Outside the camp hall was a crowd of about five hundred people, watching the mission. Kireyev and I shared the first car. As we waited to move, the crowd broke ranks and stormed us. They bounced the car on its springs and finally succeeded in turning it over, throwing me on top of the colonel. We looked at each other solemnly and with great dignity; it was truly a ridiculous situation and it was the only occasion when I detected the possibility that Colonel Kireyev did possess a sense of humor. Finally I opened the door on my side, which was upward, and climbed out as best I could. Several people helped me, but when the colonel tried to get out, not a hand was raised to his assistance. He managed to crawl out. A military jeep took us on the long ride to Salzburg to nurse our wounds and feelings. I learned that the car, a Soviet-made Ford, had later been set afire.

I was finally relieved from this duty and replaced by a member of my own group at Oberammergau. He brought with him the welcome news that I was to be sent to the USSR in January of 1949.

2 Assignment: Moscow

After leaving the repatriation team, I went back to school in Oberammergau to prepare for the upcoming tour in the Soviet Union. I asked for extra language instruction from our DP teaching staff and at this time I became friendly with one of the instructors, a Great Russian named Igor Bogolyepov.

Bogolyepov was a young man with a unique background. During the mid-1930s, he had been for several years the personal assistant of the Soviet foreign minister, Maxim Litvinov, who later was deposed following the Italian attack on Ethiopia. He was replaced by Vyacheslav Molotov. Bogolyepov was a bachelor in the Foreign Ministry, where he had learned English as part of his duties. He lived in Moscow and shared his apartment with Karl Radek, a prominent Soviet journalist and ideologue, who was caught up and jailed in the mid-1930 purges by Stalin. Radek was given ten years in jail but the history books do not reflect his ever returning from his ten-year imprisonment. Bogolyepov went on to Spain on a political assignment during the Spanish Civil War. As with other Russians who had been sent to Spain in the late 1930s, upon his return to Moscow at the end of the civil war he was immediately clapped in jail at the Lyubianka. This was common practice, the assumption being that Soviets who had been in the West were contaminated and had to be reexamined before any use could be made of them. While in Lyubianka, during his purging period, another prisoner was shoved into his cell. The new man called himself Baron Steiger. His title was not unusual: the NKVD (Soviet secret police) kept a stable of what they called their Baltic nobility, acceptable and presentable socially, masters of several languages, polished and able to mingle with Western diplomats in Moscow. Steiger questioned Bogolyepov as to why he was imprisoned and was told of the usual story of the returnee from the West. Bogolyepov

15

questioned in return as to why Steiger was there. As I remember he was told the following story.

"In the early 1930s, when the Americans first established diplomatic contact with the Soviet government, I was assigned to cultivate Americans who would be coming to the embassy. When Joseph Davies was named ambassador, I was told that the embassy had received a set of new combination locks and file cabinets, to prevent the NKVD from getting the contents of these files. At that time, at the end of the day's work, the embassy staff would merely walk out the door and lock it behind them. There were no Marine guards for twenty-four-hour security. The Soviet charwomen force, and undoubtedly quite a few others, had the run of the embassy until it opened the following morning.

"I was given the mission of getting one of the new safes ordered by the embassy, ostensibly for use in the Soviet Foreign Office. At a social event, I complained to Mrs. Davies about the backwardness of the Russians and their inability to get anything done right, due to their lack of mechanical aptitude. I asked her if there was anything she could do to get me one of these new safes (I added that I would be glad to pay for it).

"She said she would be happy to help me and would ask the ambassador to have an extra one shipped from the U.S. She called me when it arrived. I had it picked up and taken to the NKVD technicians, who took the locks apart. The techniques of opening them were learned, and from then on all American documents were routinely photographed at night, when the embassy staff was gone."

Bogolyepov stated that this was quite an accomplishment, as Baron Steiger shifted nervously on his stool and continued.

"I was in charge of these nighttime entries and the photographing, and would personally deliver the exposed rolls of film to the NKVD office. Then I was arrested and told I was holding back information; they already had everything I had given them.

"I said they must have other sources of getting at these documents but they only laughed and said I was playing games with them. I don't yet know what they meant, but here I sit. I guess that's all there is to it. But then the Russians are pretty much pigs, aren't they?"

Toward the end of 1948, I knew that I would be leaving the school, which had moved to Regensburg, and in January of 1949

I became a diplomatic courier, carrying classified mail between Helsinki and Moscow.

During that fall, I made a point of contacting the CIA men in Munich, the nearest representative to where I was living. I thought he must be at least partially concerned with the Soviet problem. We arranged to have lunch together at a hotel in the center of Munich.

He had vetted me by cable and had been informed by Headquarters that I had served with the predecessor organizations and that I would probably return to the CIA following my present three-year tour. I confirmed this but asked meanwhile if there was anything I could do for the CIA in the Soviet Union during my upcoming trips. I would be spending time in Leningrad and Moscow and this pattern of travel from Helsinki would be repeated over a period of six months.

This officer, with whom I later worked in Germany, said he would think it over and we would talk about it again before I left for Paris to pick up my diplomatic passport. We met about a week later, again in Munich. I was told "they" had talked about my offer but could think of nothing I could usefully do for the CIA. I came to realize that the newly formed agency had no plans for intelligence work within the Soviet Union nor indeed any idea of what might be done. This was confirmed to me when I was assigned to CIA Headquarters in 1951. I had thought a great deal could have been accomplished, had I known what some of the requirements were.

I mentioned none of this to my fellow students nor to my instructors, including Bogolyepov. I did know that he had come from Leningrad and that his family had been high in the Party structure in the prewar years. They had had privileges granted by the Soviet bureaucracy to their senior officials—an apartment in Leningrad, a telephone, a car, and they were able to buy food and clothing at the well-stocked Communist Party stores.

Bogolyepov knew that I was going into the Soviet Union in the early months of 1949; I asked if there was anything I could do for him. He answered that there was: "If it's possible, there is one thing. Try to find a telephone book in Leningrad and see if my family is still listed. If they are, this will mean that they are still in favor with the local party. If not . . ." He shrugged.

I said I'd try. I talked with various other instructors who had relatives in the USSR, whom they said would be willing to cooperate with us if it were possible to reach them by mail. They could then, through some third country, send mail out to an accommodation address with some intelligence about this closed society. Each one of the three instructors I talked to gave me a letter to a relative, which they had me read. I made copies, suggesting that the relatives place themselves at the disposal of people who could approach them with certain signs or questions to indicate their connection to the Western world and to the U.S. government in particular.

Just after New Year's Day of 1949 I received word that my passport was ready at the U.S. Embassy in Paris. My mother, at the time, was living in Paris and we had a chance for visits to French restaurants and some family conversation. She was staying at the Hotel Lutetia on the Boulevard St. Michel, and as she was very comfortably settled there, I didn't want to tell her, a Norwegian by birth, that during the Nazi occupation of France, the Gestapo had used it as one of their headquarters.

After a few days in Paris, the last wrinkle had been ironed out of the problem of procuring visas to Sweden, Finland, and the Soviet Union. My first stop was Stockholm, where I spent the night, leaving the pouch in the embassy code room for safekeeping. In those days, the pouch was a very heavy canvas double-lined sack, rather like a satchel with a leather flap closing it with a complicated system of straps, to which was attached the metal diplomatic seal to guarantee immunity from inspection by customs officials en route.

I went on to Helsinki, where I remained for a few days before going to Moscow. My first act in Helsinki was to buy a gray karakul hat, more a necessity than an affectation. It was bone cold, colder than I had ever known, and even more so in Leningrad and Moscow, once we were away from the moderating effects of the Baltic Sea. I couldn't imagine how the Baltic Sea could make a difference, as it was frozen solid—to the point where trucks and cars were driving on the ice, taking shortcuts in and around Helsinki.

I spoke briefly to the CIA man at the legation, but long enough to form in my own mind the opinion that he was not capable of coping with the job he had. He was totally confused about Finland itself, and his duties there. The idea of doing anything within the USSR had not occurred to him. He apparently had been given my name by Washington, but he could not imagine what I might do for him either in Finland or the Soviet Union. I believe he was still just as confused in June of 1949, when I left the courier run, as he was in January. He was a pleasant fellow, however, and when I came back to Helsinki from Moscow, he had obtained for me a French alpine stove and some C-rations to cook on the train, there being no food available on the Moscow run. I left the letters, given me by my Russian friends, in the code-room safe, as I felt my first trip would be an exploratory one. I would mail them later.

It was the night of 7 January when I checked into the airport at Helsinki, having flown over from Stockholm. A surly driver met me from the legation and took me to the quarters assigned to diplomatic couriers. After unpacking, I found a note from one of my military colleagues, saying that he and some of his friends were having dinner at the Adlon Hotel, and would I join them. Having no plans, I showered, changed my uniform, and took a cab to the hotel. My friends were there with some Finnish girls and I could see that the evening was meant to be a long one, as there was no duty for the next two days.

Sitting in the warm, relaxed atmosphere of the dining room, I noticed a vivacious young girl on the dance floor, in no way conscious of my watching her. She danced well and gracefully in spite of the fact that her left arm was gone. One of the Finnish girls at the table, following my glance, said that her name was Mielikki and that she knew her slightly. I could only say that I found her very attractive.

After a few hours, we all decided to go back to one of the courier apartments, driving home through a freezing, snowy night.

At about one in the morning there was a knock on the door and there stood Mielikki. One of the girls had asked her to come to the apartment when she was free and that's where we met. Her English was excellent and there was no difficulty in communication. Her hair was brown, rather than the usual blond coloring of the north; she had large blue eyes, and I would describe her as handsome, rather than beautiful. As we talked, she told me that when she was about ten years old, she and her mother were caught in the railway station during a Soviet air raid. It was there she had lost her arm. We became caught up in conversation and fell to talking about our personal lives. It emerged that she lived with her parents and had an illegitimate child, John Christian, whom she had decided to keep. She had long ago lost touch with his father.

I admitted that I was married and had two daughters, who with my wife were now living in Germany. As the party was becoming louder, I asked if I might take her home. We chose to walk the two-mile distance, as the snow had stopped. The sky was crystal clear, although it was still bitterly cold. We slowly made our way to the apartment at 39 Fredericks Gatan, in the middle of Helsinki, where there were many large turn-of-the-century apartments. The walk ended all too soon.

One morning, while having breakfast at the Adlon and reading a copy of *Life* magazine, a middle-aged man came to my table and asked if he might have coffee with me. He showed an interest in Americans, as so many Finns did, and it was only after we had talked for some time it became apparent that he was Mielikki's father. He invited me to visit their home. When I told Mielikki of her father's invitation, she was delighted, as she wanted very much for me to see her son and meet her sister, Marta, and her mother, Gudrun. Spending that first evening with the family, it emerged that I had some knowledge of Russian, and with that, her father began to regale me with Russian poetry. The older Finnish generation had had to learn Russian as children, when Finland was a margravate of Russia. The evening was a very relaxed one and I felt completely at ease with her family.

It was soon obvious that Mielikki and I were strongly attracted to each other. We were together during the times I was in Helsinki, when I came out of Moscow for diplomatic mail or other official business. She was highly intelligent, and aside from the strong physical feeling that existed between us, we simply enjoyed being together. I still had my quarters in the legation, but I was welcome at any time at Mielikki's home. As much as I wanted to be with her, I was also immensely stimulated being with her family.

Her father was a retired physician; we would spend an occasional afternoon playing chess. During one of these sessions, he asked me to spend a weekend at his brother's house, about two hours out of Helsinki, on the edge of one of the many thousand lakes of Finland. The house was spacious and set in a heavy forest. It was to be a large family gathering, including his brother's two sons and their wives and children. Shortly after lunch on the first day, the doctor suggested that we go to their sauna, a healthier introduction to a local custom than the Russian trial by vodka. I had become a sauna addict, and after undressing in one of the bedrooms, we donned heavy overcoats, with towels about our necks and nothing else. We left our overcoats in the dressing room and entered the sauna, where to my astonishment, the whole family was assembled, the nude children running about on the hottest top benchs. We spent half an hour steaming ourselves before going out to take a cold shower. We went out into the snow and the doctor persuaded me to jump into the icy waters of the lake. That made me a real Finn. The lack of inhibition seemed absolutely natural, and made a lasting impression on me.

In those days the Soviet airline, Aeroflot, was the only airline between Helsinki and Moscow; it made the run three times a week. The planes were old C-47s acquired from the U.S. during the lend-lease program of World War II. They were equipped to take eighteen passengers rather than straight cargo. A member of the legation drove me to the airport for my first flight into the Soviet Union, but early enough to have lunch before the plane left on its return leg. While eating, we saw the plane land and the crew come up the stairs to the restaurant.

There were five of them, but they ordered so much food that I expected that at any moment other members of the crew would appear; they ate everything in sight. In those days, the production of alcohol in Finland was a government monopoly; this included beer, which was made in three grades, numbered one, two, and three, the third being the strongest. As the Soviet crew wolfed through their lunch, they kept ordering number three. This was a powerful beer and the amounts they drank made me a little uneasy at the thought of flying with them to Moscow. Finally they finished and, belching frequently, went downstairs and to the plane. Shortly after that, the flight was called. I went to the ground level and out to the airplane, following the two or three other passengers going to Moscow. We all walked around the tail to get to the aircraft door, and I couldn't avoid seeing a large shoe-shaped hole through the fabric of the elevator panel. My stomach hurt a bit on seeing this. I found my seat and began looking for the safety belt. I should have known better; there was none and as one of the crew members walked by me, going forward, she said, "Don't worry, comrade, everything is O.K."

The flight to Moscow was uneventful and on landing at Vanukova Airport, I was met by an embassy officer. I turned over the road bag and went on to American House, which was my billet during my stay in Moscow.

3 Cold War Russia

Nineteen-forty-nine was not a good year for Americans in Moscow. Except for a couple of American newsmen, the only ones there were those assigned to the embassy. All were under frequent surveillance, sometimes so open and blatant that it was clearly intended to be seen. On other occasions, surveillance would be very sophisticated. Only after considerable experience could I "make" such a surveillance team in downtown Moscow, on a subway, or at the Bolshoi Theatre.

There were no Western tourists in those days. The few Western newsmen were pretty much limited to Moscow. Even if one of them could speak or read Russian, he always moved with care; there was always the risk of not having a visa renewed if he traveled to Helsinki or Stockholm for a vacation.

It was widely and accurately felt that all American quarters had microphones salted away in the walls and that the telephones were tapped. This promoted an atmosphere that was both oppressive and threatening. We were not allowed to talk with any Soviet citizen or official, and were reduced to dealing only with other Western embassies and legations. This all made for an incestuous kind of diplomatic social life in which people drank too much, did not get proper exercise, and in general became apprehensive and nervous.

I spent about seven days in Moscow during my first visit. American House was located on the Moscow River, about ten minutes away from the embassy. The embassy had been built during the 1920s by Soviet engineers and construction workers and was originally designed to be part of the Moscow school system. It was seven stories high; the first three or four floors were embassy offices, and the upper floors were divided into apartments for staff members and their families. Single people were practically all accommodated at American House. There, several rooms were set aside for transients, like myself, and that was where I spent my off-duty time when I wasn't roaming around Moscow or attending one of the many social affairs to which we were automatically invited. We all assumed that the Russian staff at American House was supplied by the MGB (Ministry for State Security) to keep our activities and conversations under scrutiny; later defectors to the West confirmed this.

The embassy building was in downtown Moscow, overlooking a broad square, facing the west wall of the Kremlin. From the windows you could look up the square along the narrow, sloping streets that led into Red Square at the end of which was St. Basil's Church, that many-colored onion-domed postcard church so familiar to Western travelers now. The newest hotel was the Moscow Hotel, facing onto the same square as the American Embassy but from a different vantage point. Coming down to this square from the north was one of the broad avenues and main thoroughfares in Moscow, Gorky Street, along which were many shops, stores, offices, and public buildings.

During my first week in Moscow, I made it a practice every day, regardless of the weather, to take one of the branches of the Moscow subway to the end of the line, come up to the street level, and walk back either to the embassy or American House. This proved to be a rewarding kind of exercise for me in practicing Russian and absorbing the general atmosphere of Moscow. It raised hell, however, with the surveillance teams assigned to me and these long walks, which were done at a fast pace because of the cold, had the teams stumbling and continually revealing their presence. Sometimes at a stoplight, they would catch up and stand with me on the corner, smiling weakly, until the light would change.

I had to identify Soviet surveillance patterns and methods because I needed to determine under what circumstances I might be able to mail safely the letters I had left in Helsinki. At the same time, these walks gave me ideas of where to locate deaddrops for small articles, such as a roll of film or a letter, that might be usable in the future. At the end, I was reduced to writing descriptions and making sketches of what I had learned during each walk. These I would mail to myself at the legation in Helsinki, via the diplomatic pouch that arrived about two or three times a week.

My first sightseeing stop was Lenin's tomb in Red Square, the mausoleum against one wall of the Kremlin where the May Day and November holidays were celebrated by parades with military units and the "spontaneous" organized workers. After having paid my respects to the preserved remains of Lenin, I made my way behind the GUM department store and on up to Dzerzhinsky Square, named after the first chief of the security services, the CHEKA and the NKVD predecessor organs to the KGB, the Soviet secret police. He was one of the few heads of that organization who died peacefully in bed. The square had an attractive little park, with paths lined with benches where one could sit and read a newspaper or enjoy the thin sunlight of a Moscow spring. On only one occasion did I ever see anyone going through the square, and never anyone sitting on a bench. To do so would put them too close to the headquarters of the MGB, and to that notorious place, the Lyubianka Prison. The ordinary Muscovite would always go out of his way to avoid this square and its neighboring streets. I felt quite safe in Leningrad and Moscow, having a diplomatic passport (the possession of such a passport no longer serves as certain protection).

One day during that winter, I witnessed an incident that showed me the face of political terror. I was walking in the downtown area of Moscow on a street known as Kusnetzky Most. As I walked among masses of Russians, who were bundled up against the cold, I noticed a man standing in the doorway of one of the old czarist buildings, apparently an apartment house, smoking a cigarette and gazing into the street. As I moved along, I heard the sound of a car. A large black limousine drew up to the curb abreast of me in front of the door where the man was standing. I was close enough to see his eyes open with fear; he dropped his cigarette. Two men in heavy coats got out of the limousine, crossed the sidewalk to the entryway, and propelled the man into the car. The doors slammed and I watched as it went down to the next avenue, where it turned and disappeared. I looked around and found that the streets and sidewalks of Kusnetzky Most had emptied of every pedestrian; moments before there had been large crowds. They had scattered and disappeared like minnows before a feeding trout; where they had gone I didn't know. Clearly they knew what this black sedan meant and what was happening to the man in the doorway. By the time I reached the avenue that connected with Kusnetzky Most, I glanced back and the street again teemed with people. The wide-eyed and terrified look of the man I'll always remember, but especially the disappearance of everyone from the street. Terror, part of life in Moscow, on a bright sunlit day.

That afternoon, I told a friend in the embassy what I had seen. He said a minor purge was going on in both Moscow and Leningrad; this was probably one small portion of the action, though not so small to the victims.

A few days later I flew back to Helsinki to take out the secret mail (carried in a "safehand" pouch) and pick up a new batch of classified correspondence to be hand-carried into Moscow. Just before leaving for the airport, in Moscow, I was called in by the embassy administrative officer, who asked if I would take with me an American who had been jailed in Odessa for the better part of three years and had just been released. He was a merchant seaman who had become involved in a dockside brawl and had been thrown in jail by the local police. He had languished there for several years until the embassy, after tedious negotiations, had arranged for his release and deportation to the United States. This man was on the verge of a nervous breakdown when I saw him; the first thing he said to me was, "Don't leave me alone for a minute, not even to go to the john. I just want to get out of this country."

On the plane I asked about his prison life, but he began to shake and perspire and said that he didn't want to think about it. I told him to forget it; he would soon be in Finland and on his way home the next morning. Our trip was halted in Leningrad because of bad weather and I reserved a double compartment on the train, leaving the Finland station at one in the morning, getting to Helsinki the next day. Walking about the railway station in the freezing cold Arctic night, I witnessed an incident that was typically Russian. The platform was completely deserted; the train had not yet been backed into the rail spur. My friend had not wanted to wait inside the station; he preferred to be out in the open with me.

As we walked back and forth, I suddenly heard a great deal of boisterous laughing and shouting coming from the end of the platform. In a moment there appeared three Red Army soldiers, obviously military policemen, who were hauling between them a thoroughly drunken soldier, who was singing and trying occasionally to break away from his escorts. Everyone was in good humor and they were telling their staggering friend, "Sasha, shut up. Be a good boy and come along."

Reeling along, he suddenly made a lunge and broke away, darting in front of me and falling heavily from the platform to the tracks, about three feet below. He lay there with his face on one of the rails, as the MPs, laughing all the time, climbed down, took hold of Sasha's arms, heaving him to his feet. In the process of helping him they left practically half of his cheek which had become frozen to the rail. Sasha, dripping blood, but still laughing, was once again on the platform and they noisily went on around the corner to the sobering-up room—every station had one.

This incident recalled a much more ominous and disturbing experience, while traveling on a Soviet train. I had left the Moscow station for Leningrad on a brilliant and crisp midwinter's day. The Soviets, to make a good impression, always put on a polished and highly decorated locomotive on the international train at the Moscow station, complete with a garlanded picture of Stalin below the headlight, which would take the train at high speed to the first set of marshaling yards at Klin, where they would stop and hook on a drab, ordinary road engine. On this particular day, as we were changing locomotives, I noticed a cattle train parallel to ours about three tracks away. It was made up of the usual cattle cars with the sides made of slats, with air spaces between them and the floors made in the same way to allow animal droppings to fall to the ground below. I was standing in the warm corridor idly glancing out and noticed this train was made up of about fifteen to eighteen cattle cars. As I gazed at them I was horrified to realize that there were no cattle; there were people, many of them very young. From the darkness within, their faces with large empty eyes simply stared across the tracks to the car in which I stood, as though in mute appeal. The entire train was a prisoner transport, carrying men, women, and children to some undisclosed destination. The Soviet cabin attendant in my car passed behind me at this point and I asked who these people were. He fidgeted nervously and said, "God knows, comrade, God knows. They probably got in trouble with somebody."

My merchant seaman traveling companion became a completely changed human being as soon as we crossed the border into Finland. Together we took a taxi from the railway station in Helsinki to the American Legation; he marveled at the neatness of the city, the well-to-do appearance of the crowds on the sidewalk, and was in an expansive and genial mood by the time we pulled to a halt in front of the legation. I delivered him to the legation administrative officer and he said good-bye, thanking me profusely for my attention and consideration during the trip from Moscow to Helsinki. He observed that his seafaring days were at an end, that he had a brother in California in Petaluma, where he ran a chicken farm, and that he would join his brother on the farm and never again leave it.

I had several days rest before starting another trip to Moscow and spent them happily with Mielikki. During my last visit to Moscow I had found two mailboxes where I felt I could mail letters without observation, and resolved to take the letters I had left in the legation safe back to Moscow with me.

The day of my departure turned out to be a cold, windy, snowy day with almost no visibility under the heavy cloud cover. As Aeroflot would not fly in instrument weather, I was to go on the train, spend the night in Leningrad, and then take the "Blue Arrow" express to Moscow. I was grateful that my friend in the legation had provided me with the cooking stove and C-rations. The international car was the only one equipped with berths and washstands. Actually, it was an old deluxe Wagonlits sleeping car, made in France about 1902. Leaving at midnight, we arrived in Leningrad midmorning the next day. On this departure from Helsinki, I had four Soviet traveling companions, who were returning from an international literary conference in Stockholm. Among them was a well-known Soviet author, Alexander Fedeev. They arrived at the train, escorted by an officer from the Soviet Embassy in Helsinki, totally drunk, singing loudly, and waving out the train windows, even though the temperature was far below zero.

The train drew slowly out of the station at midnight, heading for the Soviet border-crossing point at Vainikalla. There would be the usual customs inspection by Soviet officials. I had been through this experience several times, but as I held a diplomatic passport and a courier letter, I was never bothered. I decided to wait and see what kind of treatment the Soviet travelers would receive from their own people.

By the time we reached the border an hour or two later, the four Soviets were still blissfully high. They stood in the corridor, smoking and recalling their visit to Sweden. The train drew to a stop with a grinding of brakes and several customs inspectors boarded the car. That's when the holiday ended for the four travelers. Curtly, the inspectors told them to bring all of their suitcases out into the aisle, where they proceeded to rifle through them. Before the glum eyes of the rapidly sobering quartet, they systematically set aside all books or other printed material, photos, an assortment of phonograph records, and, of all things, several pairs of new shoes, presumably bought in Stockholm. This took about half an hour and the suitcases themselves were then thoroughly examined, the linings pulled out, and the handles cut open. Their inspection over, the officials bundled up all the things they had set aside and, without a further word, left the car. There was nothing the four could do but pick up their remaining belongings, which were scattered over the aisle, and pack them up as best they could. Completely crushed, they went to their compartments to sleep off the weekend and the welcome.

It was overcast and still snowing lightly when we reached the Finland station in Leningrad. Getting a taxi off the ranks was no problem and I went directly to the Astoria Hotel, the only place in Leningrad foreigners were allowed to stay. The Astoria was an Intourist hotel, so I knew I was being well looked after by the MGB, which controlled this entire organization. The Astoria was a prerevolutionary building and it displayed all the elaborate architecture of the czarist period. The rooms were large and well-decorated; mine had several pieces of statuary in it, and paintings on the walls from various museums in Leningrad. Each one carried a metal tag fastened on the item, giving a number and name of the museum from which it had been taken.

After lunch I stopped at the hotel desk and asked if they had a telephone book. Not surprisingly, there was none available. They were sorry but they couldn't help me. I then asked for directions to the Hermitage, the Winter Palace Museum of Art, and walked through the central part of the city to the museum, situated on the Neva River. This had been a palace of the czars in prerevolutionary times but had been turned into an art museum containing a veritable treasure of art, classical and "modern." While on the ground floor, checking my hat and overcoat, I noticed a door across the corridor marked "Director." I asked the cloakroom attendant if this was the office of the director of the Hermitage. He said it was. I thought, "Well, what the hell," and went over and opened the door. There was a large room in which several secretaries were working. I asked one of them, pointing to a door at the end of the room: "Is that the office of the director?"

She numbly gave me a slow nod. I passed through the room, went through the door and closed it behind me. The director was sitting primly at his desk. He looked up, his eyes widening, as he recognized a foreigner and quite possibly an American. I told him I understood he had a telephone book and wondered if I might look at it. He continued to stare at me frozenly and reached into a drawer of his desk, pulling out a Leningrad directory. I quickly walked over, picked it up, and thanked him.

I went to one of the windows and turned my back to it, leafing through the pages to where the name Bogolyepov would be. It was not there. By then the director was on his feet and moving toward me. I simply closed the book, handed it back, and thanked him again before leaving through the outer office where the girls were huddled together talking about what had just happened.

Bogolyepov's family was not listed in the phone book; this undoubtedly meant they had no apartment, certainly not a car, and were probably no longer in Leningrad. I wondered how I would break this unhappy news to Bogolyepov.

I walked back to the Astoria under cloudy skies. The snow had stopped, but it was clear that I would have to continue by train that evening. I had dinner at the hotel and attended the Kirov Ballet, which I considered much superior to the Bolshoi. Departing on the eleven o'clock train, I found the car almost identical to the one in which I had come from Finland.

The next morning, as we were pounding along to Moscow, I noticed there was only one other passenger in the international car. He had a bristly guard's mustache and was pacing up and down the corridor, stretching his legs. I was breaking out my camping stove and some C-rations and soon had a fire going and a can of ham and lima beans heating in the pot. I then noticed the tweedy stranger had moved to the door of my compartment. The aroma of my cooking was getting to him. I invited him to share my simple rations. Like a shot he came into the compartment with profuse thanks and we quickly downed the meal. He turned out to be the Australian ambassador to the USSR and was returning from a holiday in Stockholm. We spent the rest of the trip together, and once back in Moscow, I was entertained at a gourmet dinner at his residence, in return for a share of my C-rations.

I had a five-day layover, giving me time to mail my three letters. I planned to have an embassy officer, who lived near the two mailboxes I had selected, invite me to dinner. I would walk back to my quarters passing one of the boxes. After dinner I mailed the letters without observation and returned with a feeling of relief. I learned, once back in Germany, that two of the letters reached their destination and the relatives concerned were already writing to accommodation addresses in Switzerland and Denmark. (These were innocuous addressees who had been recruited to receive mail intended for the U.S. goverment, and who would forward it to us in the West.)

In the late 1940s the U.S. government received little intelligence out of the USSR and was always eager to get any information concerning rationing, the condition of the economy, and the morale of the people. It seems now, in the gaudy days of the 1960s and '70s, when intelligence is collected by a wide variety of agents and technical means as well as by satellites, that this was all very primitive at the time—it was, but it was all we had.

One winter evening in Moscow, I had a strange encounter. I had been able to get a single ticket to the Moscow State Circus, which had been highly recommended. They were hard to come by as the circus was a very popular attraction with Muscovites. Unlike American circuses, the Moscow Circus was in a single ring within a permanent structure. Otherwise, it had all the usual animal acts, highwire artists, and clowns.

Walking back to American House in the clear winter night with the snow well-packed under foot, I went down the so-called B Ring, a very broad avenue circling the middle of Moscow. The wide sidewalks were deserted and dark, as were the buildings facing the avenue. As I moved along, I became aware that I had a companion with me in the gloom of the buildings. I sensed and then heard the padding of a person walking in the snow and then a voice spoke to me in tones that were obviously those of an American Negro. He asked me how I liked the circus. I kept looking straight ahead although I was reasonably satisfied that my surveillance had left and there were only the two of us.

The man told me that in 1933 he had left his home in Philadelphia and had gone to the USSR in depression days, in the euphoria of going to the workers' republic, where everyone would be given a job. He asked if I had ever been to Philadelphia and I said that I knew the city fairly well. He asked a string of questions about the place that had been his home. He had long regretted giving up his American passport in 1933 and now had no future but to continue working in a Soviet factory on the edge of Moscow, where he was a janitor; he had married a Russian woman and had two children. I walked slowly but not slowly enough to arouse suspicion from anyone who might be watching. We parted as we approached the intersection of B Ring and the old Arbat neighborhood, as there were too many lights and street police for him to be seen with me. He asked me, if I were ever in Philadelphia, to phone his brother and let him know that he was safe and well; he wanted to send the family his best wishes and affection. I said I would; he thanked me and vanished.

Some years later I called his brother from Washington. I didn't give my name, but told him I had met Willie in Moscow and he had asked me to call and tell his family that he was all right. The shocked voice on the other end of the phone told me how much of a surprise this was. After his profuse thanks I hung up.

And then came May Day 1949. I had been in Moscow about a week before this celebration and had watched the Muscovites clean up their downtown area in preparation for the holiday. Holes in the streets were patched, store fronts painted, and banners were hung along with pictures of illustrious Russians. This was always an important time as the Russians watched to see whose faces would appear on the buildings and whose would not. As was earlier mentioned, a purge had been going on and it was not surprising that the pictures of Voznetsensky, a member of the Politburo, did not appear on the broad expanse of the GUM department store. He was among the missing and it was later confirmed that he had been shot.

The closing days of April were unusually warm for Moscow. As the first of May approached, it was clear the citizens, who had very little to look forward to, were preparing for a real holiday. Anything for relief.

May Day is a very special day. In the embassy, one could look out at the Kremlin Wall across Red Square and watch the whole parade, contrived and completely controlled during the course of the day, assembled and dispatched.

At ten o'clock in the morning the military parade and air-force fly-over would take place. This event would be attended by military attachés of countries with embassies in Moscow, the Soviet hierarchy, and selected troops of the Soviet Army. This was the event eagerly awaited by foreign embassies, with the hope that perhaps new Soviet equipment would be shown for the first time.

Space in the American Embassy, with its vantage point, was at a premium. Being an Army officer, I was invited to the apartment of the Army military attaché, Colonel Michael O'Daniel, the well-known "Iron Mike" O'Daniel, who later served as U.S. Army commander in Vietnam. By protocol he had been invited to review the military portion of the day's celebration from the reviewing stand adjoining Lenin's tomb. I was in his apartment with other officers when he left to walk over to the stand. All traffic in downtown Moscow had been stopped at seven in the morning and the streets were cleared of all but troop units and those taking part in the parade. Colonel O'Daniel went to the Mausoleum with his staff, but shortly returned, purple with rage. The Soviets all had their medals on and the "bastards" hadn't bothered to tell him. He continued to fume about their miserable, little tin medallions and emerged from his bedroom with heavy gold, silver, and bronze medals from an illustrious career covering his uniform.

"Now I'll go back and show those SOBs that I've been to war, too." With that, he stalked out.

Standing on the balcony, we watched the tanks fire up, the cavalry move off in procession, and the troop formations go on foot into Red Square, where the bands and spectators were making a tremendous noise, aided by the public-address system, which was playing records of loud, tumultuous cheering.

The military elements disappeared and the next part of the parade began to form below us. Columns of police appeared, *"plech-na-plechu,"* as the Russians called it, "shoulder to shoulder." The organized workers were next to march, including all of the various factory workers and student and sport groups, who had been waiting for hours to be finally marshaled into the street to take part in the parade.

At this point, Colonel O'Daniel reappeared and a cocktail party and luncheon began. Within an hour, the alcohol had taken effect and as lunch wore on, a glow came over us with the festive mood of the warm day.

The workers were being herded into line to pass along Red Square before Stalin, Molotov, and other prominent leaders, most of them now dead. Colonel O'Brien, another Russian language student, and I decided to see what was happening at first hand.

As we left the embassy, the police looked at us with some surprise, as we headed toward the soldiers and MGB officers, who were formed to take the "spontaneous" workers to the square. We approached the first of these troopers, and as the parade began, we ducked under their arms and joined the workers of the Moscow Light Metal Factory Number 172. They made a place for us, although they were amazed to see these two foreigners in their midst, standing out by the difference in height and clothing. Moving along, one worker reached into his coat pocket; he was immediately seized by the police; a search produced only a handkerchief; nevertheless he was led away. Two officers, who were watching O'Brien and me, fell in behind us as we reached Red Square, where the parade turned into an absolute bedlam. The police kept shouting, *"po-skoree, po-skoree"*—"faster, faster, comrades, keep your hands in the air."

We pushed our way along only to find ourselves in a girls'-school contingent. They were dressed in white middy blouses and blue skirts and there we were running along with them, with our hands above our heads. This was a standard precaution to prevent anyone from reaching for a weapon. In this fashion, we passed Stalin and Molotov, going at a fast trot, hurried on by the police until we ended at St. Basil's in the late afternoon amid a friendly and amiable throng of hundreds of Soviet citizens. We went to the Moscow River and found ourselves in the gathering dusk on the roadway bordering the river.

It was an experience we could never forget.

Heading back to American House, we paused as we noted a man with an accordion, sitting on the steps of a small frame house fiddling with various tunes, oblivious of the people passing by. When some of them stopped to listen, he suddenly burst forth into folk music and soon many young couples were dancing in the roadway and on the sidewalk. This friendly gaiety persisted and there the holiday mood continued, although behind this small house the massive walls of the Kremlin loomed, with one of its towers capped by the gleaming ruby star. Thus the people of Moscow celebrated May Day, but always under the symbol of oppression. It was the best they could do.

There was an amusing anecdote that circulated during the Moscow months through all the diplomatic luncheons and cocktail parties. The Greek ambassador, a bachelor, and a rather rotund and ebullient extrovert, had a rare encounter with the KGB. His housekeeper, working for the KGB, had also become his bedmate. The ambassador took great glee in describing what had transpired.

One evening when his housekeeper was sharing his bed, the entire plaster ceiling of the room had collapsed upon them. Typical Soviet construction, he said to me later. But along with the plaster, which had bruised them slightly, several microphones were dangling from the gap; there was the ubiquitous eye of a camera. The upshot of all this was that his next visitors were members of the KGB. They had transcribed what had taken place in the bedroom, accompanied by excellent photos of the activities. The veiled threats came out—cooperate with us or we'll expose you. The ambassador in his best form, took the photos from the KGB agents and thanked them very much, showing them to the door.

With his usual high spirits, he continued to offer these photographs of his virility and gymnastic ability in bed at the diplomatic parties he attended during the next few weeks until everyone became bored and the KGB apparently gave up on him. I'm sure there were sour remarks at their headquarters following this escapade.

This only showed what went on in Moscow and the degree to which the Soviets would push their interests and what their predilections were. In any event, the ambassador's ceiling was promptly repaired by an organization called Burobin, the Bureau for Foreigners, an instrument of the KGB, who merely replaced all of the microphones and photographic equipment.

I made eleven round-trip visits from Helsinki to Moscow and Leningrad during the first six months of 1949, and during them performed a number of operational tasks that provided our intelligence services with information about these cities which then were very restricted for foreigners. In June I went to the Helsinki Legation to have my passport routinely sent to the Soviet Embassy for a reentry visa; I wanted to make three or four more trips before my assignment was finished. To my surprise, my passport was returned with the terse comment that I was not to receive any more visas to the USSR. This action was unusual; clearly I was not welcome. I have never been back.

I stayed on in Helsinki for two more days before returning to Paris. There were loose ends of an official nature to wind up and of course there was Mielikki.

We had become very close and had spent as much time as possible together during those six months when I was in Helsinki. We now both sensed the affair was over and we probably would not see each other again. Our last moments were spent at the small Helsinki airport, where I was to take a flight to Stockholm and on to Paris. This lunch was a very sad one. By the time the Stockholm plane arrived, we had nothing left to say to each other. She knew my family situation. Before boarding the plane, we promised to write to each other. After my return to Germany, I told my wife about Mielikki; she was adamant against a divorce. I called Mielikki from Regensburg to tell her of this decision. We both really knew that this was the end and it must be this way. We never saw each other again.

4 The Gehlen Organization

The 1950s were among the most dangerous and active years of the cold war. During this span of time we saw the Berlin airlift and the Soviet blockade of Berlin. In 1950 the Korean War began; the bloodshed dragged on until 1953. Our concern about the intent of the large Soviet forces facing West Germany was great. Intelligence about Soviet capabilities and intentions became of enormous import to all of the Western powers. A great deal of attention was devoted to the embryonic German intelligence group which had survived the war under General Reinhard Gehlen.

Much has already been written about the Gehlen organization, a remarkable intelligence group. In World War II Gehlen had been chief of intelligence for the German armies in the East, facing the Russians. The closing years of the war saw the Germans slowly retreating to the West and in 1945 beginning a headlong flight to the West, away from the crushing strength of the Red Army. General Gehlen and his immediate staff, in charge of German intelligence on "Foreign Armies—East," the Soviets, kept moving. They bundled up their intelligence files and fled until they were certain they were in the American-controlled area of Germany. Gehlen and his officers then buried their files and turned themselves in to the Americans. Shortly thereafter, General Gehlen was seen by senior American Army intelligence officers. He offered the use of his buried files, with the proviso that the American Army would give his staff protection and get them back into business against the Soviets.

Before this took place, Gehlen and his immediate staff were flown to the United States, where they were billeted at Fort Hunt on the Potomac River, across from Washington. They were interrogated and interviewed at great length by a U.S. Army team. Eventually a decision was made to support Gehlen and to set him up in intelligence work in the American Zone of a conquered Germany.

During the war, the Schutzstaffel (SS) had built a military compound in Pullach, surrounded by a high wall and containing a number of family quarters, as well as office buildings. It was now in the possession of the American Army and was turned into headquarters for Gehlen. American intelligence officers lived in the village nearby and shared offices and working space in the compound. In 1949 an agreement was reached on the American side that liaison with Gehlen's organization would be turned over to the CIA. The CIA element was not very large; it was established as a base, subordinate to the CIA station in Karlsruhe. The Munich office, with a number of other staff officers, moved into Pullach, a small suburb south of Munich, and it was there that I reported for duty. The intention was to assist the Germans in gathering intelligence on the massive Soviet military presence in East Germany.

When war ends in a country and there is a partition as between Soviet and Western elements, not only is the nation divided and separated, but so are families. This was the case in Germany and later in Korea and in Vietnam. One binding fact was that both East and West Germany had a common racial and cultural past, but the West was occupied by the British, French, and Americans and the East by the hostile Soviets. Many in Gehlen's organization had originally been brought up in what became East Germany and had many friends and relatives there. This fact made intelligence operations in East Germany run by Gehlen a matter of practicality.

Toward the end of 1949, I had a telephone call from the CIA representative, Max, with whom I had spoken before departure to the Soviet Union. Could I come to Munich again and have lunch with him at the Hotel Bristol? There I learned he was chief of a CIA base in Pullach, working with the embryonic German intelligence service and the former General Reinhard Gehlen. He asked if my present duty would be finished in November and would I come to Pullach as his deputy? I wanted to get back to work with the CIA and we came to an agreement. I moved to Pullach as an Army officer on detail to the CIA in December of 1949.

It was my Pullach assignment that brought me into a formal relationship with Reinhard Gehlen. From December 1949 until

May of 1951, along with Max, I had frequent meetings with him on policy and intelligence matters, and learned much about his unusual personality and his political and personal philosophy.

When I first met Gehlen, he was forty-seven years old and had already put behind him a distinguished career as an intelligence officer for the German army during the war. Having a keen and incisive mind and a quiet and assured manner, he had risen rapidly in the Wehrmacht. By personality, he was a withdrawn and shy person, who caught fire almost only when he was engaged in discussing political and intelligence activities. He was strongly anti-Communist; at least this attitude was shared by most of the American leadership at Pullach.

While Gehlen had been condemned as a wartime Nazi by both the KGB and his German competitors, I have found no evidence that he was in fact a Nazi Party member nor that he was in any way an ideological adherent to the Nazi philosophy or to Hitler himself. Not unlike many senior German Wehrmacht officers, he was essentially politically simplistic, truly loyal only to Germany. His mind was uncluttered by ideology, unless one would describe his strong anti-Communism as an ideology. Perhaps as the best evidence in support of this picture of Gehlen's apolitical mentality was the fact that it was Konrad Adenauer who ultimately chose him as the first president of the Bundesnachrichtendienst—the German intelligence service. No Nazi, Adenauer was of course sensitive to the need that he select a man for this post who would be truthfully unassailable on that particular account.

Gehlen was short and slight in build. His face was thin and finely drawn in bone structure, and in general he had a slightly frail look about him. Mentally he was tough and resilient. A wispy blond mustache adorned his upper lip and matched his short, thin, straw-colored hair, which he brushed straight back. His clothing had a tweedy British look but his hats were typically Bavarian and he always wore dark glasses.

Gehlen was obsessed with keeping the work we carried on securely hidden from hostile intelligence eyes. He insisted on complete anonymity for himself; even after 1951 when the West German press and news magazines began to speculate on CIA intelligence support in West Germany, he stayed away from reporters, who were constantly trying to discover the dimensions of this organization and the personnel in it.

Gehlen was not a warm or charismatic member of the organization. He remained aloof and even diffident. His calm and remote demeanor was only occasionally broken through by some episode that provoked his anger; the only manifestation of his ire would be a cold gleam in his pale blue eyes. Among the American staff, we ordinarily referred to Gehlen in a friendly way as "old blue eyes."

He was a serious person and his occasional attempts at levity or simple geniality were almost painful to watch. At the same time he was scrupulously honest and we quickly learned that his word was reliable.

In these immediate postwar years, there were a number of West Germans who had been prominent in intelligence activities during World War II. Several of them were pressing and maneuvering to achieve a position of leadership for postwar intelligence work. The British had their own candidate, the U.S. Army had a candidate, and then there was General Gehlen. He outlasted them all and came out at the top of the heap as the first chief of the West German government's Bundesnachrichtendienst, the first centralized German intelligence service in the postwar era. This emergence by Gehlen as the leader in this field can only be viewed as a tribute to his iron will and dogged persistence, his singleness of purpose, and the undiluted concentration of his efforts in the direction of his ambitions and of what he felt to be West Germany's best political interests in the postwar world.

I was never close to Gehlen, but no American was. He kept a certain distance between himself and the Americans at Pullach, maintaining his isolation. He was nevertheless always courteous and unflagging in his zeal to keep the German-American relationship mutually productive and valuable. This, then, was the German leadership with whom we worked and this was the atmosphere in which we carried on our joint endeavors.

In addition to my routine functions as deputy chief-of-base, I dealt with the Germans in coverage of the East Zone and every branch of Soviet military establishments based there. Information about the introduction of new weapons, weapons-delivery systems, and anything bearing on Soviet nuclear capabilities being transferred from the Soviet Union to East Germany was of the highest priority.

We put emphasis on the acquisition of new sources in the

Soviet Zone to cover airfield, railway marshaling yards, army barracks areas and training grounds, and any other aspects of Soviet Army presence. Agents were sent east on espionage missions, as travelers, or to take up residence there and to report by deaddrop or by WT (wireless telegraph). Friends and relatives would be recruited if they were able to provide information or report by mail and secret writing to letterboxes in perhaps Sweden or Switzerland. Periodically, inspectors would be sent to the East to check agent sources and verify their status or clear up any problems that might arise.

These German agents in the East were called V-manner (men of confidence). They were listed by number and true name in a complicated system of bookkeeping at Pullach. If we learned of the capture of a certain V-mann, we could assume that he had been turned or doubled. It could be sensed in a change of his style in reporting, in his phraseology, or in his general attitude and behavior. Sometimes there would be a shift built into his communications system to serve as a danger signal to us. Inevitably when this happened, we would "play" the agent by radio to try to keep him alive, not as an intelligence-producing agent but as a human being. It was not easy and we resorted to every kind of stratagem to reassure his Soviet control that we were unaware the agent had been blown. Cases like these were always wearing.

In addition to Pullach, there were Gehlen bases in many of the principal cities of West Germany and a base in Salzburg, in the American Zone of Austria, which produced a political problem at almost every turn. One lead developed from this Austrian base that turned into a puzzling case. It seemed to involve Soviet code and cipher systems and, as such, took on a high priority. I will tell about it in the next chapter.

5 The "Count"

One day in the late spring of 1950 Max strolled into my office from his adjoining one in our staff building at Pullach to say that the Doctor was going to pay a visit; Max wanted me to be present. We went back into his office and he told me the Doctor had asked for an appointment and would bring Heinz with him.

The "Doctor" was our name for Gehlen and Heinz was his ever-present aide and equerry. The senior German staff at Pullach used cover names on the phone and in written exchanges among themselves or with us, a manifestation of Gehlen's acutely developed sense of security.

After their arrival, we grouped ourselves around the coffee table in Max's office and, as Gehlen began to talk, Heinz busily took notes of American comments, a known sign that this meeting was important. Gehlen said that his operations base in Salzburg had come up with a lead we might find significant. It appeared to relate to Soviet military and diplomatic codes and he thought we might prefer to develop this lead ourselves. He told Heinz to give us the complete story; I then began to write. In brief, an Austrian national had recently approached his base in Salzburg. The visitor gave his name as Graf Friedrich Coloredo-Wels and displayed an Austrian travel document in that name. He lived in the Soviet Sector of Vienna and frequently visited Soviet headquarters, located in the Imperial Hotel on the Ringstrasse. He claimed to know a Soviet officer in the hotel who wanted to contact the Americans. This Soviet officer allegedly had access to the new Soviet ciphers and information concerning their use. He claimed he could provide the United States with a great deal of material about this new system in return for resettlement in the West, plus $25,000 in U.S. money. He spoke only German and had thus asked the Austrian "count," who was fluent in English and several other languages as well, to approach us, which he did through the Salzburg office.

Max and I exchanged glances. We both knew that Washington would go for this lead like a hungry trout for a fly, but realized it would be difficult to check because of our own lack of detailed information about the new Soviet system. Salzburg had arranged a second meeting to explore matters more deeply and the Doctor thought we should take over at that time. Max agreed, saying he would assign a German-speaking case officer to meet with the count.

After Gehlen and Heinz had left, Max told me to cable Headquarters, propose what action we should take, and ask their concurrence and guidance. That evening we had our reply: "Cannot evaluate lead as described, but anything concerning Soviet ciphers is of great value and importance. Approve your handling this as you see fit. Please keep us informed."

The next morning we discussed this possible operation in detail. Its Vienna origins brought up the risk that the Soviets were aggressively involved, the goal perhaps being to force the CIA to parade a number of officers before them for identification. Vienna was an active center of espionage and counterespionage; it was often referred to as "the shooting gallery" because of the frequent use of violence in running operations there. But the prospect of a source in the Imperial with access to the cipher system left us no choice but to follow it through. Henry, a German-speaking case officer, would make the next meeting in Salzburg. He was briefed, told to contact the Gehlen base and to attend the meeting along with their representative. Headquarters was already bombarding us with streams of advice and questions to ask the count.

Henry returned after his meeting, looking both tired and confused. He described the Austrian as a man of about sixty-five years of age, obviously well-educated. The Soviet was identified as one Major Ivan Galkin. We immediately cabled Vienna and Headquarters, giving Galkin's name and physical description, asking for file traces. Washington had none but Vienna cabled the following: "Our files show that one Ivan Aleksandrovich Galkin, Major, is attached to Soviet headquarters. Duties unknown."

Washington, upon receiving an information copy, besieged us with more advice.

Coloredo-Wels was to go back to Vienna and report that we had been contacted and a further meeting set for about ten days later, this time in Munich. Max said he wanted me present as the count had hinted he might bring out some Russian documents. This meeting was to take place at Humpelmayer's restaurant in downtown Munich. Henry was to pick up the count at his hotel and bring him to the restaurant, where I would be waiting.

My first impression upon meeting the "count" was that he was an intelligent but slippery customer. He was of medium height, very slim, with a bony face and prominent nose, thin and highly arched. Overall, he was good-looking with an air of aristocratic elegance. His clothes were old but well-fitting and obviously had been at one time of the best quality.

Our table was in a back corner of Humpelmayer's, somewhat removed from other tables so we could speak freely. After the amenities had been exchanged, we ordered dinner. Coloredo-Wels said that first he would like to tell us something about his own background. He was an illegitimate son of the Graf Coloredo-Wels. Upon the death of his natural father some years ago, he had simply adopted the title, using it in his social contacts in Vienna. It was a respected name there, and as he put it delicately, it opened many doors to him in Viennese society. He lived alone in a one-room apartment in a run-down section of the Third Bezirk, supported by the generosity of a number of lady friends he had known over the years. I could believe this. He spoke convincingly of trips to the French Riviera, Rome, Madrid, and other capitals of Europe, always at the expense of one of his "friends."

He then began to describe his meetings with Galkin. After making an appointment, he would check into the Imperial and be taken to the major's office on the third floor. At this most recent meeting, Galkin asked if his two conditions had been agreed to: resettlement in a Western country, preferably the United States, and the $25,000. Galdin stressed that he must be shown the money before he would cooperate. He said that he would work for the Americans for about three months and then take whatever documents he was able to get his hands on and defect. As we finished dinner, we instructed the count to tell Galkin that the two conditions would be met. We also told him to make a sketch of Galkin's office and its location in the hotel and to bring a list of officers working in the Imperial, or a telephone directory.

On the sidewalk in front of the restaurant, the count assured us he would see Galkin the following day. We said he should continue to use the front entrance to the Imperial and to try to make the appointment for about ten in the morning. He looked at me closely and said matter-of-factly, "You'll be watching." I nodded.

That night I cabled Vienna and asked the station to stake out the entrance to the hotel, using the description of the count which we had previously provided them. We asked for photos of the entry, the length of time he remained in the hotel, and the direction he took on his way out.

The next afternoon a cable from Vienna arrived: "Subject was observed entering the Imperial Hotel at 1030 hours and was seen to leave at exactly twelve o'clock noon. He went towards the Schwarzenburgplatz, and we ended our surveillance, per your request."

Henry and I already shared grave reservations about the credibility of the count, his story about Galkin, whose name he could have learned in a number of ways, and the entire code ploy. Max agreed. We got off a cable to Headquarters listing our doubts and recommended that we break contact with the count. Headquarters, however, reacted violently to our proposal. Even the possibility of getting close to the Soviet cipher system, they said, required that we press our contact. We were ordered to continue it, in spite of our misgivings. I was also instructed to draw $25,000 in American currency and have it with me at all subsequent meetings. Max, Henry, and I were thoroughly discouraged at this point, but I drew the money from our finance officer, plus a leather pouch to carry it in; I also procured a .38 caliber revolver.

The Vienna Station continued routine vetting and placed the count's apartment under observation from time to time. His personal appeal to a number of Viennese ladies was apparent. He often had tea with women many years his junior; invariably the lady would pick up the check. Several of these ladies were staked out, but a dry well was struck in connecting them with any kind of intelligence activity. Charm was his stock-in-trade.

We knew that we must make Coloredo-Wels produce either Soviet documents or the fuzzy Galkin. He was receiving no money except for an occasional dinner and minor travel expenses, which seemed to satisfy him; he never asked for more.

We finally received a letter requesting a meeting at the Post

Hotel in Wels (which happened to be where his father was born). We agreed to the place and set a time, although I have never liked meeting at a time and place chosen by an agent who had a good description to pass on to any hostile surveillance or stake-out teams.

Henry and I went a day earlier to find accommodations and to check out the hotel. We went separately. As the count was arriving by train at Linz, it was possible to intercept him at the station and have him followed to Wels to see if he had a "convoy." He had none. We met in the dining room and were greeted with the news that everything in Vienna was "progressing far beyond my original expectations."

Working conversation was reserved for after dinner, when we could stroll in a nearby park and talk unheard. I was conscious of the $25,000 in my pocket and wondered if I would ever have any use for it.

Coloredo-Wels' news was that Galkin was determined to meet us very soon and had decided upon Grieskirchen, a small Austrian town, as he had once been to a spa nearby; this would be his reason for going there again. He went on to mention that when this matter had been consummated, and this was very gently said, that we might find it possible to be generous with an old man with few means at his disposal. I assured him that he would be compensated; the subject was never raised again.

At the end of our meeting, I drove the count back to Linz to the railway station and Henry returned to the hotel. It was close to midnight, but I decided to have a bowl of goulash at the local Army hotel. I parked my car and then noticed a man detach himself from the shadows in front of the hotel and move toward a bicycle. As he neared a street lamp, I had the odd sensation that he had been in the dining room of the Post Hotel that evening.

By now curfew was on and the streets were deserted, but this Austrian was obviously noting my license number. He finally bicycled down the dimly lit street. I drove after him and forced him to stop. I asked for his identification papers. He drew them from his inner pocket; he also very slowly drew a knife. At that point, I had my revolver out. I took his knife and put it in my car. His documents listed him as one Willy Froschl, living in Urfahr in the Soviet Zone. He claimed he spent most of his time in Linz where he stayed with a relative, and where he worked as a mechanic. I wrote down the address of this alleged relative on the Pfarrgasse, near the main city square of Linz, gave him his papers, and went into the Army hotel to find a street map of Linz.

It took me about ten minutes to drive to the Pfarrgasse and the street number I had written down. It was an ordinary Austrian apartment house about five stories high. The street was almost in total darkness; there were no lights in any of the windows.

I stepped into the entryway and examined, with my penlight, all the mailboxes for the name Froschl had given me. It was not there. By now it was almost one o'clock and downtown Linz was silent and empty.

Suddenly I became conscious of a car slowly coming in my direction. Standing in the gloom of the entranceway, I saw an old sedan draw up and stop opposite me. The car came to a halt; an arm and hand were extended from the rear window. I could see a pistol aimed at me; there were five crashing shots as I fell to the floor. The car pulled rapidly away from the sidewalk, its tires screaming as it turned into the square. I had no time to draw my own revolver and could only see the taillight as it sped away. Not a light was turned on in any of the apartments along the Pfarrgasse; Austrians in the 1950s, especially during the hours of darkness, were not eager to find out the causes of unexplained gunfire. I flashed my penlight over the woodwork and found three bullet holes, although I had counted five shots. It was unbelievable I had not been hit; perhaps it was intended that I simply be frightened.

Sweating freely, I found my car and started back to Wels. I decided not to report this incident; I did not want to risk being transferred back to the United States.

After a restless night, complicated by disturbing dreams, I woke up to find that Henry was already dressed, smoking a cigarette, and reading the newspaper. As I began shaving, Henry asked me if it had rained that night, as he had found my shirt, soaking wet, on the floor. I felt like saying, you should have seen my underwear.

Back in Pullach we reported on our meeting with the count in Wels. Henry and I had decided on the ride back to Bavaria that the case had to be written off. To our surprise and considerable dismay, the reply from Headquarters took the position that there was still further work to be done to resolve the matter. Apparently our hunger for Soviet cipher information was so great that our collective judgment was being clouded. Headquarters informed us they were sending out what they called the Pelican Team, which had scientific and medical methods to use in determining whether or not a person was reporting truthfully. We were to arrange for a safehouse where an extended interrogation could take place and for a complete physical, neurological, and psychological examination of the count at the U.S. Army hospital in Munich.

Wearily, we reported back that we would make the arrangements. What ensued in the next weeks turned the entire operation into a farce. The Pelican Team arrived from Headquarters. It consisted of three people, the principal one being a medical doctor, introduced to us as Dr. Clark. The other two members of the team were CIA staff officers, apparently accustomed to accompanying Dr. Clark, who had been experimenting for over a year with narcohypnosis, which he referred to as a truth process. The technique consisted of the use of sodium pentothal to put a person into a semiconscious condition, and then to hypnotize him. He would then be "regressed" to the time period in which we had an interest and the questioning would begin. Dr. Clark seemed confident that his technique would work.

It took some days to reach the count in Vienna, but once this was accomplished he agreed willingly to come to Munich and undergo certain tests. We found a safehouse and made the appropriate arrangements with the Army hospital in Munich. I had already developed some personal concern about Dr. Clark and came to the conclusion that I didn't like the man. He was about fifty years old, large and beefy, and gave a generally ill-kempt impression. He had dirty fingernails, something not usually found in doctors.

Henry and I shared the same misgivings about the Pelican Team. We agreed we should have a first-class polygraph operator standing by to take over. We contacted our station headquarters in Karlsruhe and asked for the immediate services of such a technician, and were told, as luck would have it, an experienced polygraph operator was in Munich, along with his equipment, doing some work for the Munich base. We were authorized to use him for the interrogation. Henry got in touch with this officer, named Jack, and had him come to the safehouse to prepare a room in which to carry out his examination.

When the Munich safehouse was ready, we sent for the count and immediately threw him into the Army hospital for a full medical workup. He was amiable about all this when we told him that the checkup was only to determine if he was in good health and that the subsequent examination would in no way be harmful to him. With the count in the hospital for two days of tests, we spent our time at the safehouse, not far from the hospital, and briefed Dr. Clark on all aspects of the case and the count himself. Separately, we were equally thorough in briefing Jack, on our almost certain doubts concerning Coloredo-Wels and our total misgivings about Dr. Clark. Jack responded that when he had his turn with the count, he would quickly resolve the matter. As for Dr. Clark, Jack had nothing but an ill-concealed contempt for the process, and for Headquarters even considering techniques of this sort. Henry and I fully shared Jack's opinions.

I received a phone call from the commandant of the Army hospital and was told that "our mutual friend" was in excellent health, that he had been through a variety of physical and neurological tests, and had come through them all with flying colors. He asked if I could pick him up that day, as the count was disorganizing the female staff of the hospital with his hand-kissing and flattery. We alerted Dr. Clark as well as Jack and made sure that their arrangements at the safehouse were complete.

As Henry and I drew up in front of the hospital, the count was just emerging from the front door, accompanied by a female Army doctor. She was an imposing sight, almost six feet tall and built like a linebacker. I met them at the bottom of the steps and stared in disbelief as the count smothered this woman's hand with kisses. Having made his adieus to the doctor, who turned out to be the chief psychiatrist at the hospital, he grandly swept by me with a regal nod and went to the car at the curb, where Henry waited. The lady psychiatrist, her face suffused with pleasure, turned to me and pronounced the patient fit and in every way competent, adding that she had never met a more gentlemanly or charming person in her life. Having blessed him with these remarks, she turned back to the hospital. I went to the car and we drove directly to the safehouse.

Once there, we made our introductions and Dr. Clark then began to tell what was going to take place. He described the use of sodium pentothal, and hypnosis; the count merely smiled and said that he was quite ready.

Once in the bedroom, which had been prepared for the exam, he was put completely at Dr. Clark's disposal. At the doctor's request we left the room and went downstairs to get some coffee and have a cigarette. For about an hour, there was nothing to be heard but an occasional padding sound of footsteps overhead and the murmur of unintelligible voices. Suddenly there was a shrill sound; I came alive and ran up to the bedroom to find the count kneeling on the bed, facing Dr. Clark, and speaking quickly and angrily. He said that if we didn't believe him, just put him on a return train to Vienna and we could forget the entire matter. As I watched, he flopped back upon the bed and into a deep sleep, snoring gently. The doctor turned to me and said that he had made some progress but would need quite a number of sessions to get at the core of the case. I could only nod in wonder at the bizarre situation we found ourselves in. Now, I was more than ever certain that we were being taken for a ride by the count, and in a way by the good doctor. I motioned for the doctor to come downstairs.

Henry was waiting. I told Dr. Clark that I was convinced we were dealing with a fraud and the sooner he was given a polygraph test, the sooner we could write finish to the case, get rid of the count, and get back to work. The doctor was strongly opposed to this and almost pleaded to be allowed a week in which to strip away the layers of "this psychological onion" and prove his technique. At this point, my back was up, I refused and told him that we would have an ordinary polygraph examination. I called Jack in and said the count would probably sleep for another hour and then he could put him on the box.

Per schedule, the count woke up ravenously hungry. We could do nothing further until he had consumed several GI hamburgers along with a bottle of Coke. He was led to the room where Jack had set up his equipment, and was told what the test consisted of and what was expected of him.

With the count "wired" Jack launched into the list of questions we had agreed upon, each answerable with a simple yes or no.

"Is your first name Friedrich?"

The count looked straight ahead and answered clearly, "Yes."

And so it went. There were about thirty questions which we had worked out, while waiting for Dr. Clark. After Jack had ended his questioning, we gave the count a few minutes' break and the tapes on the machine were adjusted. A second run was then made of the same list of questions. On conclusion, Jack unbuckled the count and Henry took him to another room. After they had left, Jack turned to me and simply said, "This guy's lying like a rug. He's been in the Imperial Hotel and he has worked as an informant for the Soviets but he has no knowledge of Soviet ciphers or contact with anyone who does."

After a few minutes, we went back to Coloredo-Wels. I told him it was clear he had been lying and trying to defraud and mislead us. He beamed and nodded. Controlling myself with some effort, I told him he would be given the return fare to Vienna but if he ever approached any American or allied intelligence service, we would denounce him to the Soviets as an American agent. At this he blanched. We drove him to Bahnhof and said that if he had any thought for his future, it would be in his interest to go back to Vienna and get lost.

Returning to Pullach, Henry and I framed a cable to Headquarters. Without bothering to wait for a reply, we made out a "burn notice." This was a routine intelligence procedure which was followed when an agent was found to be lying, deceitful, or fraudulent. The notice contained a photo and description and was sent to all American and allied intelligence services in Europe, stating that anyone who might approach them answering to the description should be thrown out.

We sent the Pelican Team back to Washington and were greatly relieved to see them go. I later learned that on his return flight from Frankfurt, Dr. Clark had become roaring drunk and had proceeded to assault the stewardesses on the Pan Am flight. He had to be restrained by male members of the crew. He was removed, by force, from the plane upon landing in New York and his services, such as they were, were terminated. Shortly after, we heard that the entire Pelican technique had been abandoned.

In hindsight, we had committed a cardinal sin for an intelligence officer; we had not so much been fooled by a prospective agent, but we had fooled ourselves. I realized that I had no right to educate myself in such an expensive fashion, a lesson I've never forgotten.

How to explain the five shots fired at me in Linz? I don't expect ever to have an exact answer for that incident, but can make only two surmises. One, that the gunman intended to kill me and missed with all five shots: several facts argue against this. The range from the weapon to me was not more than thirty feet and as a target I was a sitting duck in the entranceway of the apartment building. No one could have been so inept as to miss with all five shots. On the other hand, if one assumes it was a Soviet gunman, because the car went toward Urfahr in the Soviet-occupied zone, the more likely conclusion is that he meant the shots to go wild. Thinking back on the events that found me in Linz that night, they reasonably prove that the count was not a hostile Soviet agent; there was no reason for a Soviet move against me to protect him. The more plausible reason in my mind was that since I was an American intelligence officer, busy at work in Vienna and the American Zone of Austria, the Soviets merely wanted to scare me out of the area, and had found a chance opportunity in which to do it. It is thus more likely, to me, that the Soviet deliberately missed his target, than that he was so incompetent as to miss every shot. I am still stuck with the puzzle and probably always will be.

6 Headquarters

I was already deep in my fourth year of duty in Germany, scheduled to leave Pullach and return to CIA Headquarters in April of 1951. The Berlin airlift had come to an end, but the savage conflict in Korea continued with mounting casualties. There was great interest in the state of Soviet arms in East Germany. Our intelligence program there retained a high priority with the strategic planners in Washington. On the Soviet side, there was a great deal of real and notional movement of troops and transfer of Air Force units, designed to keep us both nervous and off-balance. In this they were successful. The CIA and the military intelligence services nevertheless had to keep book on all Soviet military elements, which required a constant replenishment of agent networks in East Germany and meticulous attention to the courier lines and methods of communication between our agents and various headquarters in West Germany.

My family and I were ready to go when the time came to leave Munich for Genoa, there to sail on the old Italian ship *Saturnia*. I was drained.

The voyage from Genoa to New York was absolute luxury. There were only twenty-two first-class passengers on the sailing, designed to accommodate about four hundred people. The crew members, stewards, and table waiters were in constant attendance, providing service that has long since not been available. I did absolutely nothing except sprawl in a deck chair, gaze at the sea, and wait for the next sumptuous meal.

In the early summer of 1951 I reported back to Headquarters in Washington and then found a place to live. Next came the routine administrative processing of a returning officer. After my medical examinations, I was due for a polygraph test. I thought ruefully of the count and made an appointment.

I knew basically what to expect. The more serious questions dealt with possible homosexuality, any hint of fraud against the government, and any indication of misrepresentation in official dispatches or misuse of funds. And, of course, any possible connections with the KGB, the Soviet secret police. The test ran about an hour, with two tape runs. The first one was set aside and the second one taped. When comparisons were made, my reactions to the same questions were checked to determine any evasion or contradiction on my part. I passed the test and was sent back to my holding office.

CIA Headquarters was near the Reflecting Pool by the Lincoln Memorial. Some of its buildings were located near a structure which had been a brewery; there were a few permanent government buildings perched on a hill nearby, where the director had his offices. The Office of Special Operations, to which I was assigned, was housed in one of the temporary offices; I reported to L Building, long since demolished. I was named an assistant to the chief of the Foreign Intelligence (FI) Staff (which post I myself held some twenty years later). As an assistant officer on that staff, I was in daily contact with its chief, Eric Timm, who died prematurely in the late 1950s. He was a fine and able intelligence officer; I learned a great deal from him.

Eric had been an FBI agent during the war, stationed in Spain. During World War II, Spain had close ties to the Axis powers, the Germans and the Italians. Although technically neutral in the war, Spain provided a congenial atmosphere for every kind of espionage and counterespionage activity. Timm demonstrated his flair for running complicated intelligence operations, and taking me under his wing, passed on to me his accumulated tricks and techniques that enabled a good counterespionage officer to keep his feet under him. Timm's drawling good humor and relaxed manner belied a razor-sharp mind and the kind of dedication to his country and government that, in recent years, seems almost to have gone out of style.

The work on the FI Staff was to review, constantly, all CIA positive intelligence operations worldwide. Thus, for a few months, I had an abrupt immersion into the vitals of the CIA and its work abroad. Apparently, Timm was studying me during this period. One day he called me to his office and told me that for some time there had been a need for a chief of operations in a division which concerned itself with Soviet matters exclusively. He thought I was the person for the job. I was assigned to the Soviet Russia (SR) Division as chief of operations; as such, I was the number-three man under the chief of the division and his deputy. I regretted leaving Timm's staff, but the idea of getting into active operations was too tempting to turn down. The SR Division was headed by an energetic, fast-moving intelligence officer of considerable ability, who was due shortly to go overseas and be replaced by a much less innovative and active person. Presumably this was one reason for my transfer to this division.

The SR Division was an organization whose form and status in the Office of Special Operations (OSO) generated many arguments. For this to make sense, it must be realized that OSO was composed of a number of staffs and geographic (or area, or operational) divisions. The staffs in general provided specialized assistance and advice to the divisions and to the chief of OSO. The geographic divisions were responsible for their assigned areas of the world and, in addition to their headquarters complement, carried out their duties through field stations located in the principal cities of their geographic area. These divisions exercised command authority over all CIA personnel assigned to the field stations under their control. In those early years, operations against or into the Soviet Union were necessarily based in or were run through countries lying outside the USSR. This fact put the agency's Soviet operations in almost every case under the authority of a geographic division not fundamentally concerned with the Soviet Union itself. The SR Division had its own personnel but it did not have field stations of its own. This organizational awkwardness was not solved during my first tour at CIA Headquarters and only after the agency matured a great deal did a rational and workable relationship evolve out of the differing charters and objectives of the SR Division alongside the other area divisions.

I didn't see much of my wife and daughters in the next few months as I plunged into back files, learning about the activities and programs of the division. At the same time, I was getting up-to-date on operations underway at the moment and familiarizing myself with the people who made up SR, noting what kind of intelligence officers they were and the extent of their capabilities.

It wasn't until late winter of 1951-52 that I felt ready to make changes or additions to the programs being pursued by the division. I had found that it was almost totally occupied in a program of parachuting Russian-speaking DPs, such as Ukrainians and Byelorussians, into those parts of the USSR where we had reason to believe there existed pockets of partisan resistance to Soviet authority. The objectives of these parachuted teams were almost hopeless from the outset. Two members were furnished with forged documents and false cover stories (legends) which were, it was intended, designed to enable individual agents to find jobs, places to live, and otherwise establish themselves "legally" within the USSR. If this could be accomplished, we hoped that the agent would, by recruiting friends and relatives, put together a network of collaborating anti-Soviet elements who could provide economic, political, or military intelligence from within the Soviet Union. This was also true of the Baltic areas; there were many Baltic displaced persons willing to go back by parachute to their homeland to work for intelligence purposes among their friends and relatives. However, a close review of our operational files led me to one additional conclusion: that practically every one of our parachuted agents was under Soviet control and was reporting back to us under duress. The KGB was writing their messages and feeding back information they wanted us to have, which was either false, misleading or confusing. We therefore had almost no assets, in terms of agents, within the borders of the USSR or the Baltic states.

These bankrupt efforts were going on at a real cost in lives, manpower, and money, and as an endeavor was obviously a failure, practically and philosophically. It was spectacular as we watched our courageous Polish aircrews taking off on their dangerous missions over the Ukraine at night to drop agents into the winter snows, and then to wait for the agent radios to come on the air. But in most cases the danger and control indicators appeared early in their traffic to us. These danger and control indicators were important both to us at Headquarters and to the agent inside the USSR. They could be employed in secret writing communications, but in these early years were particularly designed to be used with WT (wireless telegraph) agents, who reported exclusively by radio and who were guided from Headquarters in the same manner. The safety or control indicator could be the inclusion of a particular name in a message or the misspelling of a certain word or any other agreed-upon signal that would indicate the agent was under KGB control. Brave men, lonely fates. We were also using small but exceedingly fast patrol boats to go up the Baltic Sea to deposit agents ashore. Practically all of these were also turning out to be tragic losses.

While it was not practicable to shut down this particular activity at once and totally, it was clear that we must develop alternate methods of gaining access to the USSR and to the intelligence we needed.

As all of this was going on, we were still trying to build up officer strength in the SR Division. Some American military officers, who had been in Moscow during my visits there, were becoming available as they returned from their tours. Several of these officers were recruited for details to the CIA and to the SR Division. These were people whom I knew fairly well, and in whom I came to have great confidence, with one exception. Most of them spoke Russian fluently. Some of them are still on duty with the CIA; others have retired.

One of my early goals on becoming chief of the SR operations division was to bring this kind of intelligence operation to an end as a program. Because of the kind of mindless momentum programs of this kind acquire after a period of time, it turned out to be several years before this kind of a program could be done away with. It was clear that we had to develop alternate means of access to the USSR and to the intelligence we needed.

The one exception to whom I referred was an officer who lied about certain parts of his professional duties in such a way as to have almost disastrous results on an important agent of ours inside the USSR. This officer was discharged from the service.

One day in 1952 my phone rang; I was told a person had walked in off the street to apply for employment. He spoke Russian and wanted to work against the Soviets. The caller wanted me to talk with this volunteer. If I thought he was capable, I was to hire him and start his security processing. It was thus that I met George, who subsequently carried on some of the most significant work that we performed in handling and dealing with Soviet intelligence officers. George came into my office in J Building. We shook hands, measuring each other and coming to the mutual conclusion that we were going to get along. George was to become my best friend in or out of the agency since that day. A bear of a man, he spoke native Russian as well as French, Italian, and later German. He was and is a man of enormous energy and determination, totally dedicated to the work we were carrying on. He is several years my senior, but our friendship, both personally and professionally, has become stronger as the years have passed. We shared some time in Europe together, but our paths diverged when I was assigned to the Far East area and George remained in European affairs.

I put George in charge of our Far East branch of the SR Division as at that time we were doing some boating of agents from Japan to the island of Sakhalin, to report on several important Soviet military establishments. There we would put agents ashore from PT boats and pick them up later for return and debriefing.

In the spring of 1952 we received from the Pentagon a requirement of major priority. The Soviets had almost completed, at Provideniya Bay in the Soviet Far East, an airfield with an unusually long runway. The Pentagon needed to know if, upon completion, the airfield's runway would be thick enough to bear the weight of the size of bomber needed to carry an atom bomb. In those years the only way we knew of loading a bomb was to dig a pit, lower the bomb into it, roll the plane over the pit, and hoist the heavy and ungainly bomb up into the aircraft. The requirement came to two major items: determine the thickness of the concrete of the airfield and determine if there was a pit at either end of it.

The marching and countermarching of Soviet forces in East Germany kept us and our allies in Europe in a state of constant tension and alertness. The possibility that the Soviets were acquiring a nuclear capability in eastern Siberia took on an importance that required immediate action on our part. This intelligence task was passed to the CIA. The requirement came to the SR Division and landed on my desk.

We talked the problem over in the division and excluded the possibility of an air operation; the Soviet radar defenses were so complete and effective that we didn't feel that we could spook a plane from Alaska across the Bering Strait and get a team in *and* out. Also, in those days, the Soviets were shooting down reconnaissance aircraft. Our research on this target led to the conclusion that the only feasible way of approaching the airfield was from the sea. To no one's great surprise, we learned that the Navy ran a submarine patrol off the Soviet coast in that area, staying well beyond the twelve-mile limit, maintaining a ship-watching intelligence coverage of maritime traffic between the northern shores of the Soviet Union and Vladivostok. Each submarine was on duty for one month and was then replaced by another.

We went to the Navy to enlist their help in launching an agent team to the shoreline from their patrol submarine, retrieving it upon completion of the mission. This would involve rubber boats, silent outboard motors, and special equipment for the men to measure the depth of the concrete and to photograph the field. The Navy agreed, and the operation was on.

From our pool of DP agent candidates, after a careful winnowing process, we selected a team of four Russians. They volunteered for the mission, and our staff psychologists felt they could get along in the confinement of a submarine. The four-month training period was intense and thorough. Much of it was done in cold water near an island off the coast of Maine; some aboard a sub based in Key West, Florida. The collapsible rubber boats were designed and fabricated and the silent-running outboard motors were perfected.

The logistical and administrative backup to this operation was extensive and complex. We had to establish secure communications links between Headquarters, Pearl Harbor, several points in Alaska and some of the offshore islands near Alaska. The agent teams had to be outfitted and prepared for every contingency we could anticipate. They carried radio equipment to be used in short bursts ("squirts") to keep us informed of their progress or to advise of difficulties they encountered. There were drills to familiarize them with life aboard a sub at sea. As a last wrinkle, they had practice in what was called periscope towing, in which the rubber boat of the team was towed by a connection to the periscope tube of the submarine, while it was slowly running submerged. The sub was to tow the team close to shore, at low speed, until the sea became too shallow. The team would then cast off and go on their own to shore.

The agents were a disparate group, linked only by their common languages, Russian and Ukrainian, but there were no evident conflicts among them. As no one person seemed to emerge as a natural leader, one would have to be appointed. We feared this might lead to some resentment, but luckily nothing developed to endanger the integrity of the team as a whole.

Two of our own case officers accompanied the team on the submarine, although not on the landing itself. They were Peter and Ed, always good friends. Finally, personnel were dispatched to the points in Alaska, where the communications net had been laid down, and to Honolulu for liaison with the Navy at Pearl Harbor. The team was flown commercially to Hawaii and were put up in a safehouse until the sub was ready to start its patrol.

The day arrived and the mission began. Our own radio links came to life. Communication was severely restricted, as radio silence was routinely imposed by the Navy. Tensely we waited for any kind of word. We heard almost nothing from the sub from the time it left Pearl Harbor and approached the Aleutian chain until it was well on its way back to Honolulu about a month later.

The agent team was launched in its rubber boat one calm moonless night and the submarine was brought up until its decks were barely awash. The rubber boat was inflated, equipment and silent-running outboard motors installed, and four courageous men pushed off toward the dark shore of Siberia, guided only by the dim light of compasses, hurried glimpses of a maritime chart, and their knowledge of the shoreline gained through the intensive training period. The submarine was to rendezvous with the agent team during the hours of darkness the following night, aided by a radar reflective panel which the team would rig on the rubber boat. During daylight, the team, when it was not making its reconnaissance of the end of the runways of the airfield, was to turn the rubber boat over near the shoreline, spread a camouflage cloth over it, and remain concealed underneath until night. Aided by good luck and their own courage, the four men came through the experience intact, and succeeded in getting themselves picked up the following night by the submarine. From then on, it was a matter of straight boredom as the team played cards and chess for the remainder of the time the submarine had to remain on patrol.

Days and weeks went by. We had only "squirt," or very high-speed radio transmissions, now and then, reporting that all was well. On the homeward leg, as the patrol was returning to Pearl Harbor, a greater volume of radio traffic became possible. The mission was a success! The agent dispatch went off as planned; they had learned the concrete airstrip was not thick enough to support carrying of nuclear weapons then being developed. Both ends of the field had been reconnoitered. There was no pit at either end. We arranged a rousing welcome-home party and a special aircraft was to fly the team directly from Pearl Harbor to

Washington. Everyone was elated and in high spirits except Peter and Ed; through a mixup in commissary orders by the submarine crew, the usual supply of meat, vegetables, and fruit had been only partially loaded and there had been a steady diet of rice and spaghetti for the last two weeks of the trip.

During my tenure as chief of operations, it was the last "forced entry" mission that we took on. The entire affair ended in Washington at the home of one of the Naval officers who had been our liaison during this operation. This party was a wild affair, involving several amiable Naval types and their opposite numbers in the CIA. It was a rousing, if drunken, conclusion to a successful operation. As the Navy signal says: "Well done."

7 The Soviet Agent

The defection of a Soviet intelligence officer to a CIA station abroad always and instantly creates a condition of excitement, activity, and acute tension. The act of defection in itself can take various forms. A Soviet officer might just walk into an American Embassy, identify himself to the Marine guard, and ask to be put in touch with the embassy security officer. Or, he could telephone a CIA officer in the embassy directly, one he had perhaps met at a diplomatic function. Then again, there have been occasions when a Soviet would stroll by the car of an American known to work in the embassy and drop a note on the front seat, proposing a meeting place and time. The first contact, unless it takes place within the embassy itself, is closely monitored by other station members.

The meeting might be made on a street corner, in a hotel lobby, or in a small out-of-the-way restaurant. The Soviet would at once be taken to another location, such as a hotel room or an apartment rented solely for the occasion. The purpose would be to transfer the meeting to a location unknown to the Soviet and minimize the chance of observation by *his* colleagues in the event that his approach to the CIA was a provocation.

Once in an environment controlled by us, the Soviet would be asked for his documentation and then his reasons for contacting us. Action would be taken to verify his identification, and cable traffic would begin to flow from the station, reporting the meeting and attempting to establish the bona fides of the Soviet. Even before his bona fides could be checked, it would be determined if there were any possibility of the Soviet returning to his own residentura (station), remaining under our control, unknown to his superiors, to collect intelligence and documents for delivery to us. This was usually a rare occurrence. More normally, this first contact would wind up with the defector being moved to a more durable safehouse, where we could begin to establish his credentials and determine the scope of his intelligence knowledge.

Of all Soviet officials, officers of the KGB (the Soviet secret police), and GRU (the military counterpart of the KGB) knew exactly what their defection meant. In almost all cases there would be wives, children, or parents left behind in the USSR. It has long been standard practice for married KGB and GRU officers to be "persuaded" to leave one or more of their children in the Soviet Union for schooling, when the parents are assigned abroad. These children are a form of hostage. During the course of training Soviet officers were repeatedly told Western intelligence services were penetrated by the KGB and that any officers who defected to, say, the CIA, would be under observation wherever he went, and that one day, sooner or later, the KGB would get to him.

Yet they came. Motives varied from fear of disciplinary punishment for some infraction of their own regulations, to the worthiest motives of political maturity that simply drove the individual officer to abandon and flee the Communist system, to reject their homeland.

One such KGB officer, under cover in Tokyo as a Soviet Embassy press officer, Yuri Rastovorov, came to us one cold and snowy evening late in 1953. He contacted us through his English-language teacher, an elderly White Russian lady, who had lived in Tokyo since 1921. She knew some Americans, who were in touch with our station in Tokyo; Yuri came into our hands and the procedures described above were followed. After the preliminary debriefing, he was flown with two case officers to Okinawa, where we had a secure holding area. His credibility established, he went by military aircraft to a safehouse near Washington, D.C., to be "wrung out."

Yuri had much information to offer. As it emerged and came under scrutiny by our own analysts, more and more we were sure that he was not a hostile agent, but was telling the truth; his information was substantial and correct. As with most defecting Soviet intelligence officers, he had a wealth of knowledge that went far beyond his immediate field of work.

A Soviet intelligence officer, without regard to rank, is a very special and privileged member of Soviet officialdom. He can work and deal with foreigners as most Soviet citizens and officials cannot; after all, it is his business to study individual foreigners, especially Americans, for any evidence of weakness of will or purpose and to determine their recruitability. Because they are members of this elite group within Soviet foreign colonies abroad, they often associate only with their intelligence colleagues within their own mission. Because of the limited nature of their social contacts, Soviet intelligence officers tend to gossip among themselves regarding their work. On periodic leaves to Moscow, they would mingle socially with their peers and learn from them, through professional gossip, as well as from other friends and relatives, much information which normally would not come to them but which would be of interest to us. They would talk about economic matters, agriculture, military preparations, training, and new equipment under development.

Yuri was no exception to this. He produced a wealth of information under intensive but friendly interrogation that extended over several months. Our analysts were able to piece together a revealing mosaic of politics, plans, attitudes toward Western countries, and other official matters far beyond his normal intelligence work.

Within the CIA there were two different schools of thought on this category of person. One school was willing to believe the defector, after testing, and accept him as a willing and valuable agent. The view of the counterintelligence staff, on the other hand, was that there was literally no such thing as a Soviet defector and that a person claiming to be one should always be assumed to be a Soviet agent on a hostile mission. The doctrinaire, and faulty, bias of this staff for many years caused grievous harm to our intelligence work abroad, as well as to individuals, American and foreign.

In the case of Yuri and other defectors described in this book, the first viewpoint prevailed. Subsequent events and other defectors have confirmed his value. It is interesting to note that most of the officers who came to us in those years were in their late twenties or early thirties. They were complete products of the Soviet system, and had contact with foreigners only for professional reasons. They had little idea of what kind of fate awaited them once they had made the break. They were essentially defenseless, subject to fears and anxieties about their futures. They would brood about their families back in the Soviet Union; some would show great despondency; some would turn to drink to release themselves from feelings of guilt. A very small number would elect to redefect and would turn themselves in to the Soviet Embassy in Washington. Those who did so would be returned to Soviet control and to a fate which we could only imagine.

On our side, we would not hold a defector against his wishes. This policy made it necessary to keep him at arm's length, even after he was in the United States for an extended period, to see if he could adjust to life there, without his family and relatives. After months of debriefing, as in the case of Yuri, the defector would be ready for resettlement, which would include the acquisition of a new name and a new personal background. Thus disguised, the defector would be given assistance by the agency in acquiring whatever language skill he needed to make his way in the United States. Each would be watched closely and given help when needed. In most cases, each of them would retain a contractual relationship with the CIA because of the assistance they could give us from time to time with regard to subsequent defectors. Yuri spoke English well, having studied it in Moscow during his intelligence training. He married an American girl (a secretary in the agency) and started a successful commercial venture in Maryland, still retaining a consultant contract with the CIA.

In December of 1954 in Vienna, Austria, another KGB officer defected to us. The circumstances of his defection were influenced by the fact that he was at a drinking party with other officers during the holiday season. During the evening, his pent-up resentment against his superiors caused him to break away from the party and find his way to the duty officer at the American Embassy. He eventually had a similar experience as Yuri, but found it more difficult to adapt. He had periods of despondency and long drinking bouts by himself, but after a few years, he made peace with the world; now with a new identity, he is well established in the Washington area, has an American wife and child, and has made the transition from a Soviet intelligence officer in hiding to a respected member of a nearby suburb.

During 1953 we had another brief but very profitable relationship with a Soviet intelligence officer. This lasted several months, until the officer, finishing his tour of duty in Vienna, returned that year, under no suspicion, to his headquarters in Moscow. This man, Ivan, was well placed in his residentura in the Soviet Embassy in Vienna. Through a series of personal meetings which extended over the remaining part of his tour in Vienna, we had a number of highly productive sessions with him in safehouses in different sections of Vienna. Through Ivan, we were able to get a complete picture of the Soviet intelligence network in Austria, both in Vienna and in the American Zone. Because of the importance of this Soviet contact, I sent George to Vienna to handle Ivan and carry on contact with him.

Back in the SR (Soviet Russia) Division in Washington, I set up a small staff to support George in handling the information produced by Ivan and to provide George with everything he might need to exploit the relationship properly. At Headquarters we found ourselves hard put, in a very short while, to use or disseminate the intelligence which Ivan was producing. It was varied and in considerable volume, and we had to devise a means of passing this information in Washington to the U.S. Military, the State Department, and the White House, which would avoid pinpointing the sensitive fact that we had a single, high-level source, well-placed in the Soviet hierarchy. We contrived a way of doing this without compromising him. Conversely, this technique was not possible with regard to Oleg Penkovskiy, principally because of British style and involvement. All of his very sensitive intelligence was processed under one code word; it was clear we had a single high-quality source within Soviet officialdom. When Ivan went back to Moscow, George returned to Headquarters to prepare for an upcoming tour in Berlin.

In one particular case, with no doubt as to the reliability of the reports we were disseminating to our intelligence consumers in the Pentagon and State Department, we came across one bit of information which had quite an impact on the American defense posture. The report itself was not long; I recall it being eleven or twelve lines. It seems that the Soviets had started production on a new model battle tank; the information concerned the thickness of the frontal and side armor and the angle at which it was presented to an opposing tank. A new and higher velocity cannon had been installed in this model. This report caused such a stir in the Pentagon that our own production line of tanks underway at the time was halted, and new designs were made. These included thicker armor for our own tanks, and in turn the installation of a higher velocity and larger bore cannon. Subsequent intelligence reports from a variety of sources showed that

Ivan was accurate and was the first to provide this information at that time critical to the U.S. Army.

Having a source of this kind in the Soviet residentura itself led to some unusual and even amusing events. In discussing with Ivan the composition of the residentura, we asked him to identify all those who were intelligence officers and give us a verbal picture of their work, strengths, and weaknesses, and of course, their duties. He was thorough in carrying out this assignment, and in the course of one evening meeting at the safehouse, which was on the Berggasse in the Seventh Bezirk of Vienna, he began to dwell on one junior officer in the residentura, a Lieutenant Kostikov, who was always in hot water. He was constantly in trouble with his superiors; everything he did seemed to backfire. Ivan had to tell us of Lieutenant Kostikov's latest disaster the previous evening.

Kostikov, using one of the residentura's cars, had driven to Salzburg in the American Zone to meet one of his Austrian agents. The meeting was to take place in a small farm village, south of Salzburg, along the Salzach River. The actual meeting place was in a Gasthaus, the local bierstube. It developed that Kostikov and his agent sat at one of the tables in the dining room to drink beer and carry on their business. Kostikov was in civilian clothes; he spoke German fluently. As the evening wore on and after numerous steins of beer, they switched to schnapps and the business talk dwindled. Kostikov excused himself to go to the men's room, where he took off his wristwatch, put it on the windowsill and soaked his face in cold water. He forgot the watch in the washroom and went back to the table where the Austrian was sitting with glazed eyes. After a moment or two Kostikov noticed that his watch was missing. At once he accused the Austrian agent of stealing his watch, reached across the table, pulled him from his chair, and proceeded to knock him to the floor. Immediately, the Gasthaus was in an uproar. The proprietor called the Austrian police. The two men were fighting each other in a drunken way when the police arrived. Meanwhile, someone had found the watch and returned it to the proprietor, who gave it to Kostikov. After the disagreement had been described to the police and after talking to the two men, the Polizei realized they had a Soviet "diplomat," whereupon they excused themselves and suggested that Kostikov go back to his hotel. Still furious at being made to look foolish, Kostikov said he would drive to Vienna that night and would report to his embassy the rude treatment he had received from the Austrians.

The police left. Amid considerable confusion, Kostikov went to his car and began the drive back toward Salzburg and the road to Vienna. To reach the Salzburg turnoff, Kostikov had to negotiate a narrow wooden bridge over the Salzach River—he didn't make it. He drove off the bridge into about three feet of water at the shallow side of the river. Unhurt, but trapped in his car in the swift-moving, icy water, Kostikov sat there bawling for help. Someone heard him and called the police—two policemen came upon the scene, the same two who had reported to the first call at the Gasthaus. A farmer was roused. He harnessed two horses and, with help from several members of the village, managed to haul the partially submerged car and a very wet, cold, and indignant Kostikov to dry land. The damaged car had to be left behind, while a soaked Kostikov was accompanied to the railway station to await an early morning train to Vienna. Upon his arrival, he was called in by his chief, after receipt of a note from the Austrian police, requesting that Kostikov not be sent into other than the Soviet Zone of Austria.

According to Ivan, the detailed story had circulated rapidly through the residentura and Kostikov had been restricted to his office and billet until further notice. His ultimate fate we learned a short time later from Ivan. He had been transferred permanently back to Moscow, where he was assigned to administrative duties and reduced in rank. Presumably, his personal raincloud went back to Moscow with him.

By the summer of 1953 we had arranged, for the first time, for one of our case officers to be posted to our embassy in Moscow. He was sent there for the specific purpose of selecting and preparing deaddrops in the event that Ivan, whom we knew was preparing to return to the USSR, would agree to continue to work with us.

This officer, who was my selection and, I must say, one of my more outstanding failures, was provided with an elaborate means of communication with us. In early summer he advised us that he had found, per instructions, three clean deaddrops. These drops could conceal canisters of film or oilskin pouches to contain documents. These would be retrieved in Moscow at a later date, by other people.

After several cable exchanges, he gave a minute description of these drops, where they were and how they could be found. Ivan was sent back to Moscow in the spring on *komandirovka*—temporary duty. We told him the locations of the deaddrops and he agreed to check them out to see if he thought they were suitable. We counted on him to be the final judge on that point.

His first meeting with us at the safehouse on the Berggasse, upon his return to Venna in late spring, was a desolate one. He came into the room, and, after his usual friendly greetings, simply slumped down in a chair and said bitterly to us all, "What are you trying to do? Are you trying to kill me?"

We wondered what he was talking about and asked what was wrong. He replied, "I went to those deaddrops you gave me and in each case I found them to be totally inaccessible and completely unusable. It would have been suicide to have tried to use them. What are your people in Moscow doing? Are they working for you or the KGB?" We were dumbfounded.

After hurried consultation with Washington, I offered to go to Moscow to check this out myself and find what had gone wrong. My request was denied. I knew too much to risk going into the Soviet Union. As it turned out, a good friend in the State Department, who had served in Moscow before, contrived to find a TDY (temporary duty) assignment to occasion a visit. He agreed to check the drops, a competent man for this kind of work.

We anxiously awaited his return and met him as quickly as we could after his landing in Zurich, Switzerland. This man was a pro. He confirmed everything that Ivan had told us; the drops were impossible. They were badly described and hazardous in the extreme. We then began an investigation of our officer in Moscow. He was a bachelor and had immediately bedded down with his maid, a KGB major, and had obviously taken little care in following our instructions. His work was not only worthless, but much had been fabricated. We had Ivan's safety in mind, and he was preparing to return to Moscow on leave.

We had our own man recalled on an urgent basis to Washington, where I recommended his dismissal from the service. This was one of only two occasions where I made such a recommendation. This one stuck and he was dismissed.

In the fall of 1953 when it came time for Ivan to go back permanently to the USSR, we discussed with him the possibility of continuing collaboration with us in Moscow. He agonized over this for some time and at a subsequent meeting told us he couldn't continue his connection with us; it was too risky and he must think of his wife and children. He did say that the next time he was posted outside of Moscow or the USSR, either in the Eastern Bloc or the West, he would be willing to contact us. Accordingly, we equipped him with the means of communicating with us should he again be sent out. He memorized our instructions and, in addition, made cryptic marks in his notebook to refresh his memory, if needed. Our last meeting was one of friendship and sentiment. We were sorry to see Ivan go and I believe he was sorry to break the relationship, which, as he put it, was a way of allowing him to act like a human being, not just as a creature of the Soviet state.

We never heard from Ivan again. That is, not to my knowledge.

8 No One is Immune

In 1953 there was an episode that indicated the state of mind of some Americans at the embassy in Moscow during the early 1950s. The cold war was especially bitter and Americans in Europe, and certainly in Moscow, were aware of the tense and potentially dangerous situation that existed between the Western nations and the USSR.

Since the founding of the CIA in 1947 and until 1953 it had been State Department policy that our Clandestine Service would not have a representative at the embassy in Moscow. The reasons given were that, if discovered, it would be a great embarrassment to the ambassador and to the U.S. government, dangerous indeed for the CIA representative and, by spinoff, to the other Americans in the embassy. We had made one effort after another with the State Department, but with no success. Now, however, in the summer of 1953, we could argue that the importance of the information that Ivan might be able to provide us with after his return made it timely to reopen the matter. Subsequently we learned that Ivan was not willing to maintain clandestine contact with us in Moscow, but we felt at this time that we should at least make plans to handle him should he agree.

We staffed out the problem within the agency and secured the director's approval to raise the subject yet again with the State Department. We all felt that the benefits of working Ivan "inside" clearly outweighed the risks. We were unanimous on one point: we would not jeopardize him if it became too dangerous or if he refused contact with us.

Our ambassador in Moscow was George Kennan, who had arrived in the spring of 1953. I was authorized to begin discussions with the State Department at an appropriate level on this matter. I dealt at this time with Charles Bohlen, who was the assistant secretary of state for East European Affairs. He was reluctant and eventually came down against the proposal. He did agree to our sending someone (me) to London to see Kennan late in June, when the ambassador would be there briefly on personal business. The implication here was that if Ambassador Kennan concurred, we might go ahead; otherwise the matter was closed.

After some telegraphic exchanges with Moscow, I was told to meet the ambassador in London on 26 June, a date that stays in my mind because it is my birthday. I took the night flight from New York to London on 25 June and checked into a hotel. We were to meet the next day. The purpose of the meeting was known to the ambassador and we merely were to refine the pros and cons of the proposal. He had not expressed a position one way or another at that point. We expected to complete our business in one afternoon and I made a reservation on the night flight from London to New York the same evening.

The next morning I checked in with our London chief-of-station and filled him in on the purpose of my visit. I then went to keep my two o'clock appointment with Ambassador Kennan at Claridges Hotel, where he was staying. We retreated to a quiet corner of a writing room and I outlined our proposal and the need for it. After extended discussion, he said he thought it imprudent for such an assignment to be made. He couldn't agree with it and I should tell the agency, as well as to report that fact to the State Department.

This was a great disappointment to me. However, during the conversation I had noticed that the ambassador was very tense and nervous. He was pale, his hands trembled, and he seemed to have much on his mind. At the end of our talk, he said there was something he wanted to ask of the agency.

By this time I was only thinking of making my return flight that evening, but sat there further. The ambassador's hand was quivering and his anxiety was obvious; he stood up and slowly paced back and forth in the alcove in which we sat. "There is something you must do for me. I have here a letter"—and he then handed me an envelope; I noted that it was addressed to Pope Pius. "I have a very pessimistic view of our immediate future with the Soviets, particularly at the diplomatic level. I want you to get this letter to Allen Dulles and make sure it is passed, by secure means to the Pope in Rome." My questioning look brought the following explanation: "I fear that there is a good possibility that I will wind up someday before long on the Soviet radio. I may be forced to make statements that would be damaging to American policy. This letter will show the world that I am under duress and am not making statements under my own free will. The letter to the Pope will let him make public my position and the true situation there."

I was astounded at the grimness with which these words were delivered. But I was in no way prepared for the following: "I understand that CIA has some form of pill that a person could use to kill himself instantly. Is this right?"

I thought back to the days when we were parachuting agents into the USSR and recalled that we offered each outgoing agent an L-pill, as we called them, L standing for lethal. These were small glass vials which could be put in the mouth. One bite through the glass and the wire mesh protecting the contents would release cyanide inside the mouth and bring on death within a matter of seconds. I looked at Ambassador Kennan and wondered if he was really serious about this. He said, "Yes, I think that I must have two of these." I interrupted to say that we had such a pill and I would pass his request to Allen Dulles upon my return to Washington. I told him we would send them by diplomatic pouch. He could arrange for their receipt at the Moscow end of the diplomatic courier run. He thanked me warmly for my cooperation, but I could see the man was still nervous beyond comfort. We parted on this note and I caught the evening plane to New York.

The next day, at Headquarters, I went at once to my immediate superior in the Clandestine Service and was taken to see Allen Dulles, where I repeated my conversation with the ambassador, regarding both the letter to the Pope and the L-pill.

There was a long silence in the director's office at this point. Obviously this was a shock to those present, but it was agreed that these things could not be denied him. I was authorized to get the necessary items and pouch them to Moscow.

Later we received a cryptic cable through diplomatic channels that Kennan had received the pills. Shortly thereafter, he went to Germany on an official visit, where he made a speech with strong critical reference to the USSR. This speech resulted in his being declared *persona non grata* on the spot. He never returned to Moscow from Berlin.

Ambassador Kennan finally came back to Washington from

Europe. I made an appointment to see him and asked what had happened to the L-pills. He told me, with a curious smile—an obviously much more relieved and composed man than when I had last seen him—"I have already flushed them down the toilet."

At the time and in the years since, I have always thought that the actions of Ambassador Kennan were the actions of a very brave man. During the early 1950s the CIA was aware that the Soviets were experimenting with drugs intended to destroy a person's natural inhibitions and controls. The topic was frequently discussed in the agency and in the State Department. In the cold-war atmosphere of the time, Kennan saw himself as a likely target for a Soviet effort along this line. An extremely competent and knowledgeable scholar of the Soviets, he held no illusions concerning the kind of actions they might take if they felt their interests required it. Nevertheless, he went back to that environment of danger and was prepared to take his own life rather than let himself be used by the Soviets in a manner degrading or shameful to the United States. I personally have never had any doubt that he would have used the L-pill had he felt that his control over himself, within the USSR, was being stripped away.

9 CIA Civilian

All during these Washington years I remained an officer of the Regular Army with rank of lieutenant colonel. I had tried in the summer of 1950, while I was at Pullach, to resign my commission and accept employment with the CIA. While my letter of resignation was on its way to the Pentagon, the Korean War broke out, at the end of June. The war brought about the involuntary recall to duty of many reserve officers. Army policy was not to accept resignations from regular officers as long as reserves were being called. I was informed of this by cable, but was also told the Army would be willing to continue my detail to the CIA, which was my status in the summer of 1953, when the Korean fighting ended in an armistice.

The Pentagon notified me that I was being assigned to the Command and General Staff School at Fort Leavenworth, Kansas, in the fall, a routine progression in an officer's education. That would have ended my detail with the agency. Upon return to Washington from Pullach in 1951, I had been called in by General Walter Bedell-Smith, then director of the CIA, for an interview. As a Regular Army officer himself, he quizzed me sharply as to my reasons for wanting to resign and reviewed my record since 1945, with which he was obviously already familiar. Although my resignation could not be accepted then, he said that if I still wanted to join the CIA as a civilian at a future time when the reserve officers were being released from active duty, I should reapply. Meanwhile, I could remain in my present position.

In 1953, with this interview in mind, I asked for an interview with the new director, Allen Dulles. The agency had already made me a firm offer of an appointment at a senior grade.

My conversation with Mr. Dulles was short, but purposeful. We talked briefly about the state of world affairs and our own efforts against the USSR in the SR Division. He had a copy of my original resignation letter before him and the reply from the Secretary of the Army, giving the reasons why this could not be accepted. He asked if I wanted to resubmit this letter to the Pentagon and I replied that I did.

I was separated from the rolls of the Regular Army on September 1 of that year and went back to work at the agency the following day. The actual resignation consisted mainly of clearing out personal files and the closing out of my pay and allowance account, and receiving my honorable discharge. I signed up with the Army Reserve Corps and carried my rank of lieutenant colonel over to that echelon. Thus, I became a civilian for the first time since enlisting in the Army as a private soldier in 1936, before going to West Point. The Army had been good to me and although I didn't regret my resignation, it was with a sense of loss that I accepted my papers.

My family and I built a house in a rural part of Fairfax County in Virginia. My affair with Mielikki seemed to be receding in our memories. The constant uprooting, including the war years, was taken in stride, but the frequent moves took their toll somewhat later on. On 12 June 1953 our third and last child was born. We called him Michael.

As chief of operations of the SR Division, I traveled abroad frequently and extensively. The purposes of this travel were in general two. First, to confer with our own station chiefs abroad and to see what might be done to strengthen our work vis-à-vis the Soviet Union. Often we would agree that an SR officer would be transferred from Washington out to the field station to concentrate on local Soviet targets. During such visits I would describe for the chief-of-station and his officers the kind of operations we were finding to be successful and profitable and to encourage them to adopt some of the more successful techniques. The second major purpose behind these circuit-riding trips was to discuss Soviet operational opportunities and methods with the internal-security services or espionage services with our allies, as well as to explore with friendly nations profitable lines of effort that we might embark on together. During my more than three years as operations chief for Soviet activities, I was called on to make repeated visits to the Near East, Europe, Scandinavia, and the Far East, each trip running between three and six weeks in length. A visit to one of our field stations abroad always entailed a review of current agent activities with particular regard to those with a Soviet potential. The same applied to my dealings with friendly liaison intelligence security services, and there was often the possibility that we would agree upon some form of training for members of the friendly service. One example might show how these liaison visits abroad sometimes were conducted.

On 3 March 1953, I was having lunch with the chief-of-station in Istanbul when news came of the death of Stalin. We were at a very posh restaurant in a part of the Blue Mosque, known as the Granary. In the middle of our lunch and in a crowded dining room, a waiter burst through the doors of the pantry and hurried over to our table, where he had recognized my host. In a loud, hissing whisper, audible throughout the entire restaurant, he said, "The old bastard's dead." Having thus informed that part of the world of what had happened in Moscow, he raced back to the kitchen, beaming all the way.

The chief-of-station and I went by train to Ankara, the seat of government, where we had an appointment with a Turkish security official. This raw new city, created on the Anatolian Plain, was windswept and freezing cold. Driven snow, swept horizontally by an icy wind, blew constantly across the fields. There in a new government building I was introduced to the Turkish security chief, who with authorization of his government was cooperating with us on an intelligence matter. We were ushered into his large office and seated ourselves in the two chairs indicated. As we sat down, he began moving his hands beneath his desk, without speaking further, but smiling tentatively at me. I looked at my colleague, who shook his head slightly, and we returned to staring at each other. After a moment or two of complete silence, he broke into a wide grin, stood up, held out his hand, and pumped mine effusively. He again bid me welcome and we went on with our business.

After this meeting, we returned to the car, and I asked, "What was that all about?" The station chief told me not worry. "He was just doing a few laps on his beads counting the letters in your name to see how the last letter left his fingers. Apparently you have the right number; that's when he broke into a grin. He felt it was an auspicious name and you would bring good fortune."

Leaving Turkey, I went on to Zurich, where I had prearranged meetings with two non-Swiss intelligence chiefs who had been of much help over a period of years and whom we met at least once a year. Switzerland always proved a good country in which to have such meetings. A trip to Switzerland was always an event in itself; one could look forward to good food, marvelous cleanliness, and of course overwhelming scenery.

It was convenient on this particular trip to stop at our Berlin base (a base is subordinate to a station) on the way. The chief-of-base, an old friend, was the same officer who had been sent from Headquarters to consult with us about the "count" in Munich in 1951. He always provided stimulating conversation and we examined operational problems the agency was facing around the world. I stayed as his house guest for several days before moving on to The Hague.

Along with our own station, I had business to transact with the Dutch intelligence chief. My arrival there happened to coincide with a bizarre and, in many ways, acutely embarrassing episode involving both the Dutch and British services.

It is a matter of historical record that during World War II, the Dutch underground in Holland, or at least the intelligence arm of it, with its communications net, had almost totally been controlled by the Gestapo. The Dutch intelligence service in exile was located in London and housed by MI6. Dutch agents were trained and equipped by the British and were parachuted back into the Netherlands by RAF planes to reinforce the underground elements of the Dutch resistance remaining in the Lowlands. Anyone who has read the account of World War II espionage in a book called *Operation Northpole* must realize that almost the entire Dutch underground was controlled by the Germans. The only radio traffic coming through to London was written by the German intelligence and security services.

By the end of the war in 1945, the enormity of the Dutch intelligence debacle became apparent. Inquiry after inquiry was launched, to find out what exactly had gone wrong. Dozens, if not hundreds, of Dutch lives had been lost to the Germans. It appeared literally impossible to write up a "damage report," which could assess the amount of harm that had been done to the allied war effort in Western Europe. This ugly situation, full of rumor and counterrumor, accusation and counteraccusation between the Dutch and British, smoldered on for years, until the spring of 1953, when the Dutch Parliament decided to send a delegation of Dutch parliamentarians to London to examine all intelligence documents relating to their underground activities during the war. This Dutch delegation, even as I arrived in The Hague, was on its way to London to look into these records, to reconstruct what had happened to their wartime underground.

What transpired is not a pretty tale. The delegation was met by British representatives, who coolly informed them that, unfortunately, within the past day there had been a "serious fire" in the MI6 file room. By coincidence, all Dutch resistance records had been destroyed. In the face of this astounding piece of news, the Dutch immediately left on a return flight to The Hague. Shortly thereafter, the Dutch government expelled the MI6 representative and his assistants and closed down the British intelligence station in The Hague. All of this took place within the week I spent there. This story was told me by a senior officer of the Dutch intelligence.

To my knowledge, it was never made clear or definitive whether the Dutch intelligence disaster of World War II was their own fault, the result of sloppy work by British colleagues, or a combination of fate, circumstance, and hard German work. The fact that it happened at all, regardless of the cause, was reason enough for Dutch-British relationships to be soured for years afterward.

Summer and fall of 1953 were largely occupied in devising new techniques for getting information out of the USSR. We had stopped parachuting agents but had to find other means of accomplishing our tasks there. Third-country nationals proved to be excellent alternatives to agents-by-parachute. These operations were not easy to set up, as we had to find and screen persons who would be willing to go into the USSR on our behalf and who had the means of doing so.

This system didn't always work out, and, not unexpectedly, we would wind up with a number of "double agents" on our hands. They usually were not hard to detect and deal with. We would triple an agent, if we were able to recruit him again and send him back, undetected, to the hostile service involved. Triple agents are always kept in a special category and at double arm's length.

Doubled and tripled agents could lead such complicated operational lives that, upon occasion, it would become impossible to determine their real loyalty.

I was both amused and sometimes exasperated to read, in recent years, in the American press that a CIA agent had been "terminated with extreme prejudice," the context and implication being that CIA had executed the agent. I have never heard such an expression used by our professionals, but certainly an agent was not "done away with"; he was taken off the payroll and contact with him was broken.

This was not true of the Soviet side. The early and middle 1950s saw repeated instances of "executive" action by the KGB in Western Europe, West Germany, in particular. Knowing as much as we did about the Soviet intelligence structure through the work of agents and defectors, we were well aware of their Department V, the executive action department of the First Chief Directorate of the KGB. It was commonly called, within the KGB, the actions element under which fell the department of *mokrie dela*, Russian for "wet affairs," or bloody. The KGB assassin, Bogdan Stashinsky, was one of a number of such assassins who moved through Western Europe in those years. Stashinsky personally murdered the Ukrainian exile leader, Stefan Bandera, and Lev Rebet, prominent in the anti-Communist exile movement in West Germany. Department V later became the Ninth Sector of the First Chief Directorate in 1953, after formation of the KGB to succeed the MGB. In 1954, the name was again changed to Department 13. Whatever it was called, its work went on; murder and assassination of anti-Communist Russian exiles and defectors. Similar work undoubtedly continues today.

Stashinsky, full of guilt about his past, in 1962 defected to the West and gave a full account of all the actions he had carried out.

One KGB captain, Nikolai Khoklov, was sent on a mission into West Germany, being "staged" through Austria, from the KGB training grounds near Moscow. Khoklov had several targets assigned to him, but on reaching West Germany, found he was unable to carry out his assignment for reasons of conscience. He turned himself in to local German authorities and the Americans. His emigré targets were named and he turned over the pistol and gas cartridges he was to have used. They were concealed in a spare battery in the trunk of his car.

At this stage, two British diplomats in Washington, Guy Burgess and Donald Maclean, both members of MI6, were recalled to London under suspicion by the British secret service. They were detached from their duties in MI6, but otherwise left to themselves. Meanwhile, British security was running down leads concerning their backgrounds and security status. On 12 May 1951, both of them disappeared and, as later events developed, had clandestinely gone to the Continent, on to the East and Moscow. They had been Soviet agents and KGB penetrations of MI6 throughout their long careers.

The question remained as to who tipped them off to the fact that they were under investigation. Who told them to flee to Moscow? Clearly there was a third man involved along the line; the British Parliament went into an uproar over this scandal. Burgess and Maclean had been intimately connected with American intelligence while stationed at the British Embassy in Washington, and CIA was shaken to the core. Harold A. R. (Kim) Philby, the son of a distinguished Arabist scholar and British explorer, had then been chief of MI6 in Washington and, in that capacity, enjoyed an intimate relationship with senior CIA officers from Allen Dulles on down, and had easy access to the details of many sensitive CIA operations. Suspicion began to center on Philby as being the "third man." He too was recalled to London, where he was asked to resign from the Foreign Office and, by definition, from MI6, on 18 September 1951. To this date, the British have never explained why Philby received the courteous and considerate treatment they extended to him. His loyalty was deeply suspect and many felt he was then, and had been for some years, a Soviet agent. Nevertheless, he was allowed his freedom in England and was even given a reasonably substantial pension. Presumably, with some government assistance, he became a free-lance journalist in the London area, still retaining ties to his old buddies in MI6. Debate raged inconclusively in Parliament. At about this time a Soviet intelligence officer in Australia, attached to the Soviet Embassy, one Vladimir Petrov, defected to the Australians and definitely put the finger on Burgess and Maclean as having been recruited by the Soviets as agents during the 1930s.

Kim Philby, still ostensibly a journalist, had made his way from England to the Middle East. He kept up this facade until he sensed the net closing around him; in 1953 he decamped and fled to the USSR, where he was decorated and welcomed as a Soviet hero, and where he remains today.

He, too, was a Soviet agent, recruited during the 1930s, but unlike Burgess and Maclean, had risen to one of the top three positions in the British intelligence service.

The London *Times*, citing a secret intelligence report, allegedly compiled by the U.S. State Department in 1956, stated that Maclean, and therefore Philby, had full knowledge of American plans and strategy regarding the Korean War. They were aware of, and conveyed to the Soviets, the American determination not to carry the war against China into Manchuria or to blockade the China coast; nor were we prepared to "expand" the war, a euphemism for not using nuclear weapons against the Chinese who had massively attacked American forces across the Yalu River in North Korea. These three well-placed agents had constituted a bleeding stomach wound to American policies and strategies. Our intents were known to the Soviets and, emboldened by what they knew, they carried on their own strategies and actions with guaranteed impunity.

I had no contact with them, but there is no reason to believe now they were not completely aware of all of our Soviet work until they defected. I can also only assume that my own identity and the nature of my work was in turn passed on to the KGB. This was a thought that I constantly had with me when I went to Vienna in 1955 to take over the station.

I have been asked why, given my known status as a CIA officer and the general nature of my intelligence work abroad, I was sent in 1955 to such an intelligence hotspot as Vienna. It must be pointed out that simple identification of a person as a CIA intelligence officer does not mean that his value or effectiveness is necessarily at an end. In the first place, the higher one goes up the intelligence ladder, the less likely is he to be personally engaged completely in clandestine activity. As he goes up that professional ladder, more and more does he find himself caught up in directing the activities of other American intelligence officers, whose CIA status is either unknown or reasonably well-covered. Also, a good intelligence officer learns how to keep himself unobtrusive or even hidden, while active in his clandestine sector. These stratagems are not ideal but are really the only ones available to the intelligence officer who has become widely known to the opposition. They can be made to work.

Nineteen fifty-four proved to be a year of development and experimentation in new techniques against the Soviet target. No significant intelligence was coming to us from the scientific and technical front. All that came later. There were no U-2s flying, no satellites in orbit; they were on the drawing boards. The main source of our intelligence was the human source. There were a number of defectors during 1954 but they all were largely one-time sources, who once fully exploited were of limited use.

There was an extensive reorganization in the SR (Soviet Russia) Division in an effort to provide more effective support to those serving abroad. Preparations were made to send SR Division officers, speaking Russian, to stations in Europe and the Near and Far East. It was a time of testing and improvisation to develop doctrines that would stand up to the realities of field experience. The numerous defectors provided a continuous and substantial flow of intelligence. As the year came to an end, I realized I would be going into my fourth year as chief of operations and should give some thought to a foreign assignment again. I was now waiting for the right assignment. On that note, 1954 ended and 1955, a year of great importance to me, began. I was sent to Vienna.

10 Vienna: The Occupation Ends

The year 1955 began with a spate of Soviet defectors, plus a few from Soviet Bloc countries; some of these were intelligence officers. As a result, there was an uncommonly high flow of significant intelligence during these early months. The handling, debriefing, and resettlement of the defectors kept most of the division busy for the first few months.

The SR Division had no personnel permanently stationed overseas; plans were underway to arrange such assignments—a real breakthrough. One day early in 1955 the chief of the Clandestine Service called me to his office. I found my division chief there. They told me that I was to go to Vienna as deputy chief-of-station and chief of operations; the positions were held by the same person. I was to propose a replacement to take over my SR duties and I was to start working with the East European (EE) Division. My suggested replacement was approved, and I spent less and less time in the division as I went to the EE Division to read files and become familiar with their programs and operations. At the beginning of April I moved into the EE Division permanently. Progress had been made in convincing the chief of the Clandestine Service that SR officers should be stationed abroad permanently in certain key countries, where there was a large concentration of Soviet intelligence officers. Preparations were underway, country by country, to implement these plans.

As I looked back on the four years in SR Division, I felt some satisfaction in what had been accomplished. We had backed away from the wasteful and, in many ways, tragic program of parachuting agents into the Western reaches of the USSR, with such calamitous results. At the same time we had begun sending so-called legal agents in to the USSR. We had "run" our first Soviet intelligence officer, as he worked in place as our agent. The sizable number of intelligence officers who had defected to us had provided information of unique value to the U.S. government, and had provided the CIA with the identities and background of other Soviet intelligence officers, who were likeminded and whom we might successfully approach. We had made a breakthrough with the Department of State. There was always hope that another Ivan would come to us and be willing to work in the dangerous confines of Moscow. Later events were to fulfill this hope.

In Virginia, I was having more and more domestic problems. My wife and I recognized there was a fundamental incompatibility between us. We decided a tour abroad in Vienna might give us a fresh outlook and a chance to overcome our differences. We sailed from New York on the SS *America* early in April of 1955. Our car had been shipped with us, making it possible to drive in a leisurely manner to Vienna. My mother accompanied us, as a dependent, and stayed for about ten months; not an easy person to live with at best, her presence did not help an already unsteady marriage.

We docked at Bremerhaven, Germany and the car was unloaded and cleared. At Salzburg, I checked in at our base to coordinate with the Vienna station. Temporary reservations had been made for us at the Hotel Bristol on the Ringstrasse, a hotel very familiar to me from previous visits. From Salzburg to Linz, we followed along the northern slopes of the Salzkammergut, one of the more spectacular drives among the many Alpine lakes. Passing through Linz, and taking a detour to the Pfarrgasse, the memories of my repatriation days there came flooding back and the surprising encounter with a gunman in 1950. Going east we came to the crossing from the American to the Soviet Zone of Austria, where our documents were examined first by American Military Police and then by illiterate young Soviet soldiers who, with rifles slung over shoulders, and unable to read English or Russian, would check our documents upsidedown.

Each car was logged out of the American Zone and the departure time was forwarded to our MPs in the American Sector at the border-crossing point into Vienna. This was to protect Americans from just disappearing into the Soviet Zone. Each car was given a two-and-one-half-hour period in which to arrive at the guard post. If within a reasonable length of time, a car had not checked in, an MP jeep would double back to find out what had happened. There had been cases in which Soviet patrols, in their own zone, had stopped nondiplomatic travelers and held individuals for hours at a time, a harassing technique.

Our rooms in the Hotel Bristol had windows facing on the Kaerntnerstrasse, one of Vienna's main thoroughfares and shopping centers. The Vienna State Opera was directly across this street. It had been bombed and badly damaged during the last days of the war when the Soviets shelled the center of the city. The pride of the Viennese, after nearly ten years of reconstruction, the opera house was nearing completion, and the Viennese were anticipating its formal opening in all its new splendor in the fall.

I reported directly into the CIA station and began to familiarize myself with its organization and composition. We had extensive office space in a former Austrian Army barracks area, the Stiftskaserne on the Mariahilferstrasse. There were also offices in the Allianz Insurance Building on the Waehringerstrasse, not far from the American Embassy. In the embassy proper there was only the chief-of-station, his secretary, and our communicators.

The man I was to replace had his office in the Allianz Building. He had amassed a great deal of leave and was anxious to turn his duties over to me. After an overlap of about a week, no further joint work was needed and he went on his vacation. I again buried myself in files and ongoing operations, including many activities not directly related to the Soviets, but dealing with Soviet Bloc countries.

There were at the time international meetings going on in Trieste between the four major powers occupying Austria: the United States, the USSR, the United Kingdom, and France. Occupied Austria was divided into four zones, one for each allied power of World War II. Vienna was divided into four similar sectors, the First District being international. This district was controlled successively, with each country having a one-month tenure as chairman of the Allied Control Commission. The Hotel Bristol was in the First District; a few doors down the Ringstrasse was the Grand Hotel, the family billets for the Soviets. Soviet intelligence headquarters, including the KGB and GRU, were across the Ring in the Imperial Hotel, which brought to mind our time with the "count," or perhaps I should say, his time with us.

By early summer, there was a great deal of excitement at the prospect of the Soviets finally agreeing to a treaty with the Austrian government, which they and the other three powers would sign, giving Austria back its sovereignty and freedom. This would bring about the removal of all occupation troops, and the return of offices and facilities which had supported the occupying powers. The only representation to Austria would be through each embassy.

In July of 1955, the American ambassador to Austria, H. Llewellyn Thompson, the American negotiator at the talks in Trieste, was able to cable Washington that the Soviets were ready to sign a peace treaty with Austria. This was accomplished with all four powers participating, with the stipulation that within ninety days after signature all military occupying forces and their supporting echelons would be removed. National representation would revert to an embassy and perhaps a consulate.

This meant the departure of thousands of soldiers by each of the four powers, their military headquarters, air bases, supply installations and other service establishments that had been created by the massive occupying forces. Our intelligence apparatus in Vienna and the American Zone would have to be dismantled and cut back from several hundred staff people to a few score, who would then be housed in the American Embassy on the Boltzmanngasse.

For the American military element, it was a relatively simple move. Supplies and equipment would be packed and shipped to West Germany. Our own station went through a weeding out, as we cut down. We also relocated station officers who were to stay, under suitable cover in an independent Austria, without the benefit of military cover. It was some comfort to realize that my Soviet counterparts, in their headquarters at the embassy, were undergoing the same traumatic compression.

As American military headquarters and personnel in Vienna left for Germany or to return to the States, many more private homes were vacated and became available for ordinary rental on the free Austrian market. We were able to find a large house, which I needed, in the Eighteenth Bezirk of Vienna in a very stylish neighborhood called the Cottage. Our house on the Hasenauerstrasse was old and formal. We moved about the middle of October, just after the signing of the treaty. About two blocks from our house, the Soviets had leased the Cottage Hotel, a fenced-in large billet of apartments for their families and, in some cases, their children.

As the final October date drew nearer, all four powers were evacuating office buildings and other facilities which they had used. When the long-awaited day arrived, there was an extremely moving ceremony, especially for the Viennese, as the four powers lowered their flags which had flown over the Allied Control Commission Building in the Schwartzenburgplatz for ten years. Each country had had a special parade company of troops flown in, accompanied by a military band; they would march through the square as each flag was lowered and the national anthem played. The Platz was jammed with Viennese. As each country, preceded by the military band, marched out of the square, cheers rolled out and the Viennese realized the occupation was really over.

The last country to march in was the Soviet Union. They stood at attention as their anthem was played and they waited for their flag to be lowered. The Soviet soldiers on the roof of the building were obviously having trouble and their strenuous efforts to lower the flag caused the Viennese, to whom this had a special wry significance, to laugh until the entire crowd roared with them, to the Soviets' embarrassment.

As their unit marched out of the square, an Austrian couple, standing in front of me, began commenting in German about the large glockenspiel they carried, with ribbons fluttering from each arm. The man, turning to the woman, commented in a loud voice that in the old days when the Russians had a victory march, there were not ribbons on the end of the glockenspiel, but skulls. I could believe this.

The summer of 1955 was not entirely caught up with administrative problems with the shifting from military to civilian cover. The Vienna station had long maintained several Austrian surveillance teams, replenished with new blood from time to time to keep down the risk of being penetrated or identified by the Soviets. The members of these teams included Hungarians and Czechs, who had been in refugee centers and were long residents of Austria. From July to October we kept them almost fully employed in pinning down the movements of known Soviet intelligence officers, when the newly established Soviet Embassy was rearranging its personnel organizations and finding ways of accommodating a large KGB and GRU residentura. In terms of percentage, the Soviet intelligence organs would be about four times larger in manpower than our station. Our surveillance teams helped greatly in determining, among the two different Soviet residenturas, who would remain in Vienna and who would leave. We wanted to find out where these officers would live and which of their agents, from occupation days, they would keep. We wanted to identify and study these agents from the standpoint of how susceptible they might be to recruitment by us. We wanted to know what kind of intelligence requirements the Soviet case officers were passing on to these agents, but they would also try to slip one of their people onto our list to find what requirements *we* had. To know what your opponent needs badly is to know where he is weak. The sword cuts both ways.

It came to our attention that in midsummer there would be a high-level strategic meeting in Moscow between representatives of one of the major neutral powers of the world and their Soviet counterparts. The delegates of the neutralist power, after spending about ten days touring various capitals of Western Europe, would go to Moscow to conduct these negotiations. Before leaving Western Europe, the seven-man delegation would go to the Salzburg area to rest. This served a double purpose: to give them some seclusion and quiet surroundings in which to plan their strategy during the upcoming negotiations. The State Department requested the CIA to do all that was possible to learn the nature of the positions and objectives of this delegation. This requirement wound up in the Vienna Station. The neutralist party would stay at Schloss Fuschl, on the Fuschlsee, about twenty kilometers outside of Salzburg.

Schloss Fuschl is a gingerbread kind of castle, built on a promontory jutting out into the Fuschlsee. It had been used during the war by Field Marshal Hermann Goering as a personal vacation spot. Now it had been taken over by the Austrian government as a small hotel and assigned to the tourist trade. The neutral delegation had requested certain rooms and suites for specific dates. They would spend about five days there, after which they would fly to Moscow from Berlin.

The two chief delegates were to be given the royal suite in this small but luxurious schloss. It consisted of a very large living room with a dining table at one end, a large fireplace, many pieces of overstuffed furniture, and a large round table in the middle of the room, the most likely spot where the delegates would have their talks. There were two bedrooms off this central room, each with a bath. We wanted to install a radio transmitter in the living room, so that voices conferring around the table could be radioed out and recorded on tape. This would not be too difficult. There were several small fishing lodges available for rent, across the lake from the schloss. The flat expanse of the lake promised good transmission. The main problem was: how to gain access to this suite so that we could work with our own technicians and install a radio that could be turned off and on from a distance.

This would have to be accomplished a few days prior to the arrival of the delegation. We worked this out by borrowing from another European station a case officer and his wife, both of whom were soon to retire. They were a distinguished-looking couple, obviously "wealthy." They were to make reservations on their own for this particular suite and were to occupy it, ostensibly on a holiday, for three or four days, with the assurance that they would be gone by the time the delegates arrived. The management of the schloss was politely insistent that the Americans had to be gone in time for the staff to prepare the suite for the next guests, VIPs indeed. They agreed, made reservations accordingly, and spent several days, with cost no object. It was thus possible for them to have visits from "friends" during their stay; these callers would, of course, be our technical team, who would install the radio. This impressive case officer and his wife arrived and checked into the VIP suite. On the second day, "visitors" began arriving to see them. The technical team determined that the large central table would be ideal for radio transmission; it was near a window that faced toward the fishing lodge we had rented. The total range was about half a mile; the lake was not large. Transmission tests were made at this time between the schloss and the lodge and conditions were found to give excellent reception. The lodge was fitted out with sleeping bags and whatever would be needed by a couple of men on a fishing holiday. There the automatic recorders were installed. Each cottage was quite remote from the next; in fact it proved a problem to bring in the heavy wet cell batteries for power for the recorders, there being no electricity.

The installation of the radio in the pedestal of the table went off without a hitch; tests showed that the link between the radio and recorders was operating ideally. After these tests, everything was left in place and our couple left two days before the delegation appeared. The next day, cleaning teams from the hotel staff readied the suite for the next occupancy; we were again able to test the equipment by listening to the conversations of the maids as they worked.

The following day the delegation settled in with the two leading members occupying the bugged suite. The conversations came through loud and clear as they sat around the table, whether to relax or go over State papers. This they did for several hours each day and their negotiating positions with their proposals and objectives came out perfectly through the mass of conversations. We cabled summaries back to Washington from our Salzburg Base and furnished the State Department with the information they needed. Verbatim copies followed in the pouch. The operation went off smoothly and at the end of the visit, we all returned to Vienna with the technicians and transcribers. I asked the head technicians if we would have to retrieve the radio. He looked at me and slowly responded, "Well, it's not all that expensive, so I think that we can just leave it there."

"Is there any likelihood that it will be discovered in the near future?"

He said, "No, there's no reason to believe so. But in about six months the batteries are going to smell like dead fish and at that time, they'll find it. But we'll be long gone."

We left it at that and heard no more about the operation.

As for the intelligence itself, which had aroused such interest at the State Department and elsewhere in the government, the neutral country's primary demand at the upcoming conference was that the Soviets provide the technical skill and money to finance the first steel mill ever to be built in this country, and that it be of a considerable size. This demand was met and accepted during the meetings in Moscow. They also wanted assurances from the Soviets that MIG-21 fighters would be available in large numbers at a reduced cost; pilot training and spare parts would be part of the package. This, too, was later agreed to. The third objective was to have Soviet support on what they thought would be an upcoming confrontation with a neighboring state; they wanted support against this state. This, subsequently, also was agreed to by the Soviet Union. All of this information was in the hands of our diplomats and other parts of the Executive branch, long in advance of its being made public; our strategic plans in that part of the world were adjusted accordingly.

This was accomplished in five days along the shores of the Fuschlsee and under the blue sky of the Salzkammergut during an idyllic two weeks in summer.

While preparations were being made to leave Vienna and the occupied zones of Austria, we concentrated a great deal of attention on the Soviet Embassy on the Reisnerstrasse. We surmised that they had to move all of their residentura, which during the occupation had been under various forms of Soviet military cover, into their embassy. Many officers of the KGB and GRU would be holdovers from the occupation era, but others would be new arrivals from the center in Moscow. We set up a number of observation posts near the embassy and kept our surveillance teams in the general vicinity. Gradually a picture of the stay-behind residentura took shape.

Under close surveillance scrutiny, the comings and goings in their residentura began to take on specific patterns. One of them was the use of a public telephone box about two blocks from the embassy. It was the nearest one and, like careless people everywhere, the Soviets would use this phone to make their operational calls to set up meetings with their agents. The situation begged for a radio transmitter in the telephone box, linked to automatic tape recorders in a nearby apartment.

While making innocent phone calls, some of our officers examined the inside of the box carefully and gave our technicians the dimensions and particulars they would need to prepare a transmitter for installation in the box. It had a peaked roof, like a miniature circus tent, but the ceiling inside the box was flat. There was a vacant space between the ceiling and the roof itself. This was the logical place to install a transmitter and still provide easy access for repairs or to replace batteries. Several night visits to the box found this to be the case, and we prepared a cavity for the radio.

We waited for a cold and rainy night to minimize the chance of a passerby observing the work going on. Two technicians squeezed into the box in the early-morning hours and made the installation in about ten minutes. They went on the air and the listening post reported they had picked them up with full clarity. Now, all we had to do was sit back and wait.

The next day, during the late afternoon, three officers, whom we knew to be KGB men, were observed on different occasions leaving the embassy, and in each case they headed for this telephone box. Our surveillance squads were alerted and the conversations we picked up began to make sense. The numbers which the Soviets would dial presented no problem; we had means of checking the Vienna telephone system to locate the number being called. The conversations over the phone posed a different problem. It was clear an operational meeting was being set up, as the Soviet might say in German: "All right, Gunter, I'll meet you at the same bierstube in an hour and a half."

Surveillance of the Soviet would reveal the name and address of the bierstube, plus the fact that he had added an hour to the time when he would meet his agent. In actuality, the time would be in a half hour.

We would observe the meeting and, at its conclusion, "take" the Austrian agent to his home. We finally approached an agent at his apartment and identified ourselves as Americans. We told him we knew of his relationship with the Soviets. He was very shaken and there was little difficulty in getting him to work for us and not inform his Soviet case officer—in effect, "doubling" him back into the KGB. He reported questions given to him and we would prepare replies to be passed back. Subsequent polygraphs of this agent indicated that he was telling the truth, and had not revealed his connection with us to his Soviet control. Thus, the KGB officer would report that he had achieved a penetration of the American Embassy (where this Austrian was employed) and go to his meetings with confidence. This play went on for some weeks, but we noticed that the Austrian was becoming increasingly edgy. We told him of our observation and he admitted that he was terribly nervous. He said he was in mortal fear of the Soviets and of what they might do to him if they learned of his double status. He asked if he could cut out of the scene. He would keep in close touch with us, but at the same time drop out of sight from the Soviets. He had relatives in Linz, where he thought he could find a job. We had a final meeting, after which the perspiring but relieved agent left.

All good things come to end and so did the radio tap on the telephone box. As best as we can reconstruct, the Austrian telephone service, apparently on a routine check for needed replacements, went into the vacant space and found our transmitter. They disconnected it and that was the finish of our access to the residentura's clumsily arranged communications system between their case officers and the agents involved. But we came out ahead, as we had doubled a number of Soviet agents. We have no reason to believe the Soviets ever found out about the tap on this box, although the technique was well known to them, unless they had their own penetration agent in the Austrian telephone offices. If our knowledge of their track record in matters of this kind is of any significance, I would judge this a good possibility.

For a long time in the past, it had been an accepted doctrine in the CIA that an officer could not work directly against a KGB or GRU officer. Such face-to-face encounters were to be avoided. There were stringent regulations that required reporting of any kind of contact with officers of Soviet intelligence organs. Such contacts were never followed up by our officers; he would be ordered simply to report any attempts by a Soviet to press a contact with our own people. Our general posture was one of defensiveness and certainly one of a passive participant in any encounter with a Soviet intelligence officer. It was considered impossible to continue a contact for any length of time without losing more than he might gain from such a liaison.

While I could understand the reasoning that lay behind this doctrine, I didn't agree with it. During my time at Headquarters in the SR Division, I had constantly worked to make it possible for Russian-speaking SR Division officers to be sent abroad on permanent duty for that very purpose: to contrive face-to-face meetings with Soviet officers, to study them, and put them on the defensive. Being in such a position, the American officer could scrutinize his opponent and make his own estimate of his weaknesses and sensitivity. Only from this position could we learn enough about an individual Soviet to judge whether or not he had significant weaknesses, psychological or ideological, that might make him an able and willing collaborator over a period of time. I wrote some reports on this general theme and discussed them on a number of occasions and at great length with my chief in Vienna. He was a very capable officer and one for whom I had a great deal of personal and professional respect. He became enthusiastically seized with this approach to our opponents, and made an appointment for us to talk about it with the ambassador, Llewellyn Thompson. If he did not disapprove, CIA officers, known or unknown as being such, would seek out our

Soviet opposite numbers and attempt to draw them into a personal or social relationship. We felt the ambassador should know what we were trying to do, how, and why. We would be bound by whatever restrictions he might put on us.

We met at the station chief's house one evening. He lived on the Sternwartestrasse in the Cottage area, a few blocks from my own home. We sat before the fireplace exploring the pros and cons of this operational philosophy, weighing the benefits and risks in pursuing it. After several hours of scrutiny of all alternatives, Ambassador Thompson agreed that we could go ahead, but the number of officers must be limited and he was to be kept informed of contacts we made. This was a victory; I was told to go ahead, with one other station officer of my choice. As I spoke workable Russian, I chose one member who was fluent in German and was, in my opinion, a mature case officer able to handle an experienced Soviet officer. We briefed Headquarters and got a guarded and, I believe, reluctant approval.

With the doctrinal barriers lifted, the question was: how to begin? We had photographs of most of the members of the Soviet residentura and a fair amount of personalia about each of them. Some of us had individually met one or two at official receptions, which seemed to be the playground in which we must work to establish our initial contacts.

It had been clear to me for some time that the Soviets themselves had no reluctance to be seen in the company of Americans, whatever our backgrounds or position. This was understandable. They were, after all, directed to cultivate Americans officially, to study them for possible recruitment. Officers of senior rank or mature in experience were quite self-confident in dealing with an American official, especially a known CIA officer.

I recall one stag reception given by the Austrian government, held in the rococo white and gold ballroom of the Palavicini Palast on the Herrengasse in the First Bezirk. There were about one hundred and fifty men present, in evening dress, representing practically every embassy in Vienna, and many senior officials of the Austrian government. I recognized the chief of the Soviet residentura, Sokolnikov, from our surveillance photos and walked over to introduce myself. He was very amiable and we chatted briefly before I drifted to another group. I noted that surrounding Sokolnikov were several members of the American

Embassy. I could hear their conversation; they were talking of the recent riots in Poznan in Poland; Sokolnikov was handling them with sophistication. One of our embassy officers said to him, "Mr. Sokolnikov, just what do you do in your embassy?" Sokolnikov looked across at me and, with a self-assured smile, raised his voice for my benefit and answered, "Oh, I do in my embassy exactly what your Mr. de Silva does in yours."

We nodded to each other and that's how our connection began.

We knew that besides volleyball, the two outdoor sports the Soviets seemed to enjoy the most were hunting and fishing. I had always been an enthusiastic trout fisherman; for the fishing season, I had a lease on a four-kilometer stretch of a well-stocked trout stream an hour and a half out of Vienna. It was part of the Schwarzau, a beautiful, tumbling alpine stream, which poured down from the foothills of the Alps. One drove from Vienna to the village of Gloggnitz, there turning northwest to my leased stream. The Austrian Forest Service, which supervised all such leases, were vigilant and efficient; they insured there was no poaching. Only the leasee was permitted to fish along with any invited guests. The water was crystal clear, flowing over rocks and along fast-moving gravel-bottomed stretches into still, deep pools before starting another rapid fall. It provided every challenge for trout fishing and was stocked with excellent rainbows and browns, and even graylings.

To make direct contact with opposite members in the residentura was not too difficult. I had chosen Jerry as my partner in this endeavor. An avid hunter, he especially enjoyed shooting duck, pheasant, and boar. In season, these were plentiful in the twisted and wandering waterways of the Löbau, across the Danube from Vienna proper. It was agreed that I would take on the Soviet fishermen and Jerry would take on the hunters. We were both on the diplomatic list of the embassy and were invited to many of the frequent social events. These diplomatic functions provided perfect stalking grounds for us, just as they did for the Soviets. At the next large stag event I went to—the Austrians were very long on stag evenings—I glimpsed Sokolnikov talking to one of his colleagues. Again from our photographs, I recognized his deputy, Mr. Grishin. Grishin was several years older than Sokolnikov, and was probably five or six years my senior. I went over to them. Sokolnikov saw me coming, smiled invitingly, and I greeted him.

"How is your work going these days?"

"Probably the same as yours, Mr. de Silva," he returned.

I asked, "Don't you ever do anything to get away from the office? Do you ever go hunting or fishing?"

"Ah," he replied. "I love to shoot duck. Grishin, here, he's the fisherman."

Later on that evening, I cornered Grishin.

"Mr. Grishin," I said, "Mr. Sokolnikov mentioned that you're the fisherman in your group. I have a four-kilometer stretch of trout stream not far from here and I wondered if you'd like to go with me sometime. I'll get a chance to practice my Russian; you can work on me with your English."

Grishin was obviously prepared for just this gambit.

He said, "What do you propose? Where is your trout stream?"

I described its location. We agreed on the following Sunday and exchanged home telephone numbers. It was set up that I would give him a call on Saturday and tell him when I would pick him up.

Grishin had clearly been briefed to expect an invitation of this kind; he had Sokolnikov's permission to go out alone with a Yank intelligence officer over the weekend. I figured: well, it's a case of he wants to study me and I know that I want to study him. We'll see how it turns out.

That weekend began a long series of fishing expeditions *à deux*. I called Grishin on Saturday and we agreed to get an early start at about eight o'clock in the morning from his home.

He was waiting for me as I stopped my car at his door. He had packed some lunch for himself and a few extra things to share with me. His lunch was very appetizing, as I remember, and included herring, sausage, and bottled water. I had brought some Austrian cheese, American beer, hard-boiled eggs, and good sour Austrian pumpernickel bread. Also a jar of ripe olives, which were entirely new to him.

Grishin's fishing equipment was good. It was worn but well-kept; it had been used a great deal. Mine was similar. I told him he would have a good stretch of water to fish that day and if he were lucky he might land a grayling.

"Graylings? I've never been able to take one of those. Are they really stocked in your stream?"

I told him, "There are quite a few, but I've only taken one in all the times I've been fishing here. Maybe our luck will change today."

"Noo, poyekhali!" exlaimed Grishin. "Let's go."

We stowed our gear in the back of my car and took off on the road past Schwechat Airfield toward the Semmering Pass. The Schwarzau lay at the foot of the pass. Late spring in any part of Austria is a glorious season. Everything was green, and the fields made a broad expanse of softly waving grass. Farms began to appear with cattle and horses grazing in abundant acreage. Every farm had its own colony of ducks and geese, clipped wings preventing flight, and, as we passed, there was a loud outburst of honking and gabbling. These geese were formidable watchdogs, as I had found when walking about the Austrian countryside.

There was little conversation between Grishin and me except to remark on the beauty of the landscape and the wonderful weather. He mentioned nothing about himself or his background, nor did he speak of Russia or his family. Nor did I. The atmosphere was friendly with intermittent, short exchanges about the local scene.

We passed through the village of Gloggnitz and turned off to reach my portion of the stream. Grishin brought out a local map and quickly put his finger to the spot where we were driving. He attentively looked over the landscape to make sure he had a picture of the terrain in keeping with his map, which I observed was a Soviet field artillery fire-control map. After all, Gloggnitz had been in the Soviet Zone during the occupation.

I stopped at a middling-good part of the stream for our first try. There were much better places, but I thought I'd let him start casting to see how he operated. Watching as he put his gear together, after we pulled off and stopped at a wide spot in the road, I noted that he was very much at ease with his equipment. I put my rod and reel together, we buckled on our creels, and I heard Grishin humming to himself. We separated as Grishin went upstream and I turned down; we agreed to meet in about a half hour and move on to another section.

The remainder of the morning was spent in this fashion, with little discussion, as we moved from spot to spot. By lunchtime, Grishin had caught three good-sized rainbow trout and I had two rainbows and a brown. Brown trout had only recently been introduced into Austria and were unknown to Grishin. I explained they were widely found in the United States and would give a stiff battle on the hook.

At noon, we sat on a bank near the stream and spread our lunch on a cloth I had brought. It was an idyllic Austrian scene, with the brilliant blue of the sky reflected in the clear waters of the swiftly moving stream. The clouds moved in various patterns before us; it was an ideal day. Grishin remarked he had not had as agreeable a day's fishing since he had left the Soviet Union. I didn't ask where he had fished, but added that it was one of the better days I'd had on the Schwarzau, as well. After lunch, he stretched out on the grass, while I made a few more casts, with no success.

During the afternoon, we went to one of the better places for trout and waded in the cool waters in shade and in sun until about five o'clock. Comparing our catches, Grishin had taken four more good-sized fish and I had three. He was pleased with such a good day and that his catch was larger than mine. As we had learned that my Russian was better than his English, we spoke English on the drive back, talking about some of the places we had fished. As we neared Vienna, Grishin became more chatty, saying that he had thoroughly enjoyed our expedition. I had also found it to be relaxing (and promising) and suggested that we go again in a week or two. He said he would like that.

I dropped him off at his house, and after shaking hands warmly, he told me he would phone when he could get away for another trip.

Grishin and I went to the stream about a dozen times during the summer and early fall of 1956. I'm sure that he always wrote a report on the events of the day, as I did. The important part was that he kept coming back, showing increasing enjoyment at each of our outings. After the second or third trip to the Schwarzau, we began to exchange casual comments about our backgrounds and early lives. It seemed that Grishin had been born in Moscow, and educated there. He had gone through the usual military schools before entering the GRU (military intelligence); Vienna was his first foreign post. He was essentially a serious man, although he had a wry sense of humor. He enjoyed a joke, but preferred more philosophical conversation, and it was only at a later date that we discussed anything political. I found him to be a pleasant companion and believed he felt the same about me. These outings, I think, provided a release from the tensions I knew existed within a Soviet colony abroad. I didn't press him and he seemed to unbend a bit. This was what I had hoped for.

As the months wore on, Jerry, my partner, established his own contacts with two members of the Soviet residentura, who were ardent hunters. In their outings, they often shot game out of season, while Jerry rigidly observed the game laws. He was born Viennese and had become an American citizen during his teens. With his Austrian background, he knew all the customs and traditions related to hunting. A different-style jacket was worn, depending upon what game was to be shot, and he was always correctly dressed for the event. This side of Jerry amazed his Soviet friends, as I observed on one hunt that I joined. He spoke German with a Viennese accent, not lost on the Soviets, whose German had been acquired at school. I urged him to make his contacts last throughout the winter months as well, writing personality descriptions after each outing.

The weekends Grishin and I spent together became increasingly relaxed. Our conversations were longer and more revealing, as we dipped into our backgrounds, exchanging views of life in Austria, our attitudes concerning the world at large and the period of history we were living through.

Driving back from the Schwarzau in late summer, Grishin lay back in the passenger seat of the car, extended his legs, and began to talk about the United States. He asked if his opinions were generally right and would I correct him when he had his facts wrong? He questioned me about how we lived, how people found jobs, how they used their money, and what kind of work "people in our class" had available to them. I answered him honestly and felt a sense of mild excitement that he was beginning to talk about matters such as these, which were verging on the political.

During the early fall of 1956, our conversations ran along the same lines but with a growing exploration in depth, on Grishin's part, of my political views, and his own, as well. At that time there was growing ferment in the Hungarian political picture and we frequently referred to the events of the summer in Budapest. His comments and questions were not sharp or aggressive, but were more ruminating and musing, as he searched for answers to questions that perhaps he had not been able to articulate before. I felt sorry for him. On one particular afternoon, as we were returning from the stream, he blurted out, "You know, Peer (we were on a first-name basis, his name in dimunitive form being Valya), the trout season is coming to a close—I wonder how else we can meet during the winter?"

I replied, "We'll figure out something; I've looked forward to these fishing trips and I think it would be a pity if we lost contact."

"I agree."

But then quite suddenly he asked, "You know what my position is in my embassy?"

I gave him a sidewise look as we drove along and replied, "Yes, I do, Valya. And you know mine, too."

He leaned his head back and spoke, while still gazing straight ahead.

"Yes, I know your position as well."

We rode silently along for a while and then he continued.

"You know, in my system, one never knows when one will be transferred. It could happen quite abruptly or I could be here for a couple of more years. I've been here about a year and a half and I'm eligible for reassignment at any time. Yet again, I would like to stay."

I told him that I was only a little over a year into my tour in Vienna, and that I would probably be there for at least another two years.

He went on: "If I'm suddenly transferred, I'll do everything I can to get in touch with you before I leave. I want you to know that."

Jerry and I often compared notes. He made the suggestion that it might be a good idea if he invited the Soviet and American hunters and fishermen to a stag evening at his home. We settled on a date and Jerry sent out the invitations. The dinner was to be on a Tuesday, 23 October 1956.

About eight of us gathered at Jerry's for drinks and a dinner of venison. The evening was a memorable one. Everyone was relaxed, the drinking didn't go beyond bounds, and the three-language conversations were easy, animated, and stimulating. Jerry's radio was tuned into the Austrian station, Rote-Weiss-Rote, to some pleasant background music. Just before dinner was to be served as we were all standing and sipping our drinks in the living room, the music suddenly was cut off and a voice began speaking urgently in German.

"We interrupt for an important announcement. In Budapest, at this moment, extensive demonstrations are underway involving Hungarian students and young people, who are attacking Hungarian government buildings, in particular, the radio station and the AVH Headquarters."

Conversation in the living room died out at once, and everyone listened to the news, as it continued.

"Some student demonstrators have been killed by gunfire, and there are reports of crowds in various parts of Budapest moving toward the central squares of the city."

We all looked at each other as the radio continued.

"There are some reports, not yet confirmed, that Soviet troops and tanks have been engaged in actively opposing the demonstrators with small arms and machine guns."

I walked across the room and turned the radio off. The entire group was silent. The atmosphere in the room was oppressive, leaden. Finally, Sokolnikov, the senior Soviet member at the party, stood up and said, "I think it better that my comrades and I return to our embassy. I hope you all understand."

We all quietly agreed and began shaking hands. The Soviets went to get their coats and we escorted them to the entryway. Grishin caught my eye and, ashen-faced, he took my hand and shook it firmly and warmly. He then turned and joined his colleagues as they went out into the night. The Hungarian Revolution had started.

The next day our ambassador announced to the embassy as a whole that there was to be no further social or diplomatic contact between the American Embassy and the Soviets until it had been resolved at the Washington level what our attitude was to be. He especially called me in to say that because of our association with certain Soviets, all of that would have to go in the "deep freeze."

A few days later, as the situation in Budapest and throughout Hungary worsened and the first part of the bloodbath began, my phone rang one evening. I answered it; Valya Grishin was at the other end. He told me in a rapid and hushed voice that he was at the East Bahnhof across the Danube in Floridsdorf. He was on his way back to the USSR; he had received his orders only a few hours before and he and several other officers "of our service" were returning to Moscow. Nobody knew that he was calling me and he couldn't speak very long. He thanked me again for all of the fishing trips, and, as he put it, "the wonderful experience we had together, the conversations and the friendship." I told him if he ever came to a Western country again that he could always address a note to me in care of the American Embassy, in whatever city he was, and it would reach me. He thanked me again in warm and urgent tones and said good-bye.

That was the last we ever heard from Valya. I know he was just on the verge of making that ultimate step to join us, until that fateful evening in October 1956.

The Hungarian Revolution changed the nature and level of American and Soviet relations, particularly in Vienna, to such a degree that direct and personal contact with Soviet intelligence, such as we had been trying to accomplish, became impossible, as a matter of American policy. Our relations with all Soviets, except at the most formal diplomatic level, were at an end and remained that way for the rest of my tour in Europe, lasting until August of 1959, when I left Vienna for a further post.

11 A Cautionary Tale

Following the end of the four-power occupation in 1955, the American Embassy assumed its place as the center of American representation in Austria. It was a gray four-story sandstone building of classic proportions, shaped like a shallow U. Our offices were on one of the upper floors. The building, before the Nazi occupation of Austria in the late thirties, had been an Austrian school for diplomatic studies. Its function had gone back to the days of Franz Josef, when Vienna was the hub of the Austro-Hungarian Empire of over thirty million people.

My own family life deteriorated badly in the spring of 1956 and by April my wife and I had agreed to separate. She returned to the States, taking the youngest child with her. I kept the two girls with me until the end of the school year in June. All of this coincided with the announced departure of the station chief, who was winding up a two-year tour in Vienna. He was due to go to another European post, and I was to succeed him.

I had always felt that the residentura had fairly good access to our comings and goings. We knew of minor and small-scale operations in which they had procured embassy telephone books and lists of employees, together with home phone numbers and addresses; we knew they were constantly using this information to achieve penetrations into the embassy proper. Their pressure in this direction was relentless and unceasing. The case of Sam is only one example.

Sam was an embassy officer, who had been hired after the American occupation ended the previous year. He was Jewish, and it was for this reason that he found himself caught up in a rather unpleasant game with a KGB officer.

From time to time, we would have a cup of coffee in the embassy snack bar. That was as far as it went; our social and business paths seldom crossed. He was a round-faced, rather heavily built man who always seemed somewhat on the tense and nervous side.

One morning my secretary came into my office, closing the door behind her. She came over to my desk and said in a low voice, "Sam is outside and wants very much to see you. I think he's been crying."

He walked hesitantly into my office and took the easy chair I offered him. I gave him some coffee and asked, "How are you Sam? What's up?"

"I'm in trouble and I need help," he blurted out. He sipped some coffee and put his cup down clattering.

I got up and walked to where he was sitting, put my hand on his shoulder, and suggested that he simply take it easy and relax.

"What's the problem, Sam?"

He gazed distractedly out the window. He seemed to have trouble forming his thoughts, gulping several times and clearly trying to control himself.

"There's this Russian, you see. He phoned me at home the other night and told me he was a Russian official and he wanted to talk with me. I told him there was nothing to talk about; he insisted and said if I refused he could make trouble for my relatives in the States. He went on, saying he knew I was Jewish and there were ways of making things unpleasant for me if I didn't meet him."

I asked if the Russian had given any name and Sam replied he hadn't.

"He told me to be at a certain bench in the Volksgarten behind the Burgtheatra at four yesterday afternoon."

Sam became jittery again and I waited a bit before speaking.

"Did you go to meet him?" I asked.

"I figured I had to. I was scared by what he said on the phone. I don't want anything to happen to my relatives. I had no idea what he might do, so I went there yesterday. After a few minutes a man walked up and told me his name was Boris. We sat together on the bench. He's a big guy with a very mean face and a slow way of speaking. I was afraid of him right away. He looked at me steadily and I couldn't meet his eyes; I had to keep looking away."

Tears formed in Sam's eyes and I walked over to the window. "What did he say to you?"

"He told me to bring copies of any correspondence that came

to my desk the next time we met. He said there were important things he wanted me to do for him later, but first he wanted to know what I did in the embassy."

I asked him what happened next.

"I told him I didn't know—I simply didn't know. He pressed me further and I agreed to another meeting. He said, fine, be at the same place at the same time on Monday. I went home and couldn't sleep all last night. I decided I had better have a talk with you."

"I'm glad you came to me, Sam. First, do you think you can go to this next meeting without being too nervous about the whole thing?"

"I don't know. I can't see what good it will accomplish, but I guess I can see him. I'll do whatever you ask me to."

"O.K., here's the pitch. Go to the Volksgarten meeting place. Pay no attention to anybody around you. Look at his face, his hands, the way he dresses, and note particularly the way he speaks. See if he wears rings or any unusual kind of clothing and try to see if he has any gold fillings in his teeth [always a sign of Soviet affluence and status] or any special mannerisms."

I went on.

"Tell him you've thought the matter over and want to avoid any kind of trouble, that you'll bring him a few papers, but nothing important crosses your desk. He'll ask you for another meeting and when this one is over, return to the embassy and act as you normally would at that time of day. Don't rush to my office unless something urgent has taken place with your friend, Boris."

Sam interrupted vehemently to say, "He's not my friend—he's not my friend."

I told him that I understood, but he should drop by to see me in a leisurely fashion after the staff meeting on Tuesday unless some important point came up over the weekend.

Sam agreed, sitting there forlornly wondering what he had gotten himself into.

I took him to the door and told him not to worry; we'd be looking out for him every foot of the way. He seemed to feel better and slipped out the doorway and down the stairs toward his own office.

This all sounded interesting, but not unusual. Many Soviet intelligence officers had approached American officials because of their Jewish origins. The line in those years was always pretty much the same. "You're not trusted or appreciated by your superiors because you are Jewish; you can do more to help the cause of world Jewry by cooperating with us than in any other way. Besides, we know about your relatives and it will be better for them if you help us out."

Calling in a few case officers, we agreed to have one surveillance and photographic team put together to cover the meeting at four o'clock. We would photograph Boris and one of the surveillance squad, after getting details of the meeting, would go to our operational post, overlooking the Soviet Embassy, to wait for Boris's return.

The next morning I saw Sam briefly in the hallway and assured him there was nothing to worry about. He seemed rested and relieved and looked as though he had finally had a good night's sleep. I promised him everything would work out and added that, if possible, he might ask Boris for a telephone number where he might reach him, if necessary.

The time for the meeting came and passed. We had word from our photographic team that they had several good photos of Boris; they would deliver them to me that evening. The surveillant, who had gone back to the Soviet Embassy, picked out Boris entering the front door at about six P.M. The time intervals checked out with the account that Sam later gave me.

After the daily embassy staff meeting on Tuesday Sam came to my office. I looked at him questioningly and the words came out in a torrent.

"This guy told me that I should always remember how the Jews are oppressed in the States and I'm looked down on by people in the embassy. He said the work I could do for him would help all the Jews. It didn't make any sense, but he kept talking about this for fifteen minutes. He then asked if I had thought over his proposition. I said I'd be willing to give him a few papers, but they were of no value and I'd bring them to the next meeting. Oh, he gave me a phone number, without my asking, in case I wanted to get in touch with him."

Excellent photos of Boris came in which we compared to our gallery of officers in the Soviet residentura. These were obtained by surreptitious streetside photography and from passports of individuals to which we had access. Even the Soviets had to go through airports and cross borders at railway connections and surrender their passports, just as we did. He turned out to be Nikolai Petrovich Fomin, at least that was the name used on his passport to enter Austria. Fomin had been assigned to temporary duty in Austria from Moscow; it was obvious that Sam had been his target.

The chief of the surveillance team told me he was quite impressed with Boris's appearance. He had a really menacing presence, and Sam had been quaking like a rabbit under the steady eyes of a wolf.

Before the meeting on Tuesday, Sam was again showing his nerves and asked how long this would go on. I assured him it would soon end. There were two or three more meetings when some innocuous papers were passed. Meanwhile, our surveillance squad was "taking" Boris about Vienna, as he apparently occupied his free time in performing operational chores for the Soviet residentura.

One morning, not to my surprise, Sam came to my office, saying he couldn't take it anymore. He asked if I would speak to the ambassador and have him relieved of duty in Vienna and sent back to the Department of State as soon as possible. The ambassador had been kept up-to-date about Sam's problem. After an exchange of cables, Sam, a bachelor, soon was on a plane out of Schwechat and away from Boris. That was undoubtedly the happiest day he had ever spent in Vienna. On our side, we had not only identified another KGB officer and his operational style, but we had given support and protection to an American who felt threatened and in trouble.

The door leading into my offices in the embassy was across the corridor from the embassy cipher section. I had a nodding acquaintance with the members of that office and knew perhaps half of them by first name, but had no official contact.

One morning my office door burst open and one of the embassy code clerks strode in, a young Jewish boy, whose name I recall as being Irving. He had simply brushed by my secretary and, once in my office, shut the door firmly behind him and came to my desk.

"Something happened last night, Mr. de Silva, something you wouldn't believe. I've got to tell you the whole story; I don't know what to do and you're the only person who might help."

I calmed him down and put a cup of coffee (indispensable in this business) in his hand. Irving was a tall, rawboned young man of about twenty-three years, a bachelor, who spent his leisure time with a younger set of Americans and Austrians. They never presented a problem; we envied their carefree attitude and obvious enjoyment of being single and in Vienna. In staccato and nervous bursts, Irving told his story.

Several months before, after work one afternoon, Irving and his friends were at one of their regular haunts, the Regina Hotel garden café, for a glass of beer, where they planned their evenings. This was almost a ritual. A well-dressed older man had been sitting at a nearby table, noticeably paying attention to this group of young people, who were laughing, talking, and enjoying themselves. As they were about to leave, he got up and came to their table. He was wearing a neat, dark blue suit and one of those hats "with the brim curled up all around"—a homburg. He spoke German with an accent and introduced himself as a Belgian businessman who frequently came to Vienna, and it would please him very much if he could pay for their drinks. Irving and his friends, who didn't make much money, were only too happy to have this friendly stranger pick up the tab; he joined them for a final round of drinks.

Some time passed and on four or five occasions, this group of young people found Monsieur Michel joining them. He came to be something of a patron; they looked forward to having him pay the bill when their paths happened to cross. He never asked anything of them and simply seemed to enjoy their company. At the close of a short evening social hour, he would tip his hat and disappear into the First Bezirk.

As time went on, M. Michel learned that Irving collected classical records. Irving lived alone in an apartment not far from the West Bahnhof and his time at home was spent in reading and listening to the phonograph. One evening his phone rang; he was surprised to recognize M. Michel's voice. He had just arrived in Vienna and told Irving he had found a couple of French classical recordings that he might like and could he drop by and leave them? Irving gave him the address, and in about half an hour there was a tap on the door. Handing Irving a parcel containing the records, M. Michel entered the apartment and put his hat and gloves on a table. Irving was opening the package when M. Michel crossed the room to where he was sitting and said, "Irving, there is something you should know about me."

His demeanor and tone of voice were entirely different from

anything Irving had noticed before. M. Michel reached into his inner coat pocket, took out an envelope filled with a large bundle of American banknotes, bound by an elastic band. He dropped it on the table in front of Irving's startled eyes. He then reached into his other pocket and drew out a passport, saying, "I'm not a Belgian businessman. I am a Soviet intelligence officer and my name is Aleksandr Shchukin." There it was in Russian and French, describing Mr. Shchukin as a Soviet diplomat.

"I know that you are a code clerk in the American Embassy. This is ten thousand dollars for you in return for half an hour of your time, in which you will tell me all about your work in the code room in the embassy."

As Irving told me this, he was rubbing his hands together nervously. He said he couldn't have been more surprised if M. Michel had crawled into his chair and turned into a serpent. All he could think of saying was that his parents were in Vienna, visiting from the States (which was true) and that he expected them at any moment.

Shchukin said that he understood, but they must meet the next evening. Irving thought distractedly and finally told him that he would meet Shchukin at a shop in the arcade in front of the West Bahnhof at eight o'clock. He was already pushing Shchukin, who had scooped up his money, toward the door.

"You've got to leave now. If my folks arrive, I won't know what to tell them."

That was the essence of the story Irving told me in an agitated fashion that morning in my office. I had no reason to question this approach. It would be easy to verify the meeting, which was set for that night. But it was particularly interesting that the Soviets would drive so aggressively for the jugular, in the sense of going straight for an American cipher clerk. This fact, in itself, reflected their acute need for information about our diplomatic ciphers.

We arranged with some friends in the Austrian State Police, after informing them of the circumstances, to have the meeting surveilled, to have them pick up Shchukin, and then wait to see what transpired. Everything went off as planned near the West Bahnhof. As soon as they met, the police dropped down on them both, like a net. One police officer led Irving away around the corner and turned him loose, while two others touched the brims of their caps and asked for Shchukin's papers. With great composure, he smiled at them both and handed over his passport, which they examined, noting it listed him as a Soviet diplomat. They returned his passport, saluted, and excused themselves. Our sources confirmed that he spent the night at his embassy and left Schwechat Airfield the next day on an airliner bound for Prague.

Irving came in the next day to thank me for bailing him out of a difficult situation; luckily his tour in Vienna was coming to an end that month. He received permission to leave a few days early and return to the States with his parents, who were still in Vienna on their vacation tour. I thanked him for helping us in what could have been a much more serious matter.

I have never known a KGB (or GRU) officer, who was himself Jewish. They possibly had staff officers who are Jews, if only for the possibility that such an officer might give them an entrée to Jewish targets. From conversations that took place in various residenturas with which we were familiar, a Jewish person, under intelligence scrutiny was generally the object of interoffice derision. Invariably, he was the "Zhid," the Yid. The KGB approach to both Sam and Irving, attempting to play on their supposed inferiority, and their presumed insecurity within the American governmental structure, provides further one simple example of the wholly cynical way the KGB would study people for recruitment purposes, and how they would bring pressure to bear on individuals they thought defenseless.

12 Bugs and Radios

One of our indigenous Austrian agents reported in with what he thought might be a useful piece of news. A friend of his, a Viennese real estate agent, had told him that he had a new client, "one of the senior Russians in the embassy." It was none other than our friend, Sokolnikov. He was looking for a new house in Hietzing, in the Thirteenth Bezirk. The real estate agent had really gone to work on this one, anticipating a big fee if he found the right place for this Soviet. He didn't know Sokolnikov's KGB status, but our agent did.

After several meetings with our man, he assured us that the realtor was a friend of long standing; he could trust him. When his friend had found one or two properties in which the embassy expressed interest, he was to let us know. We ran some investigative checks on the realtor and found him clean. Our own agent was another matter. If we approached the realtor through our agent, that would blow him to the realtor as an employee of the Americans. We questioned him on this point; he volunteered nevertheless to recruit his friend for us. This was done. The real estate agent seemed to have no reservations about this connection; we put him on a nominal retainer on a monthly basis and polygraphed him. Even beyond Sokolnikov, a realtor could be valuable in numerous ways in the future.

Through our own technical staff in the station, we began dickering with Headquarters for an appropriate radio transmitter for use when the time came. The exchanges were endless and in general unsatisfactory, as far as we were concerned. It always seemed that way when trying to get a fairly simple working item such as a short-range clandestine radio transmitter. Endless questions were raised as to where the transmitter would be used, for how long, what was the likelihood of its being discovered, and on and on. In any radio operation of significant potential, the risk of hostile counteraction was always high. Our Headquarters rationale seemed to run that for a low-level radio operation of little importance and sensitivity, our most sophisticated equipment could be made available. On the other hand, for a potentially high-level activity with significant risks, only nonsensitive and nonsophisticated equipment could be used, for fear of compromise of some of our advanced techniques.

We were blessed at the time, in the Vienna station, in having on temporary duty as chief of our communications section, a senior communications officer whose grade was considerably higher than normally would be found in a station of our size. He was there in connection with other technical work then underway. This officer, whom I shall call Norwood, was a remarkable personality in his own right. A genuine down easter, and a very decent and likable person, Norwood's conversations with me would invariably consist of "Ah, yup," or "nope." Technically, he was very highly qualified.

He came to my office one day and said that he had been watching the problems we had encountered with Headquarters in our cable traffic concerning the radio transmitter. He had been giving the matter some thought and went on to describe how he thought he could make a good small transmitter that would serve my purpose and would work for about half a kilometer in range. This came as a relief after the endless exchanges with Headquarters over a minor request. I told him to go ahead, let me know what he needed and when he thought it might be ready.

He launched into what, for him, was a veritable stream of conversation. "It's ready now. I made it over the weekend and this is it."

I had not noticed as he came to my desk that he had placed on it a nasal inhaler tube, the kind one buys in a drugstore. It was about half an inch in diameter and about two inches long. It lay there by my lamp and Norwood said once more, "That's it. Let's go across the hall and test it."

We went to the communications area, passing through several reinforced concrete walls and the heavy doors that protected the area. Norwood had hooked up the receiving end to a tape recorder. He flicked the tape to forward and at once his conversation with me in my office came through with complete clarity. He had been experimenting with this design for about a year, back at Headquarters, but had never been able to promote any interest in it. He had been told that, in practice, it wouldn't work and they already had "on the drawing board" something that would meet their needs. I told Norwood that, as far as I was concerned, it would work for our purpose and asked him to put the equipment aside until we needed it, which would be soon. We stopped cable traffic on this technical requirement and nothing more was said.

In a few days the realtor reported in excitedly. He had found a house in Hietzing that satisfied both the Embassy Administrative Section and Sokolnikov. It was a large house, occupied at the moment by a Canadian diplomat, who was to be transferred in a week. He felt that Sokolnikov was really interested and would probably sign a lease even before the Canadian left.

We knew from experience that senior Soviet intelligence officers very frequently held operational meetings in their homes with subordinate members of their staff, as they talked over their work and planned future activities. We had learned elsewhere that if meetings of this kind could be monitored, they could provide leads to agent identities, perhaps enabling us to double a Soviet agent back into his own residentura. However, when Soviets acquired property of this kind, at the earliest possible moment they would have someone from the residentura occupy it to insure that there was no other entry. There was only a very short time when the house would be empty; we had to arrange a delay between the time the Canadian departed and when the Soviet "watchdog" appeared. The realtor thought he could easily delay the move, perhaps with a mixture of carelessness and a premature departure of the Canadians. We located a listening post approximately three hundred meters away; this we rented and occupied to prepare for Sokolnikov.

In the few days remaining to us, we had to run field tests on Norwood's device, under conditions that simulated those in Hietzing, with regard to distance, types of surrounding construction, and extraneous electrical noises that might exist. After looking over various staff houses and their locations, it turned out that my own house on the Hasenauerstrasse was best suited for trial as a listening post. A friend, an American foreign correspondent, lived in a house at about the necessary distance from mine. We had frequently lunched together, he knew my status, and we had been mutually helpful. He was certainly not an agent of ours, but enough of a friend, I hoped, to do me a favor.

I went to see him one evening and said that I'd like him to help me out on something that wouldn't take much of his time, but was important to me. Taking the small transmitter, I told him what it was and that I would like to leave it behind his radiator that evening to test its range and effectiveness at my own house. I asked if he could spend the next half hour in the living room, moving about and talking to himself, playing some records, as we made our tests. He said he would be glad to help. I placed the device on the floor behind a radiator and told him I'd be back in about an hour to get it. The technicians were set up with their recorders at my house and we spent the next thirty minutes listening to some clear Mozart, as he played a favorite record. I returned at the end of the test, thanked my friend, and picked up the tube. He asked no questions, but said again that he was glad to be of help.

There was nothing further to do but wait until we got the green light from our realtor, plus the keys to the house, the evening following the tenant's departure. Our listening post near the target was set up; our technicians would enter the house, install the radio and get out. We had rented a small panel truck to park across the street with two of our men in it to watch both ends of the street and to give warning, by a separate radio link, to those working in the house and those at the listening post. The day came with little advance notice. The Canadians were to leave the next afternoon, but the Soviets thought they were to be there until midmorning the following day. We would have one night in which to do the job, which should take an hour at most. We had to find a location for the radio, install and test it, and leave the house exactly as we had found it.

On the evening of our entry, the two men parked the truck and settled down for a long night. Everything was checked and found to be in order. Two men from the technical staff were to make the entry with keys provided by the realtor, and when the job was done, would lock up the house. They were then to join us at the listening post, although we didn't anticipate any action until the next day. I kept up with developments during the installation and listened to reports from the men in the truck on the general traffic and passersby in the area. The street was almost deserted after ten o'clock in the evening. At the appointed time, word came from the truck that our men had entered the gate into the dark garden surrounding the house.

"We can see them now. They're at the side doorway; they've gone in and closed the door."

Protracted silence. Suddenly, after a half hour, we began to hear various sounds of scraping, knocking, and body movement. Norwood's transmitter was a success.

Then we heard a very loud crash, followed by a period of absolute silence. We looked at each other. Someone remarked it sounded like gunfire, which it did. The men in the van came on the air with considerable agitation.

"We just heard something inside the house that sounded like a gunshot. Nobody is coming out the door and we don't know what happened."

To our great relief, after about three minutes, the truck men came back on the air, saying that both men were coming out from the side door of the house.

"They're through the gate and strolling down the street."

Shortly they joined us and we gathered around to find out what had happened in the house.

They were both jittery; one of them said, "There we were, trying to find the best place to install the equipment. A large paneled room on the ground floor seemed to be the most obvious place to be used as a study and where Sokolnikov would hold operational meetings. There was a piece of paneling near the window, which would be a likely spot for a couch and an area in which they could sit and talk. We took a piece of the paneling out, put the radio in, and then switched it 'on' to give you an idea of how things were progressing."

We told them we had received the transmission.

"Then it came time to clean up. We had to do some coloring with our markers as there were scratches on the paneling. We started walking back in the darkness and me, great boob that I am, backed through a doorway. I guess some doors had been removed from their hinges to get furniture out and one was leaning against the jamb; I managed to hit it and it toppled to the floor, making the crash you heard."

For about the next eight months, we had a stream of remarkable intelligence as Sokolnikov held frequent operational meetings with his staff in that room. We learned the identities of a number of local Soviet agents and were able to double several of them. We also acquired a great amount of positive intelligence. Sokolnikov and other members of his residentura and sometimes embassy staff officers would meet to review world affairs and current Soviet policy. On our side, the Political Section of the embassy and the Department of State in Washington were impressed with the substance and volume of the reports.

At the end of eight months, the batteries went dead and transmission ceased; we felt that Sokolnikov had never been aware of the plant. We had been careful at all times to turn off the transmitter, with a signal from the listening post, when Soviet sweepers were at work in the house, as was routine from time to time. Unlike the batteries that were used in the transmitter at the Schloss Fuschl, these didn't emit any odor to call attention to the radio.

There was a follow-on development to this operation, which showed one of the sad peculiarities of bureaucratic institutions, of which the CIA is one. Norwood's radio transmitter was a marvel of miniaturization and efficiency. It worked perfectly, and did everything we wanted. It suffered from only one defect: its assembly and use had not been approved by Headquarters. After Norwood returned to Washington, I learned that he was sharply reprimanded for making this unauthorized transmitter, and just as sharply rebuked for permitting me to use it operationally. It may have been that only my strong letter of commendation of Norwood's initiative and skill kept him out of more serious trouble.

13 Hungary, 1956

In February 1956 an event took place in Moscow, unknown to the outside world at that time, that would have a dramatic and profound effect throughout the world, and especially in Hungary later that same year. Before the Twentieth Party Congress, Nikita Krushchev delivered his famous speech on de-Stalinization, and the cult of the personality. The speech was secret, and its existence, let alone its content, was not known to the Western world for several months. I first learned of it and read it during a routine consultation at Headquarters in the spring of 1956.

The chief of our Clandestine Service regularly saw visiting station chiefs from abroad and when my appointment came, he told me of the speech, and how a copy of it had been obtained from an East European Communist who happened to be our agent. It had been reproduced and was being studied in the State Department and the Executive branch. There had been no publicity; he asked me to read it over the weekend and to come in the following Monday and give him my opinion of it.

Krushchev's speech was astonishing. I read it and reread it. I thought of the anti-Communist riots in East Berlin and in East Germany in 1953. Would this speech head us all into another period of political convulsion in the Communist world? My own feeling was that this was now inevitable and this was essentially what I reported on Monday. The chief agreed and told me before I returned to my post that he had a special interest in what would be taking place in Budapest, which lay so close to Vienna. He instructed me to devote extra attention to the gathering of political intelligence on the Hungarian scene during the rest of my tour in Vienna.

Returning to Vienna, I held a meeting with our station officers, covering the trip to Washington and the Khrushchev speech, the general content of it and the remarks of our service chief. We had already been told officially, by cable, of the existence of this speech and that we and other European stations would be getting excerpts of certain portions of the speech for our own study. The ambassador had also been informed through his own communications channels; we had several long discussions about the significance of the Twentieth Congress speech. The impact of this event was being felt worldwide by the Communist Party as a whole. The Chinese Communist Party rather shakily announced their own policy of "let a hundred flowers bloom, let a hundred thoughts contend," clearly a move of political conciliation toward their own people. Even that far from Europe, there was restlessness; the leadership was trying to respond and control it.

It should be noted that the text of the Khrushchev speech had come into Western hands as a result of a CIA operation elsewhere in Europe. Because of its intelligence origins, there were different schools of thought concerning its validity. There were those who felt the speech had been floated into Western hands deliberately, as a ploy to confuse Western policy makers. Others felt the text of the speech was genuine, that it had in fact been given before the Twentieth Party Congress. We generally accepted the latter view. In the Vienna station we stepped up our intelligence operations in and out of Hungary and particularly into Budapest, where the political ferment was concentrated. The news reporting by American and other Western journalists and visiting correspondents took on a different tone. Political meetings of students and young workers in Budapest became more and more frequent and the subject matter discussed, particularly at the Petofi Circle, a literary discussion group, became more challenging to the authority and fundamental doctrines of the Hungarian Communist leadership. We had a young Hungarian university graduate, who, while living in Budapest, had official reasons for making visits to Vienna. He was one of our best and most accurate sources, as it turned out. He attended some of the meetings of the Petofi Circle, and was present at the dramatic and important meeting of that group on 27 June 1956, which concerned the executed Hungarian Communist, Laszlo Rajk. The rehabilitation of the martyred Rajk, the impassioned speech by his widow at his graveside, and the increasing demands for the resignation of Rakosi as First Secretary of the Central Committee of the Communist Party were typical of the incendiary topics discussed at the Petofi Circle. The Poznan riots had already occurred; the Communist leadership in Budapest could feel the ground moving under its feet. During the summer and early fall of 1956, they maneuvered endlessly, rejuggling the cabinet, shifting party chiefs around, consulting with Soviet advisers, and visiting Moscow for guidance, as well as receiving numerous delegations from the Soviet Union. The students talked among themselves with increasing freedom and audacity.

It is a well-known phenomenon in the field of intelligence that there often comes a time when public political activity proceeds at such a rapid and fulminating pace that secret intelligence, the work of agents, is overtaken by events publicly recorded. As the summer of 1956 wore on, we all sensed that this was what was happening in Hungary and this I reported to Headquarters. The excellent Western press, based in Hungary, was reporting in great volume about the explosive and rapidly moving developments among the workers and students in Budapest and throughout the Hungarian countryside. Of great interest to everyone (Hungarians included) were the attitudes and intentions of the Soviet Army divisions, based in Hungary itself. There were two of them, one in the central area near Budapest, the other somewhat to the west between the capital and the Austrian border. As far as we could determine from agent reports and information given by friendly travelers to the areas, Soviet troops, with their dependents, were staying close to their compounds and had even reduced their training and field exercises to an all-time low. They were keeping out of sight.

When Rakosi resigned his leadership of the party in July, Erno Gero replaced him. Gero was almost as thoroughly detested as Rakosi had been, and there was open speculation in Budapest as to how long he would be able to hang on. That matters such as these, so highly critical of the Soviets, could be openly and repeatedly discussed in the cafés of Budapest was an incredible development, both to the Hungarians and to observers in the West. Our intelligence sources could document what we read and lend credence to these reports, often after the fact of their being reported by an alert and aggressive Western press corps in Hungary. Our Hungarian university sources confirmed the published reports and were able to give us a three-dimensional view on how these events actually transpired in Budapest, also informed and prescient opinions as to what would happen next.

Hungary, 1956

On 23 October 1956, the dam burst. I have already recounted that I had been at a stag dinner in Vienna on that evening, with our Soviet opposites, after a season of hunting and fishing together, in the hopes of further cultivating intelligence contacts. That night the tinder-dry atmosphere in Budapest broke into roaring flames when the Hungarian secret police (AVO) and Soviet military elements fired on crowds of unarmed Hungarian students, killing and wounding many. An observer at this scene later told me that an animallike roar swept through Budapest as the citizenry came off the sidewalks and into the streets, and moved against the Hungarian organs of repression. The Hungarian Revolution had begun, unorganized, spontaneous; a torch lit to the cause of freedom.

Within a matter of hours, a number of the hated AVO in border towns near Vienna, such as Hegyshalom and Goer, were disarmed and in many cases beaten to death. The wildly happy Hungarian populace at the border area tore down the barriers and opened the way to anyone who wanted to cross into Austria or go to Budapest. The ambassador called me in and told me none of my staff was to go near the border, let alone cross it. Fortunately, he did not extend the ban to agent activities and within hours we had a number of Hungarian-speaking sources moving into Hungary to learn what was taking place with the Hungarian police, Army, and Soviet military elements. All of this was, at the same time, being done by the Western press, based in Vienna, but there could not be enough information. Every bit of news was welcome and every interview important. One of our agents, fluent in Hungarian, German, and Russian, found a small Russian military unit parked in a field near the town of Goer. They were staying by their vehicles and cooking food over fires. He approached them and said in Russian that he was from the West and asked them what their general attitude was about the events going on. He reported they were reluctant to talk, but one replied, "This isn't our affair—our orders are to stay out of everything." He reported they were not deployed for combat or to take up military positions. This reticent attitude on the part of the Soviets was reflected elsewhere in Hungary where Soviet troop units were located. Meanwhile, the Hungarian population was forming farmers' cooperatives, workers' councils, and student discussion groups. The uniformed Hungarian police were interfering with no one and were showing a common bond with the population. The Hungarian Army, where it was to be seen, had sided with the populace as a whole.

The Hungarian Revolution has been thoroughly covered by journalists and students, then and in the years since. There was no intelligence impetus given to the Revolution; it was spontaneous in every respect, although clearly the Hungarians hoped for U.S. help. Our function during those tumultuous days revolved around matters such as Soviet Army morale, Soviet military intentions, and developments in Budapest and the surrounding countryside.

In the first week after 23 October we were approached by certain Hungarians, whose roles became important. These contacts developed in the principal Austrian towns close to the Hungarian border. The men we met were all employees of the Hungarian State Railway System. They described how their railway system included a telegraph net from one switching point to another, from one station to another, throughout the entire length and breadth of Hungary. This system functioned through the metal of the rails themselves and each railway station had one or more telegraphers at work. They used this network to keep track of their rolling stock, advise of problems along the lines, and inform other stations of changes in the makeup of trains or in requirements for rolling stock.

What they wanted us to know was: at the rail crossing points in the eastern part of Hungary, where the tracks went into the Soviet Ukraine, their colleagues on the Hungarian side of these crossing points had begun informing them of transportation requirements being levied on them by Soviet railway officials just across the border. These were detailed and voluminous: a certain number of flatcars by a certain date, goods wagons (boxcars), passenger cars, all to be assembled at certain points at certain times. These transportation orders were sizable and were coming in torrents from the Hungarian border-crossing points. We immediately cabled all of this detailed information to Headquarters; our analysts there put it together and came back with the somber appraisal that the Soviets were calling up rolling stock for eleven armored or infantry divisions from the Ukraine and points east to be moved into Hungary at the earliest possible moment.

We informed our Hungarian friends that the Soviets undoubtedly had the firm intent of putting down the revolution by armed intervention. These were very sad days, even as the Hungarian people freed themselves from the Communist regime; we sat powerless on the sidelines watching the Soviets prepare to crush the revolution.

Meanwhile, the Soviets were carrying on the fiction of negotiating with the Imre Nagy government, purportedly to move all Soviet troops to the USSR. We knew to the contrary; they were moving troops to suppress the new Hungarian government. Our policymakers in Washington, by virtue of this intelligence from the Hungarians, had at least seven to ten agonizing days in advance to decide what, if anything, the United States might do to help the new Hungarian government or how the United Nations might help. There was never really any chance that anything could be done; we all sensed this. Time was too short and the circumstances too difficult. There was no common border with Hungary except through Austria, which under the 1955 Peace Treaty had to maintain its neutrality. It was U.S. government policy to respect that neutrality; there was no way of assisting Hungary through Austria or even by overflying it with aid of any kind. Hungary was literally surrounded by Communist bloc countries.

The days of Hungarian freedom rolled by inexorably. We watched helplessly as the Soviet juggernaut approached from the east and prepared itself for the attack. The movement and deployment of eleven Soviet divisions couldn't go unnoticed by the Hungarian population as a whole; wild rumors, which unfortunately were solidly based, swept the country from one end to the other. Everyone feared new Soviet intervention. Some speculated that the Soviets simply wanted to make a show of strength by coming into Hungary in force, but that they would then leave, having shown the world they were going of their own free will. Most Hungarians, out of long experience with Soviet duplicity, were simply fearful of the future. They were not, however, afraid to organize themselves to oppose Soviet intervention. They faced the certain onslaught with rare equanimity and courage. This was true throughout the country, as a whole, according to our sources and Western newspaper accounts, which were still being freely circulated and sent abroad.

By Saturday, 3 November, Soviet military deployments had apparently been accomplished. Soviet troops and armored columns controlled all the main highways leading out of Budapest to the east and in the direction of Yugoslavia, and had reached as far west as the Hungarian border towns facing Austria. Infantry elements in force had closed around Budapest, although they had not yet made any move to enter it. Budapest itself was alive and rampant with rumors, as its inhabitants gathered equipment, weapons, and food against any contingency.

In Budapest, the Soviets carried on their game of negotiations with the Nagy government. They requested a Hungarian negotiating team, to include senior Hungarian military staff personnel, to meet with them on the island of Czepel in the Danube River, to have further talks concerning the status of Soviet forces in Hungary and their ultimate withdrawal. These cynical gambits had no substance whatsoever; they were only intended to draw the leadership of the Free Hungarian Government into a trap, which was sprung the night of 3-4 November. The negotiating team, including the senior Hungarian army officer, General Pal Maleter, vanished without a trace.

These closing days of October and the beginning of November had found all members of the station literally living in their offices around the clock, with occasional forays out for operational purposes to meet with agents. My function was to manage the overall effort. This kept me at my desk, or roaming the halls, checking in with other embassy elements as to what their flow of information was. During these exhausting and emotional days and nights, the cable traffic from Headquarters and other stations in Western Europe came in a deluge. To keep all of our officers fully informed as to directives, responses and the various kinds of advice and evaluations we were receiving, I set up an "In" cable book and an "Out" cable book in my outer office. From these books, which were on a table surrounded by a few chairs, all officers were to keep themselves completely informed of all correspondence being received and sent. As a consequence, my outer office was occupied day and night by people reading the traffic and sometimes commenting together about the situation. Mainly, there was silence as they sat absorbing the developing tragedy. They all knew what to do with regard to their own contacts and sources, and worked on their own, preparing cables and dispatches; it was in that form that I saw the results of their efforts before they were sent out.

There was a short- and long-wave radio in my office and I had the frequencies of English-language broadcasts out of Budapest and other parts of Hungary. During this crisis, we had been given the services of temporary-duty officers from Washington and other stations; the communications section organized themselves on a twenty-four-hour basis, with at least two communicators always on duty. One of the main problems I had was to see that everyone got enough rest to keep themselves going; they were all gray with fatigue. From time to time I would have to order someone to go home and sleep for a few hours.

Early in the morning of Sunday, 4 November, I was asleep on my office couch when I was abruptly awakened by one of the communicators on night duty.

"They've started it in Budapest. The Soviets are attacking."

He spoke in a low, agitated voice, partly from fatigue, but mainly with emotion at what was taking place. I put my shoes on and went to inform everyone who happened to be in the station of this development. I told them I was going out and would be back in half an hour.

I drove from the Boltzmanngasse, down the Waehringerstrasse and parked near the Votivkirche. It was about six in the morning and still black, but the sidewalks were filled with Viennese, standing, listening to the outdoor loudspeakers that the city had installed on lampposts, carrying the news from Radio Budapest in both English and German. One of the first broadcasts out of Budapest went as follows.

"Now Imre Nagy, President of the Council of Ministers of the Hungarian People's Republic, is going to address you."

"This is Imre Nagy speaking, the President of the Council of Ministers of the Hungarian People's Republic. Today at daybreak Soviet forces started an attack against our capital, obviously with the intention to overthrow the legal Hungarian democratic government.

"Our troops are fighting.

"The government is in its place.

"I notify the people of our country and the entire world of this fact."

Other broadcasts followed in rapid succession. The battle of Budapest had begun.

As the streetside loudspeakers, in metallic tones, continuously poured forth the developments in Hungary, I observed reactions that changed forever my previously held view of the Viennese people, generally a cynical, cold-hearted lot. Looking about me at the people on the sidewalks, as the news crackled out overhead in bursts of English and German, I saw the Viennese, singly or in small groups, standing in silence so as not to miss a word. Almost without exception, tears streamed down their cheeks. The people of Vienna wept for the Hungarians in Budapest and did so in public and without any shame. I had never been so moved. The Viennese are a breed apart from the rest of Austria: aloof, self-seeking, and often rude. That day they displayed a kind of humanity and compassion that I had never thought they possessed. Beginning with the siege of Budapest by the Soviets and lasting all through the troubled weeks and months to come when refugees poured into Austria and mainly to Vienna, they offered the Hungarians all they were able to give, and opened their homes to them. My respect for them never failed again.

"Radio Budapest: Russian attacks started at four A.M. Russian MIGs are over Budapest. Goer is completely surrounded by the Russians. Szekesfehervar does not answer. AP, Vienna, if you have something, please pass it to me. The government waits for your answer: the news of the capture of the Hungarian military leadership was confirmed by the government spokesman, Mr. Hamori."

Another one a bit later: "Since the early-morning hours, Russian troops are attacking in Budapest. Please tell the world of the treacherous attack against our struggle for liberty. Our troops are already engaged in fighting. Help! Help! SOS!"

And still more: "In our building we have youngsters of fifteen and men of forty. Don't worry about us. We are strong. When the fighting is over, we will rebuild our unhappy country.

"We hope the United Nations meeting won't be too late."

From *The New York Times* of 4 November 1956: "Dateline New York. The Soviet Union early today vetoed a United States resolution proposing the United Nations Security Council censure of the Russian military attack on Hungary."

The Hungarian tragedy had really only begun.

14. The Refugees

The days and weeks following the sacking of Budapest and other Hungarian centers could be called "the time of the refugees." Hungarians by the thousands came across the border into Austria, at night, fleeing the reimposition of Communist rule in their country. For a long time after 4 November, ten to eleven thousand refugees nightly crossed the dark border into Austria, where they were generously received and given food and medical attention.

There were frequent outbursts in the Western press that a Soviet Army company or battalion, flags flying and bearing their weapons, had defected from the Soviet invasion forces and crossed into Austria. Invariably the stories would relate that these units had been interned and were being kept under Austrian guard at a secret camp. One place mentioned was the old airfield at Tulln, not far from Vienna. There was a rash of these reports; each one found its way into the wire services and back to Washington and the CIA.

We were besieged by cables, asking about these nonexistent troop units and these hordes of Soviet defectors; where they were, why hadn't this been reported, and did I need extra help in screening them? The simple fact was there were no hordes of defectors during the revolution nor in the weeks and months following the crushing of the revolt. Only one defector, a lieutenant in the infantry, who spoke Hungarian, was able to mingle with the refugees and find his way to the American Embassy, where he turned himself in. He was quickly removed from Austria and flown to an interrogation center in West Germany.

I explained repeatedly that the Hungarian refugee flow was so anti-Russian and anti-Communist in composition, and the refugees so emotionally and ferociously bitter about their treatment at the hands of the Russians, that a known Russian in their midst would certainly have been beaten to death on the spot. It would have been almost impossible for a Russian to have made it alive to the border, let alone to a safe place in Austria in that mass of aroused Hungarians. These rumors of Soviet defectors died hard and the news reports made interesting reading. The furious pace of the time made it unnecessary for the news services and press representatives to retract stories that were simply false, and were later proved to be imaginary. Headquarters was caught up in the fever of the times and became avid fans of this school of creative journalism. They bombarded me for information; when I explained in tortured detail why there were no Soviet defectors, I only received peevish replies that I was not being aggressive enough and I undoubtedly had poor liaison with the Austrians if I could not find out where these Soviets were being kept. Even when I went home for consultations in the summer of 1957, long after the myth of mass Soviet defections had been dissipated, I was still met with querulous questions from friends at home, high and low, as to why I had booted the whole problem of these notional Soviets.

Early in November, one event gleamed like a ray of friendly light in a wild storm at night. It was an incident related to me by the Austrian chief of the Staatspolizei in Vienna. On Saturday, 3 November, a Swiss citizen arrived in the vicinity of Vienna, having driven his car from his home in Zurich. In Switzerland, every able-bodied male of military age is considered to be a citizen soldier and, by Swiss tradition, keeps his uniform and rifle at home. When the time comes for his annual training, he simply dons his uniform and reports for duty. The name of this Swiss was known to me but has long been forgotten—a pity. He packed his uniform, put his rifle in the car, and headed for Vienna. At a later debriefing, he revealed he had arrived on 3 November. He turned east and headed for the Hungarian border, which was still open and unpatrolled, even though this was the eve of the new Soviet attacks on Hungary. The Swiss was motivated simply by an overwhelming urge to help the Hungarian Freedom Fighters. He was personally outraged by the Soviets and impressed by the courage shown by the Hungarians. He left his car in one of the nearby fields, changed into his Swiss Army uniform, shouldered his rifle, and marched into Hungary, determined to find a band of Freedom Fighters whom he could join.

The Refugees

Daylight found him in a Hungarian village, striding purposefully along. No one bothered him, but before long he ran into a Soviet patrol, who promptly took him into custody. After some initial confusion to determine who he was and where he had come from, they radioed to their headquarters they had a uniformed Swiss soldier and what should be done with him? The Soviets wanted nothing to do with Swiss involvement and told the patrol to turn him over to the Hungarian police, who also didn't know what to do with him. The Austrian Red Cross was called—communications still being open—to whom they explained the situation. They agreed to send a representative from each country later that afternoon, to a certain border-crossing point, now closed and in control of the Soviets. The Swiss would be turned over to the Austrians, eyes closed to the exchange.

This soldier, now in neutral Austria, had to be interned. The Swiss was furious. He had come to fight, no one wanted him, and he had been kept for hours in detention. He demanded to see the Swiss ambassador at once.

Frantic phone calls between Nikolsdorf, the Austrian bordertown, and Vienna, resulted in the decision to escort him as quickly and diplomatically as possible across the border to Switzerland. An Austrian policeman drove his car, which had been found in the field, followed by a sedan in which rode the Swiss national, a Swiss military attaché, an Austrian army officer, and an Austrian police official. He was taken to the border and quietly turned over to his own people. He was completely disgusted and thoroughly irritated at the failure of his mission. The Swiss were relieved; the Austrians were relieved; the Hungarians were relieved, and it would appear that the Soviets were relieved.

Almost every evening a few hundred refugees would appear at the American Embassy, arriving in the early hours, almost aimlessly as though they had no other place to go. They would mill about, some standing on the embassy steps making impassioned speeches to the others; sometimes they would leave a note or make a request to the Marine Guard at the embassy door. They created no disturbance, but their need for friendship and understanding from the Americans was almost pathetic. These were people who had been torn from their families and their homes; they had no idea what the future held for them. In most cases, they had only the clothes they wore or that the Austrians had given them. Contributions and help from all over the world had only begun to trickle into Austria; it was later to become a flood. The ambassador usually sent out a ranking member of the Political staff to speak with the group and ask for questions. Some of these were barbed: why hadn't we helped? Didn't we know the Hungarians had counted on us for assistance? They were not always easy to answer but the answers were accepted without any show of resentment.

Practically all of the Western embassies reinforced their staffs and their consulates to deal with this vast human tragedy. Most embassies volunteered help for the refugees, especially those who wished to immigrate to their countries. In addition to the United States, offers were made by Great Britain, Canada, Australia, France, Italy, Switzerland, the Scandinavian countries, and others to provide material assistance in the camps which the Austrians had set up and to arrange for relocation centers in their own countries to help them find work and places to live.

The American Consulate behind the Rathaus on the Lichtensteinstrasse was reinforced with scores of screening and visa officers to deal with the lines of refugees that formed early every morning. Because many of the Hungarians, who came for processing, ultimately to be settled in the United States, had volunteered intelligence information to the visa officers, who were ill-equipped to handle this, I set up several rooms in the consulate, staffing them with Hungarian-speaking CIA officers. There, these volunteers were interviewed. They knew they were talking to intelligence officers; voluminous and detailed information was obtained concerning the organizational structure and identities of the AVO (Hungarian secret police) and the Soviet intelligence and security organizations in Hungary, particularly in Budapest. Many of these refugees had been pressed into service, involuntarily, by these intelligence organs and knew about their methods of operation, their intelligence requirements and agents. There was one group, however, who deserve special mention.

In Budapest, under the governments of Rakosi and Gero, most Western visitors, especially journalists, were housed in the Duna Hotel in central Budapest, under strict AVO and KGB scrutiny. As with newspaper people everywhere, the journalists would tend to congregate in the evening at the hotel bar. The AVO had considerately provided the bar with a number of beautiful Hungarian women, popularly known as the Duna girls. I saw many of them during the refugee period; truly lovely women. Generally blond, always voluptuous, they were sophisticated and intelligent; their purpose was to make friends with Western, and especially American, correspondents. Most of them were technically prostitutes, but their calling had in no way touched their looks; as a whole, I had never seen a more stunning group of women.

As the Duna girls turned up in Vienna, singly and in pairs, they came to the embassy to volunteer information about the AVO and KGB links they had had. They were taken to the Security Office on the first floor; it was quickly apparent that this operation should be handled by us. The girls wanted nothing but to offer information.

By that time, I had a number of officers on temporary duty from Washington. I assigned one Hungarian-speaking officer to sit in the embassy Security Office and interview these girls. Vic was a short, quiet, friendly man of about fifty years of age. His sole distinguishing feature was his extremely bushy eyebrows.

Vic's anteroom soon became a social center for the Duna girls as they waited for interviews. He was essentially shy, but he had to pass through the waiting group every morning, and he couldn't control his eyebrows as he blushed and elbowed his way into his office.

He spent several weeks talking with the unending stream of girls, each one lovelier than the last, and at the end of the day, Vic was limp and exhausted. The net result was a mass of highly valuable counterintelligence information, but the experience took its toll on Vic. He told me later, "That was the hardest duty I ever had in my life."

Around the middle of November, the embassy was notified that the then-Vice-President Richard Nixon intended to visit Vienna, as an American gesture of sympathy and friendship to the Austrians and to the Hungarian refugees. The visit of a Vice-President abroad always entails much preparation and planning for security, accommodations, entertainment, protocol visits to the host government, state dinners, and all the activities that go on in the diplomatic world. Mr. Nixon's visit was no exception; Ambassador Thompson arranged for him to stay at the Residence, a large and sumptuous home in Hietzing. This visit didn't please the ambassador and he didn't conceal his view that it was ill-timed and almost certain to be construed as a provocation by the Soviets. Cable exchanges between Washington, Vienna, and Moscow indicated that Ambassador Bohlen, then in Moscow, felt the same way. Thompson and Bohlen attempted to have the trip canceled or at least postponed for several months. The response, apparently from the White House, was flat and final: Mr. Nixon was to carry out certain affairs for President Eisenhower and would inform the ambassador, upon his arrival.

This led to a rather strained atmosphere preceding Mr. Nixon's arrival, reflecting on all of the U.S. staff. I was singled out by "Tommy" Thompson and told not to be aggressive in my work against the Soviets, lest there be some unforeseen incident that could turn the visit into an occasion for Soviet political reprisal of some kind. I didn't share his trepidation, but set up our schedules accordingly.

In reading the cables, giving the composition of the Nixon party, I noted the name, Robert King. In the early days of World War II I had known a Robert King, then an FBI agent in San Francisco. We had become good friends in connection with our joint work involving Soviet espionage against the atomic-bomb project. I cabled to see if this was the same person and learned that he had been informed I was in Vienna and that he would look me up.

The Nixon party arrived with the usual excitement and confusion that accompanied such visits. Two aides, including Bob King, were to stay with Mr. Nixon at the Residence. During early visits to the embassy, Bob came to my office and I spent a number of hours debriefing him on everything I knew about the events of the recent weeks and the present situation. He passed on much of this conversation to Nixon during private talks with him. There was a formal reception, to which I was invited; Bob had arranged that I have a few minutes alone with Nixon to give him a firsthand briefing. This seemed to nettle the ambassador and he later quizzed me extensively as to what took place with the Vice-President. The subject was innocuous enough, but only served to highlight his nervousness about the visit.

Nixon ranged widely throughout Vienna, going to our processing center at the consulate, calling on various Western embassies who were sharing the responsibility for resettlement of the vast number of refugees, but keeping protocol calls and receptions to a minimum.

The Refugees

One evening, as the Nixon party left the embassy, Bob King dropped by my office, and asked, "Hey, are you going to be home tonight?" His question was casual and friendly; I thought perhaps he might be free and we could get together.

"Yup, I'll be home all evening. Haven't a thing planned."

"Great. I'll probably be calling you later on."

I said he'd find me home with my feet up.

I was living alone with only a housekeeper, as my family had gone back to the States. I had a small but comfortable house on the Dr. Heinrichmaierstrasse, with a spacious and very beautiful garden; a huge chestnut tree on the left side of the house towered over the roof and provided shade for a small patio. The back part of the garden was loaded with flowers and apple trees that were covered with blossoms in the spring and later bore delicious fruit. It was a relaxing place to read and listen to music, during infrequent moments of leisure.

I reached my house at about seven-thirty and had dinner, looking forward to a quiet evening and a talk with Bob.

Time wore on and at about eleven o'clock, since I hadn't heard from Bob, I went to bed. The jangling of the telephone in the middle of the night roused me to instant wakefulness. It was Bob; he spoke to me in his easy Alabama drawl.

"You know where I'm staying and if you feel like joining me tonight, get dressed and come on over right away, but wear some warm clothes. I'll explain when you get here. Can you make it?"

"I'll be right there. Give me fifteen minutes."

It was cold and damp in the middle of November at two o'clock in the morning. Driving into the Residence grounds, I noted considerable activity, muted though it was. There were no loud conversations or noises, but I saw perhaps half a dozen strange cars, mostly bearing Austrian official license plates. I went inside and was grabbed by Bob and taken to a corner at the entranceway.

"The old man's going down to the Hungarian border. No cameras, no press. He wants to see the situation for himself, get an idea of what these people are going through. Do you want to come with us?"

I was eager to go (the ambassador had made the border "out of bounds" with no exceptions) and shortly found myself in the back of one of four sedans, rolling through the dark streets of Vienna. After we were underway, I noted that my companion was none other than Dr. Max Pammer, Chief of the Austrian State Police. Max was an old and good friend. He had made the arrangements for this visit to a border farm, and had mentioned to Bob there was an American he knew would like to go along, if there was room. He said Bob had smiled at him and said, "You probably mean Peer de Silva, don't you?" He told Max he had already asked me and that I'd be riding with him.

We moved rapidly through the bleak night, southeast of Vienna, until we reached the town of Andau, a few kilometers from the Hungarian border. It was pitch black, only a few lights visible, some distance ahead of us. I knew the general topography of the region; there were a number of large farm holdings, several of which were up against the wire fence that separated Austria and Hungary. In Andau, a number of heavy farm wagons, drawn by tractors, were waiting for us, each wagon filled with hay. We broke up into small groups and got in the wagons, burying ourselves in the hay. It was biting cold and I thanked God for the sweater and heavy Austrian lodenmantel I had grabbed at the last minute. The lodenmantel is a multipurpose Austrian-designed utilitarian overcoat. You could sleep under it, make love on it, and keep warm in it. That night it was keeping me warm.

As this strange convoy started out across the fields, I looked up into the clear, starry night, as we lumped over the furrows, and thought of the thousands of Hungarians who, at that moment, were waiting to take that final step across the line into Austria, where they would be safe.

In even deeper darkness there loomed, low and close to the ground, more farm buildings. We could see some fences and hear the movement of cattle in the barns. We rounded a corner of a farm building and saw a single naked lightbulb, over a doorway. We stopped; there seemed to be nobody else on the face of the earth at that moment. A figure jumped down from the first wagon and opened the door. Light flooded out, the man leaned inside and spoke rapidly and softly in Hungarian. He turned, came back to his wagon and I could hear him say in German, "There are two of them in there now. They have just come across and are very tired."

There was more hushed conversation. We were told to gather near the lighted door. I could see Nixon's figure, as he approached with an interpreter and stepped inside. I was standing in the doorway and could see the room, which was small and dominated by a pot-bellied stove in one corner, together with some stools and cushions. It was warm; there was a large old-fashioned percolator on the stove, which gave forth the wonderful aroma of Austrian coffee. Sitting on stools in the center of this small room, there were two young women in trousers, worn shirts, and jackets.

One girl was about eighteen and the other about twenty-four. They looked wan and exhausted, but they gave off an aura of peace and serenity. The interpreter turned to Nixon and said, "The girl I spoke to said she speaks some English. She learned it in school. Her friend speaks only a little German. Both of them were employed in a machine-tool plant in Budapest."

The older girl's English was not at all adequate and the interpreter was the mediator between Nixon and the girls.

Nixon said in a soft voice, "Please tell them who I am and that I came to welcome them to freedom, and to listen to anything they might care to tell me."

The interpreter translated this; the older girl smiled and gestured to a stool. He told Nixon she was offering him a stool to sit on, if he wished. He sat down, resting his arms on his knees, looking at them intently. The interpreter went on.

"She wants to know if there is anything the Americans are going to do to preserve the freedom of the revolution."

Nixon responded, "Please tell them there is nothing the United States government can do at this time except to help people like them and provide them all with a future of promise and hope."

The girls listened carefully and then replied, "Please tell your Vice-President that we understand. Please tell him also that we appreciate his care and his thought. We know he represents the American government and the American people when he tells us these things. We don't want to be discourteous, but now all we want to do is rest. Then we will go on to his country and be good companions in freedom when we get there."

After the translator had finished this statement, Nixon stood up, walked over, and shook hands with each of the girls. He said good-bye, wished them good fortune, and assured them they would be welcome at the consulate as soon as they felt able to make the trip to register for immigration to the United States. An aide took their names and that information was passed the next day to the consulate. As a matter of personal interest, I checked the consulate files about a week later and found the girls were being processed for entry into the United States.

Returning to the farm wagons, we could dimly see several other figures coming across the Hungarian fields to the borderline wire. We headed toward Andau, but saw the door open, as new refugees entered the room we had just left.

At the Residence, a worried and pacing ambassador was waiting. I glimpsed the Vice-President's face, as he entered the door; he looked tired, serious, and withdrawn.

I said good night to Bob, thanked him for asking me, and went home to a rather troubled sleep.

The remainder of 1956 and the early months of 1957 found us largely caught up in intelligence work revolving around the Hungarians and the continuous stream of refugees still coming into Austria. It was also a time to reestablish networks within Hungary; there was no lack of Hungarians who were willing to go back across a border, which was not a tight Iron Curtain, as it had been. There were many sympathizers, who had remained in Budapest, and while it was dangerous for those involved, it was not difficult to find relatives and friends who were willing and productive collaborators. Budapest was still a crucible in which the real strength of Communist ideology was being tested.

The weeks following the revolution were enough to embitter perhaps all of the entire Hungarian population. Cardinal Mindszenty had achieved the stature of a national hero; even his taking refuge in the American Embassy (then a legation) was understood and supported. The last premier of the Hungarian State, Imre Nagy, following the attack on Budapest on 4 November, had taken refuge in the Yugoslav Embassy. He remained there for several weeks while János Kadar, who had assumed leadership of the country, negotiated with him through Yugoslav intermediaries regarding his future. In previous years, Kadar had been imprisoned by the Soviets and released only a few months before the revolt. He had come to power as an instrument of the Soviets, following the overthrow of the free government of Imre Nagy. One story that was repeated again and again, in all of the debriefings of Hungarian refugees of official backgrounds, who had given other reliable information, was to the effect that it was a commonly held view in Budapest that Kadar, during his Soviet imprisonment, had been physically

The Refugees

castrated by the Soviets. He was viewed more in pity than in anger; it was felt the Soviets owned him body and soul.

In the case of Imre Nagy, Kadar announced publicly that the Soviets had guaranteed him safe conduct from the Yugoslav Embassy across Hungary to the Yugoslav border. The Yugoslavs agreed to accept Nagy as a refugee. When the time came for Nagy to be taken to the Yugoslav border, he left the embassy and entered an official Hungarian car. A few days later it was announced by the Soviets that Imre Nagy had been shot. So much for a Soviet pledge of safe conduct.

Closing thoughts about the Hungarian Revolution of 1956 must be dominated by one central fact: In approximately ten days or less, the militarily dominated satellite state of Hungary, with Soviet armed forces on its soil, had risen against this Communist leadership, had destroyed it, and had set itself up as a free and neutral nation. This had never happened before. The tragic fact that the Soviets moved quickly and effectively to subdue the uprising in no way lessens the importance of what the Hungarians did for themselves in the face of Soviet terror and armed might, although they started from total disorganization without any external help whatsoever. A common canard of the time was that Radio Free Europe had instigated the revolt, that "fascist" elements in the West had supplied the insurgents with weapons and leadership and that CIA had really masterminded the entire situation. It was, according to the requirements of Soviet doctrine, a counterrevolutionary manifestation.

They couldn't afford to recognize the revolution for what it was: a revolt of the people to rid themselves of a Communist government. Whether or not the leadership in Moscow believed their own fantasies, we had ample evidence at the time that Soviet troops in Hungary at the beginning of the revolution and the eleven divisions that crushed it and remained after it were under no illusions whatsoever. They came expecting to find American troops and other Western elements throughout Hungary; instead they found ordinary workers, students, and farmers. They knew they had been lied to and that they were acting in no better capacity than Janissaries in putting down the Hungarian people.

If there was one single phenomenon that made the whole overthrow a possibility, I would describe it in this way. After the AVO and Soviets fired on the unarmed demonstrators, the population of Budapest and other major urban areas simply rose up in disgust and anger to throw off their tormentors. They rapidly found out that each one of them could safely and with confidence speak freely to his neighbor, his fellow student, his workmate, and his fellow soldier. Not only could they speak freely and without danger, but their neighbors and friends, they learned, had felt exactly as they did. This knowledge swept through the population like a prairie fire. The common bond that this created enabled them to form a sense of popular will, which was to sustain them through the terrible days and weeks of the Soviet invasion. They had learned that the spirit and passion for individual liberty remained in the Hungarian spirit throughout the country. This, I believe, they have never forgotten and exists today, however quietly it is concealed.

15 Transition

The emotions generated by the Hungarian Revolution of 1956 did not end overnight. There was a long and traumatic elision that lasted well into 1957. Thousands of refugees entered Austria and were resettled by a sympathetic group of Western powers. We performed a variety of services in handling this mass of humanity. We, of course, had to winnow out secret AVO deserters, who had crossed with the multitudes into Austria, and Soviet agents who had taken advantage of the crowds to start out on intelligence missions in the West. It is doubtful that we were completely successful in this endeavor, but we were able, especially with the help of Austrian security authorities, to identify and neutralize a large number of hostile agents.

In the spring of 1957 I found I was more than interested in one of the secretaries in the station. We had known each other for some time, as we had mutual friends and socially were invited to many of the same parties. She was the wife of one of my station officers, but they had led an estranged life for several years. Her husband was also a friend of mine and still is, but it was clear that I was strongly attracted to Marilyn. My own marriage was completely on the rocks; my wife had moved to Florida, where she had taken up residence, prior to divorce proceedings. Upon receipt of her divorce papers in early summer, she married an Army colonel, whom she had met in Virginia. The arrangements regarding our three children were complicated, but over the years they have become accepted and amicable.

The spring passed; Marilyn and I were to be married that summer. She and her husband had long before planned to divorce and they had agreed to this upon her return to the States, after five years in Vienna.

It is usual in our service for officers serving abroad to be given thirty-days' home leave for every two years of foreign service, duties permitting. In my case, I had been overseas since April of

1955 and was well qualified for home leave. Only the hangfire problems of the Hungarian Revolution kept me in Vienna until that summer; I planned to return to the States in July. Marilyn had preceded me to the States to spend the required six-weeks' residence in Reno. Her decree became final early in July, and after meeting in San Francisco we were married in a civil ceremony in Monterey, California.

Headquarters knew of these intentions and that I was going to cut my home leave short because of the still-turbulent situation in Austria. After a short honeymoon in Carmel and a visit to my family in San Francisco, and a few days spent with Marilyn's many relatives in Boston, we flew back to Vienna in early August.

We left New York for Copenhagen, which is a fascinating city and at that time of year sheer beauty. It was a city undamaged by war and populated by people whose natural friendliness and gaiety were apparent everywhere. On one occasion we asked a cyclist at a street corner directions to a certain museum. The cyclist, an elderly man who spoke fluent English, at once hopped off his bike and walked along with us to point out the way. It was a warm summer's day and we invited our volunteer guide to a sidewalk café for a glass of beer. He accepted gladly and we spent a few pleasant hours together. This was typical of the very enjoyable Danish people. Our stay in Denmark was brief as I had to get back to work.

The flight to Vienna was uneventful until we reached Schwechat Airport. There, a large group from the station was on hand to meet us. In something of a carnival procession, we drove through the drab streets of south Vienna to the bandbox house where I was living, on the Dr. Heinrichmaierstrasse. There they had put up welcoming posters and had mixed a punchbowl of what the Viennese called "bowle," a mixture of light wines, afloat with either fresh strawberries or peach slices. This typical Viennese mark of welcome ended the day of coming home.

There had been no significant changes in the embassy or the station during my absence. A new ambassador was shortly to arrive. During my consultations at Headquarters, which had lasted about five days, he had been at the agency for a day of briefings about our activities in Vienna and I had spent that day with him. The departure of Llewellyn Thompson, with whom I had had a spotty relationship, didn't find me desolated. His new post was the embassy in Moscow, where he later distinguished himself, negatively, in the Penkovskiy case. The new ambassador, H. Freeman Matthews, turned out to be a man with whom I formed a strong personal friendship, which has lasted over many years. He was at the time one of the four career ambassadors in the Foreign Service. Of middle height, "Doc," as he was commonly called in private, had a shock of white hair, pink cheeks, and an appearance of exuberant health. He was an enthusiastic and very good tennis player and, finding out that tennis was my game, thereafter asked me to play every weekend at the embassy court behind the Residence. A small group of officers met him at Schwechat and returned to the embassy, where the new ambassador met the principal embassy officers.

He then turned to me and said, "Peer, let's hop in my car and drive out to the Residence. You know it pretty well, don't you?"

I said that I did, but couldn't bring myself to tell him that in Thompson's day the tennis court had been turned into an extra parking lot for use during official functions. Thompson was in no way a sportsman. His form of relaxation was poker.

We drove out to Hietzing, the embassy administrative officer accompanying us, and pulled up in front of the imposing house, surrounded by a large park. The ambassador was not interested in seeing the house, but wanted to see the tennis court. We went through the door to the foyer, on through the living room and winter garden and out to the lawn. To the right was the wire fence surrounding the tennis court. The court had long been out of use and sat there, covered with oil stains and wheel ruts, looking very abandoned and hopeless. Ambassador Matthews looked at this scene for a grim moment. He then turned to his administrative officer and said firmly, "Today is Tuesday. I want to be playing tennis on this court by Saturday."

He played tennis the following Saturday; I was in the group of doubles. He could never get over the idea that the court had been used as a parking lot. During the next two years, he would occasionally comment acidly on the fact that this was just as bad as if the embassy silverware had been sold.

A chief-of-station has many and varied relationships with his ambassador, whatever the country. At this point, my experience with ambassadors had been limited to Moscow, Vienna, and, to a lesser extent, Germany. Later on it was to include close contact and professional relationships with ambassadors in several parts of the Far East: Korea, Hong Kong, Saigon, Bangkok, and Australia.

It goes without saying that, just as there are strong and weak CIA station chiefs abroad, there are strong and weak ambassadors. Some are timid, with an evident insecurity; on the other hand, most are confident and strong men, able in their leadership. I feel that most ambassadors under whom I have served have been men of high competence, probity, and courage. There were a few who were simply vapid and indecisive, but these were by far the minority. These few I could leave quite alone except for infrequent occasions when I needed official approval for an action involving policy, or when I would brief them on major station activities.

One classic example of caution, bordering on timidity, comes to mind. In Moscow, one Oleg Penkovskiy, who was to become famous as a Western agent in the highest levels of Soviet officialdom, made a direct approach to the American Embassy in Moscow to form a secret intelligence liaison with us. This development was viewed with the greatest suspicion by the ambassador. The upshot of Colonel Penkovskiy's courageous but perilous approach to the embassy was that he was sent away and told not to return. He left but went to the British, where he formed a contact. He let the British know his real purpose was to contact the Americans and he sought their help in arranging this. The British moved a little more aggressively and the relationship between Colonel Penkovskiy and the Americans, with the British being part of the equation, came into being. For sixteen months intelligence of the highest caliber flowed from Colonel Penkovskiy to the Americans and British. This is a matter of historical record and has been many times confirmed in terms of its strategic value. The fact remains that Penkovskiy was literally turned away while trying to make contact with us. This is a good example of excessive caution when presented with a rare opportunity. An approach such as Penkovskiy's could have been a Soviet provocation, but it could have been examined at closer range. Incidentally, his CIA case officer was my old friend George, whom I had hired in 1952.

Relations between an ambassador and station chief are, in the first instance, affected by the fact that each has his separate private channels of communication to Washington. This has sometimes provided grounds for a feeling that there may be a split in the line of command, anathema to the Department of State. Only the way in which the station chief conducts his business with the ambassador and the candor he brings to the relationship can ease this potentially abrasive arrangement. Each ambassador abroad has the absolute right to demand data such as names or other identification concerning agency sources abroad. It is to the credit of all that they seldom do, but rely upon the personal relationship and his accumulated experience with the way CIA functions abroad. Any station chief knows that if he crosses swords with an ambassador or withholds essentially important information from him, he will be the loser. At any stage, an ambassador, with any reasonable cause, may send a cable to the State Department, asking the immediate removal of the chief-of-station or any other member of his staff; this would be acted upon at once. This absolute power is rarely used. From my experience in watching our work abroad, I have seen it used only once. The agency choices in filling senior posts abroad are of such a caliber as to keep the association stable and friendly. Both sides are generally represented by experienced officers, long past the stage where petty considerations intrude.

I have been fortunate to have been stationed with ambassadors who were mature, hard-working men of broad vision and outlook. The exceptions can be forgotten; one simply had to work carefully and make certain there was no cause for offense or affront. An ambassador who was offended by a mode of conduct or personality could cause a feeling of distrust or insecurity within his staff to an extent that could create real difficulties in the workings of the station. Embassy staff officers, after all, take their lead from their ambassador, however friendly they might be individually. Everyone in the station was expected to conduct himself in ways to insure an easy working relationship at all levels in the embassy. There were inevitably petty jealousies and attitudes that had to be dealt with on both sides, with the station chief acting as peacemaker, but with an understanding ambassador this was not a great problem, only a constant factor to be considered.

The question has often been asked me in Vienna and since: Did I ever think I was known to the Soviets or to hostile intelligence services as being a CIA agent? My response has always been: "Absolutely. In all of my foreign assignments, I was always posted under my true name and was well known to the KGB.

Through them, I had to assume I was also known to all their satellite intelligence services; the Czechs, Hungarians, Poles, and East Germans."

This has always been a sound working hypothesis, I have found. I early formed habits and techniques on my own part, which would keep an air-gap between my personal life and my life in the clandestine sector, in which I would be performing secret acts. I was usually in charge of officers who carried on most of these activities, but there were times when I would be personally involved.

As far as I was concerned, it devolved down to keeping space, and often time, between my performance of clandestine work and my routine in the embassy and at home. This was to avoid hostile surveillance, care in the use of telephones, and taking all necessary precautions for protection during a clandestine meeting—a proper employment of what we call "tradecraft." This required that specific clandestine actions didn't become identifiable through habitual use, and were changed from time to time to keep an adequate distance between myself, my contact, and those who might be trying to identify us both. I remember Sokolnikov in the Palavicini Palast: "Oh, I do the same thing in my embassy as your Mr. de Silva does in yours."

Often we work in liaison with a friendly foreign intelligence service. This can be dangerous in the sense that the service you are working with may be penetrated by the KGB. There was a dramatic case in this regard. We had a working relationship with the Austrian State Police, who conducted extensive internal security activities. The principal officer, assigned to carry on liaison with my staff, was their number-three man. My officer was Jack, who had deflated the "count" by polygraph in Munich in 1951.

We were careful in our handling of our contacts with their service, knowing the routine risks in dealing with a foreign intelligence service. It was not until 1962 that we learned how dangerous it had been. I was in the Far East, but these are the circumstances related to me. A Hungarian intelligence officer had defected to the Austrians and asked at once to be put in touch with the CIA. We accepted his story and agreed to take him to the United States. He was in mortal fear of his life. The Austrians put him in maximum security in a police facility under their control. Two days before he was to be flown to the United

States, this man was found writhing on the floor of his room, crying out in agony and screaming that he had been poisoned. He died within a few hours. Access by Austrians to this person had been strictly limited. An examination of the circumstances leading up to the death led inescapably to one Austrian official. He was the number-three man and the person, during all of my years in Vienna, who had been the daily liaison with my staff. Investigation proved him to be an agent of the Czech intelligence service. It was he who killed the Hungarian, with poison supplied by the Soviets.

An experience in World War II taught me, at a very early professional age, a lesson in personal vulnerability. The year was 1942, in the San Francisco Bay area. I was then in charge of investigating Soviet espionage activities directed against the Radiation Laboratory at Berkeley, which was the spawning ground for the atomic-bomb project. In our circles, it was common knowledge that the Spionmeister, directed by the Soviet Consulate in San Francisco, was one Steve Nelson. Born a Yugoslav, he was a professional, a graduate of all the principal intelligence schools in the USSR. He lived a long life and died quietly of old age, but not before he had performed monumental tasks for the Soviets. Steve was never prosecuted, because he was spying for the Soviets, our ally. We had Steve under close surveillance, both personal and technical. At one stage, he moved from Oakland to a small house near the Berkeley campus of the University of California. We knew about this move, but nevertheless one day in the mail I received, at home, a U.S. Post Office change-of-address notice, telling me formally of his change of address from Oakland to Berkeley, signed by Steve. One must smile.

Nineteen-fifty-eight saw other changes in my life. Our first son, Peer, Jr., was born in Vienna at the Rudolfinerhaus on 13 May. We found our house too small at this time and moved to a large villa in Grinzing on the Hungerbergstrasse. Grinzing is one of the Bohemian areas, known for its many weinstubes, its heurige wine, and zither music, recalling the days of *The Third Man*. This villa was spacious, with French doors opening from the living room on to a balcony from which we had a panorama of Vienna. The garden was filled with trees, a few statues placed among the shrubbery, and a riot of color from the many flowers, with dahlias of every hue dominating the scene. The days in this house were some of the happiest we have ever had.

In spite of the fact that Ambassador Matthews was a much more amiable man than Ambassador Thompson, U.S. government policy in Vienna was still dominated by the Hungarian events of 1956. By directives from the State Department, there was still no social contact between American Foreign Service officers and the Soviets. The ambassador had no alternative but to follow this policy, and our earlier promising interplay of contacts with our opposite numbers in the KGB could not be resumed. On the Soviet side, their ground rules had changed; they sought us out at diplomatic functions and frequently would phone our homes or offices, trying to set up a contact. "Doc" Matthews commiserated with me, sensing the profit to be gained by aggressive contacts on our part with the Soviets, but could do nothing.

Our basic operations consisted mainly of servicing agents traveling to and from the Soviet Union for short visits, as well as strengthening our information sources in Budapest and the surrounding countryside. The latter was not too difficult; there were many Hungarians still eager to assume risks to put their finger in the Soviet eye in their homeland. In the station, we had a small group of officers who dealt exclusively with Hungarians, with their own surveillance teams and technicians. The Soviet Union, in the wake of the revolution, was attempting to rebuild its position in Hungary and consequently was reinvesting large amounts of Soviet Army and other matériel in the country. The training program they had previously conducted for Hungarian Army and Air Force officers was resumed. This provided us with another means of access to Soviet strategy, doctrine, and equipment. The revolt had deeply shaken the Soviet confidence, not only in Hungary, but in all its satellites. They knew there was a limited amount of reliance they could place in their Hungarian "allies." Nevertheless, there was intelligence to be gained and we mined that lode for all it was worth.

The early months of 1959 wore on. I became increasingly conscious of the fact that I was finishing my fourth year in Vienna. One beautiful day, as the Russians say, the incoming pouch brought a personal letter to me from the deputy chief of service, then Richard Helms. It contained what I had been expecting. This was my fourth year, he wrote, and it was time to decide where I should go next. He asked if I had any preferences, which was not usual in our service; one was simply told what his next post would be. That night I talked with my wife about possibilities for our future.

By this time, we had given a good deal to the work in Austria and Central Europe and were perhaps more tired than we cared to admit or even knew. We both agreed that we should shake the dust of Central Eruope from our feet and find a new area in which to live and work. Marilyn had been a secretary with the CIA since 1949, and was fully familiar with life in the agency abroad and how administrative matters were handled. That evening we sat on the floor of our house on the Hungerbergstrasse and leafed through a world atlas. It brought to mind my experiences in Tokyo just after the war in 1945 and we began to concentrate on the pages dealing with the Far East. In those days the American military and diplomatic presence was strong in the Far East from Korea all the way to India, and we both felt that a tour in that part of the world would be the thing.

The next day I replied to Helms' letter, for which I thanked him, and said that we thought an assignment in the Far East would be a change and give us a new perspective. We had thought of such exotic places as Hong Kong or Bangkok and, while I didn't mention them, they were in my mind as I wrote my reply, giving my general views about going somewhere in this area sometime in 1959.

It seemed to me to be the fastest exchange of letters on record between Headquarters and myself. About two weeks later I received a letter from Helms, stating that I had been "selected" to head the station in Seoul, South Korea. This was not my idea of one of the pleasure palaces of the Orient. I was to remain in Vienna through the World Youth Festival in July but was to leave at its end, with short consultations in Washington and then an immediate departure to Korea.

I went home that evening and found Marilyn standing in the foyer, as I came in the door. I told her that we had our new assignment and said, "I'm only going to say it once and you won't like it. We're going to Korea."

Her reply was completely unexpected.

"That's terrific. It should be a fabulous place. I know we'll love it."

And we did. Looking back upon the Korean years, they were

among the most exciting ones we had spent with the agency abroad, but this lay in the future. At the moment our thoughts were filled with preparations for the remaining months in Vienna and getting ready for our new assignment in a really distant and foreign environment.

There was no essential change in the nature of my work, following the Hungarian Revolution, until the end of my tour in August of 1959. Agent work was never drudgery for me, although others have found it so. In general, we went on building up agent networks in Hungary, especially in Budapest, and elsewhere in the Soviet Bloc. There were always defectors.

The World Youth Festival was a Soviet postwar creation, intended to demonstrate the solidarity of the Communist movement based in Moscow. It was essentially a series of conventions, held every second year, and up until 1959 had always been held in the Soviet Bloc countries or the USSR itself. These so-called festivals were strictly propaganda operations on the part of the USSR. The Soviet government had used pressure on the neutral Austrian state to secure Vienna as a site for the 1959 propaganda circus. The Austrians were in no position to deny them. The Vienna festival was Moscow's first venture to sponsor the festival out of the Bloc, and its aims were obviously high: to demonstrate the ability of the Communist party of the USSR to unite students and young people in free countries of the West behind the Soviet Communist movement and, by so doing, bring political pressures on the free Western countries. Very heady goals indeed. We soon learned that the Soviets were leaving nothing to chance; vast amounts of money were to be poured into the Soviet effort to mold and control the student leadership in Austria and in all participating countries.

We, for our part, had a great deal of cooperation from student organizations in Austria. The Vienna Station had been appointed as the center of CIA coordination to deny the WYF to the Soviet Union as a political propaganda victory. The Soviets, as it turned out, made a fundamental error in choosing Vienna as the site for the WYF. They had myopically ignored the fact that Austria had been occupied by the Red Army a scant four years previously. People had not forgotten the bitterness and harshness of the Soviet occupation. The marks and wounds of that occupation still existed, and millions of Austrians retained hateful recollections of the postwar years under Soviet control. Then too there was the more recent vivid experience of the Hungarian Revolution and the Soviet role in it.

The vast majority of Austrian youth were almost instinctively anti-Communist and anti-Soviet. The presence of many young Hungarians, who had taken up residence in Austria following 1956, was a significant factor as well; they banded together with their Austrian compatriots to form cohesive groups, taking part in the many events that were scheduled for the World Youth Festival. There were debates, marching, nighttime rallies, and many public demonstrations during the five days of the festival, winding up in a final parade, with bands and flags flying, in the Vienna soccer stadium. The Soviets intended that their representatives, well organized and financed, would dominate all these events and end up in the stadium to ovations and popular acclaim by the Viennese public. Most of the Austrians had financial and other support from labor unions and social groups. Rarely were we asked to give small amounts of money for such things as posters or material for armbands. Student leaders from other Western countries would come to us for advice; financial support came from national sources. They wanted moral support and encouragement from us; of course they got it. Their enthusiasm was tremendous. It was infectious, and quickly spilled over to members of the station assigned to working with non-Communist student groups, as they arrived in Vienna to take part in the week's festivities. Some stayed in youth hostels, others used local campgrounds and many were taken care of by student associations from the University of Vienna.

The most memorable result of this festival was that, from the Soviet standpoint, it was an absolute failure. The Westerners outdebated the Communist youth groups; their meetings were more intelligent and cogent and their Communist adversaries were outdone at every turn. The Communists were not shouted down, to the credit of the Western students. Their delegations were given equal time at the many meetings, street marches and rallies, but the audiences were clearly opposed to their Soviet sponsors.

The last day of the WYF was on a Saturday. The closing ceremonies of the festival consisted of an enormous rally and parade in the soccer stadium. The Western groups, and especially the Austrians, drew thunderous, rolling cheers and applause from the packed stadium. But when the Soviet and Soviet Bloc contingent marched from the tunnel into the stadium, the entire body of spectators simply sat on their hands. The silence was acute. We later learned a number of Soviet officials in the Vienna Embassy were transferred back to Moscow and relegated to obscure posts.

In August 1959 we packed our effects and after farewell parties with American, as well as Austrian, friends finally ended a four-and-a-half-year tour and flew to London to take the boat train to Southampton, where we boarded the *Queen Mary*. From New York, my wife and son went to her home in Boston, while I went to Washington for a week's consultation.

They joined me in Washington at the end of the week and we flew to San Francisco, sailing on the *President Cleveland* for Yokohama, beginning a series of Far Eastern assignments that were to comprise, in effect, the second half of my life in CIA.

16 Korea

Once again we headed up a ship's gangway and boarded the SS *President Cleveland*, sailing that September afternoon from San Francisco to Yokohama, looking forward to eighteen perfect days of rest, with the sun overhead reflecting on the endless expanse of blue water as we gravitated from our cabin to our deck chairs beside the pool and to the dining room or poolside buffet luncheons. After a one-day stop at Honolulu there was a straight run to Yokohama.

Reservations had been made for us in Tokyo at the old Imperial Hotel, the low gray-stone structure so strikingly designed by Frank Lloyd Wright, located in downtown Tokyo close to the Imperial moat. Our plans included a few days layover in Tokyo, where I had some Korea-related business to take care of, but there would be some time for sightseeing. A friend, working for an American business firm, having spent his boyhood in Japan with his parents and being fluent in the language, was to show us an older and more traditional side of Tokyo. I also wanted to see the new Tokyo, since I only remembered it as a burned-out wasteland after the terrible fire-bombing raids during the closing days of the war in 1945.

The ship plowed along and as we sat stretched out, my eyes closed to the warm sun, I mused about the briefing given me at Headquarters in Langley about our station's earlier ejection from Korea. It was complex and almost comical. A Central Intelligence Group had been attached to the United States armed forces during the Korean War from 1950-1953. Their main duties consisted of interrogations and debriefings, running short-range reconnaissance operations behind the Chinese and North Korean lines, and reporting order-of-battle information concerning the Communist Chinese and the North Koreans. When combat ended and the truce began in 1953, the CIA group was then assigned to the U.S. Eighth Army headquarters in Seoul, a part of the United Nations Command.

The American Embassy in the immediate postwar years was reestablished in the Bando Hotel in downtown Seoul. The embassy eventually moved across the street into a large but dreary-looking office building in which I would have my offices. My assignment in Seoul was to establish an official CIA presence in Korea once again, to reopen an intelligence liaison with the South Korean government, and in general to refurbish a CIA-South Korean relationship which had been broken by a bizarre episode of a few years before.

In the immediate postwar period, the agency group was still flying agents from the south to North Korea, as well as boating them up the Yellow Sea to make their way behind North Korean lines. To give support to this activity, the CIA maintained a training site on a small island southwest of Seoul on the Yellow Sea. South Korean agents were trained, equipped, and ultimately were smuggled into North Korea to carry out their assignments. The CIA and South Korean officers lived at the site, with other personnel and agents in training. The camp was heavily wired off and guarded by roving armed patrols along the shores facing the Yellow Sea.

On one cloudless afternoon, shortly after the cease-fire, the guards noted a launch heading in the direction of the island. Syngman Rhee, president of Korea, was entertaining a party of friends on this launch, slowly sailing down past the training camp's shoreline. Through some monumental foulup, the officers in charge of the CIA training site had not been informed that President Rhee would be passing their beachfront that day. At the sight of this unidentified boat, which continued on its way after many warning shouts, the guards opened fire. Fortunately, no one was hit. President Rhee's party turned back to the port of Inchon, and once ashore, Rhee demanded to know who had been shooting at him and his party. By the time he drove from Inchon to Seoul he had the answer; it was the CIA. Without hesitation, Rhee called in the American ambassador and told him this group would be given seventy-two hours to leave Korea. This was done and the station, to a man, flew off into the rising sun.

Now in 1959 the agency was opening once again an "overt" station; that is, a station declared as such to the Korean government. We had, of course, maintained a small covert presence in the country during the years of our banishment. My title within the embassy would be special assistant to the ambassador.

A CIA station abroad does not hang out a shingle with its initials on it, nor list itself in the phone book. However transparent it may be in fact, there is always a "cover" shielding a CIA presence in a foreign country. Quite often this cover is very complicated and sophisticated, resulting in a CIA station operating completely undetected during its work overseas. More often than not, however, "cover" would be relatively nominal, and would consist of the agency station being a part of an official American entity, such as an embassy. Presidential directives were explicit in describing the subordination of the CIA station chief to the American ambassador, if cover were to be established within an embassy. Furthermore, the ambassador had full rights to know anything and everything being done by an agency station in the country of its assignment; it only remained for the ambassador to set the limits of what he wanted to know and what he didn't care to hear about. Woe betide the CIA station chief who misled his ambassador or concealed from him matters of real importance.

My business in Tokyo finished, we took off one September morning from Haneda Airport in a drenching downpour, the leading edge of a typhoon approaching Japan from the south. Flying west, we soon could look down into the gray, swirling mass of clouds and wind as the typhoon battered its way north; an awesome sight. Reaching the Korean mainland, we came into clear skies, passing over mile after mile of mountains and valleys until we descended to Kimpo Airport on the outskirts of Seoul.

The embassy administrative officer was on hand to meet us and he steered us quickly through customs and out to a waiting car. The road to Seoul ran through expanses of rice paddies and now and then past farmers' huts with their straw-thatched roofs, the homes of three or four farming families, often related by blood or marriage. Young children waved from the roadside, their parents and elders not far away in the paddies. This short but first impression of the country in which we were to live three years was one of the warm friendliness of the people but also of the still-primitive conditions in which they lived.

As we crossed the bridge spanning the Han River, the outskirts of Seoul still showed war damage to buildings and streets. Once in the city, just across the bridge, we were plunged into a maelstrom of traffic; buses, bicycles, handcarts, horse-drawn carts, and Korean and U.S. Army trucks. But everywhere there teemed masses of people; the Orient.

We were to live temporarily in an apartment in one of the two embassy compounds, which accommodated the greater part of embassy officers and their families. The compounds had been established by the Japanese before World War II and held the homes of families of officials of various Japanese banks and commercial enterprises in Korea. In addition to the newer apartment buildings constructed by the U.S. government since the Korean War were several houses originally built by the Japanese, in the long, low style typical to Japan, with rooms separated by shoji doors covered with rice paper. These softly sliding doors with no means of locks kept Marilyn awake for many weeks, imagining, at the slightest nighttime sound, the entry of a "slicky boy," as midnight thieves were called. Even with high walls encircling the compound, topped with barbed wire and broken glass and the twenty-four-hour guards walking through the grounds day and night, occasionally there would be an entry into a home. These night visitors greased themselves to avoid capture; they were ever-present, and were infrequently caught. They seldom caused harm, but their reputation for coming and going like wraiths was well deserved.

From the airport we went directly to our apartment and unpacked the small amount of luggage we had with us and later that day I reported to the ambassador, then Walter Dowling, a respected and competent professional in the Foreign Service. Our arrival coincided with his departure to become American ambassador to West Germany. He had been responsible for the negotiations with the South Korean government and for the reinstatement of the CIA in South Korea with myself being the first senior representative since the debacle at the island training site. Seated in his office he asked questions about my background and CIA experience, impressing me as a strong and dynamic personality. He had arranged for a series of meetings the next day with senior Korean officials and, as he was in the process of making his good-bye calls, he took me along with him. In this way I met many of the principal officers of the cabinet, the police, and the armed services, by whom I was received courteously but with a distinct reserve. This attitude was not lost on Ambassador Dowling. As we drove from office to office in

Seoul in his limousine, he said he had noted the cool atmosphere, and considering the way in which the CIA had been thrown out of Korea, I would simply have to wait out a period with the Koreans until they were assured of our mutual interests and my own respect for Korea.

After about a month in Seoul, I detected a lessening in their coolness and thereafter was able to work with the Koreans in altogether more friendly terms.

In Washington, en route to Korea, I had been impressed, at both the CIA and the State Department, by the depth of American official concern regarding the stability of the Rhee government. South Korea occupied a key and critical place in American Far Eastern policy, surrounded by Communist China and the Soviet Union, acting as a buffer to Japan, our major ally in the Far East. This concern was centered on one question: Was the Rhee government becoming so widely unpopular with the Koreans that an internal upheaval was becoming likely or inevitable in the short run? At that time we had about fifty thousand American troops, plus Air Force units, in Korea and we were apprehensive about their safety in the event the South Korean government were to fall into such disarray that the North Koreans might be tempted to strike again. This made it necessary for us to ascertain how widespread and how publicly offensive was the corruption within the Rhee government. Was the population as a whole becoming alienated? Were the repressive aspects of the government pushing the people toward massive civil disobedience or civil opposition? Occupying the special position we held in South Korea, how could we move the Korean government in directions consonant with American policy?

It may be said that our policy instructions constituted gross interference in the internal affairs of South Korea. The realities of international politics, the welfare of our own country, and the welfare of the Korean people argued that we use our very real leverage, born out of fighting side by side with the Koreans in a long and bloody war, not to mention the equities which grew out of our massive economic and military aid since the Korean War.

Ambassador Dowling and later his successor, Walter P. McConaughy, knew of my intelligence brief; both of them welcomed our participation in the collection of what was essentially political intelligence; our American role in Korea was, in truth, intended to strengthen the independence and integrity of the

Republic of Korea. For many months it had been common knowledge that Syngman Rhee, who had given so many years of his life in his fight for an independent Korea and had been so long in opposition to Japanese rule, was rapidly sliding into senility; it was equally clear that certain members of his Liberal Party and ministers of his cabinet were manipulating him, taking advantage of his growing inadequacy.

On the day Walter McConaughy went to the Kyung Mu Dai, President Rhee's official residence, accompanied by a group of senior embassy officers, formally to present his credentials as ambassador to Syngman Rhee, I could observe at firsthand a president in glowing physical health, but with almost no attention span or ability to concentrate on problems of state.

To get the political information we needed—as distinct from the kind of intelligence provided by agents such as I had been accustomed to in Austria—was not difficult in itself. What was difficult was to winnow out rumor from truth and to recognize that many sources of information came from political opposition groups who were intent on damaging the Rhee government. The ominous fact was that President Rhee's Liberal Party was riddled with financial and political corruption, which was well known to the Korean populace at large. Beyond this, the ruling party had become increasingly repressive and authoritarian in order to maintain its control and authority over the people. The corruption and repression had made the Korean nation increasingly sullen and hostile to its government.

My first month in Korea found additional CIA officers arriving from Headquarters, including one fluent in Korean and Japanese. They were immediately assigned to selected intelligence objectives and soon we had a valuable collection of informed political observers in the universities of Seoul and in key government ministries. These were not agents in the classic sense; rather they were "special connections" whose main motive was to maintain a privileged contact with the U.S. government. They largely confirmed the information already flowing into our embassy of widespread bribery and intimidation of other political parties by the government.

Under the Korean political system existing at the time, it was possible for the vice-president to belong to a different political party from that of the president, and this was the case during

Rhee's tenure. His vice-president was a well-known Catholic layman, Chang Myon, also known by his Christian name of John Chang, who headed the Democratic Party, which was the major opposition party, and was always severely restricted in its activities by Rhee's Liberal Party. Chang Myon himself was under constant surveillance and frequently under what amounted to house arrest. His leading supporters were often assaulted by goon squads under control of the Liberal Party, although it is doubtful that in his last months Rhee was aware of the extent of this pressure. Chang Myon had been the target of several assassination attempts and on one occasion had been shot through the hand. He was effectively silenced, although he enjoyed wide popularity among the people, and there were few doubts as to the result of a free election were Syngman Rhee to die or step down.

It soon came to my attention that the American Embassy had no contact whatsoever with Chang Myon; it had simply been assumed that this would be viewed by President Rhee and especially the ruling clique in the Liberal Party as a mark of hostility toward Rhee and a deliberate provocation on the part of a member of the embassy. Checking with Ambassador McConaughy to ask if he would object to my establishing a contact with Chang Yon, I was told he saw no reason why I shouldn't, but he ventured that the embassy Political Section undoubtedly had adequate relations with him. A look of surprise crossed his face when I informed him that as far as I could determine, no contact had been made with Chang Myon at any level.

Toward the end of 1959 the Korean government held a Christmas reception for the diplomatic corps in the large ballroom of the Bando Hotel. Chang Myon seldom attended any kind of official function and I was surprised to find him standing alone and ignored in a corner of the ballroom. I made my way through the crush of people to where he stood, introduced myself, and said I was a recent arrival in Seoul. In his excellent, cultured English he replied that he knew my name, that I represented the CIA, and expressed his pleasure at meeting me. As we talked, he went on in a bland, level voice asking if he could perhaps see me privately in the near future, as he had a number of important things he felt the American government should know. Perhaps I might find time to visit him at his home? We agreed that he would phone me when he could and we both smiled as we casually moved apart.

During my relatively short but significant relationship with Dr. Chang, there never was a time when he could have been termed an American agent, in the professional meaning of the word. Rather, this mild-mannered intelligent and gentle human being was truly a Korean patriot, who correctly saw only ruin and bloodshed for his countrymen under the continued rule of the Liberal Party. His confidential liaison with me was, in his opinion, a proper and honorable link to the United States, which after all had once saved a free Korea from extinction and which once might again be called upon. On no occasion did Dr. Chang ask a personal favor of me nor did he by direct work or inference seek money or anything of value for himself. A gentleman by instinct and preference, he was destined for rough treatment at the hands of the coup government which ultimately toppled him.

A few days later my secretary buzzed me to say that a Dr. Chang was on the phone and would I speak with him. I picked up the receiver and after a few amenities, he asked me to join him for tea that afternoon. At three o'clock, my driver, armed with detailed directions, drew to a stop in a narrow street on the eastern edge of Seoul. Chang's house presented a blank stone wall to the street, pierced in the center by a heavy wooden gate. As I got out of my car, the gate opened and Dr. Chang stood in the entranceway to greet me. We went inside, where I found myself in a small garden, bounded on three sides by the wings of his modest but comfortable home, and on the fourth by the wall fronting on the street.

It was already early winter, but the day was mild and he suggested we sit in the garden and have tea. He led me to an arbor where there were two benches and a circular table. A moment later, his fifteen-year-old daughter, Angela, brought a tray of tea and cookies. After Angela had gone back to the house, we sipped tea, as Dr. Chang began to develop the conversation. I encouraged him to do the talking, asking for some background on Korean politics and the organization of the government, especially his role initially. Quietly and deliberately, Dr. Chang explained to me the theoretical role of the opposition and how politics actually worked in Korea. As leader of the opposition, he and his party were systematically harassed and threatened by the president's party. He hastened to assure me that President Rhee was not a bad man and had given much of himself to creating a free and independent Korea, which had so long suffered under Japanese rule until the end of World War II and under foreign occupation since. Nevertheless, he said, Rhee had become a very old man and no longer had the mental alertness and toughness that he had brought to the newborn Republic of Korea in the years just after World War II. He was increasingly senile, unable to grasp the complexities of ruling and administering part of a divided country which had long been under pressure from the Chinese, the Russians, and the Japanese. He bitterly described how the members of Rhee's cabinet had formed a cabal which actually ran the country for their own benefit and the benefit of their hangers-on. Although Rhee was still a powerful figure in Korea, he was unaware of how his country was being exploited by this group of ministers. He told me of the extent of financial and material corruption within the government and, as he described it to me, it appeared pervasive, enormous, and widely known and resented. At this first meeting, and in subsequent conversations with him, he gave me chapter and verse on details of corruption, abuse of political power, and physical oppression of Koreans who were not in the president's party, but were considered to be enemies of the Liberal Party.

He described his own position as being tenuous, but that reports coming to him from all different sectors of the population and military establishments had led him to the conclusion that he, along with his party, enjoyed wide popularity. He referred to the parliamentary elections to be held in March 1960, only a few months hence, confident of his party's expectation at least to double its representation in the parliament. "We can hope that it will be that way," he said with a wan smile, "but we have already received numerous reports from sympathizers within the government that the balloting will be rigged and that plans are already well advanced to insure a Liberal victory by a landslide."

He rose and paced slowly back and forth, speaking softly all the while. "What I'm really afraid of is that Rhee and his party will use these elections to crush me and my party once and for all. If this is successful, Korea will be left in confusion and open to a situation which will give the North another chance to do what it could not accomplish in the war between 1950 and 1953."

The shadows were lengthening in the little garden. Chang said that we must see each other often and that he would give me as honest and complete a picture of the dangers facing Korea as he could. Unsaid between us was our mutual recognition that a Korea in turmoil would pose a threat to the United States even as it would to Japan. Chang commented on my situation in Seoul. I would be followed from time to time and I must accept that members of the government would speak critically of me in their contacts with members of my embassy. He smiled gently, "You must realize you're the first American who has spoken to me in over a year. They all seem to be afraid of the thought of appearing critical of Rhee's government by being friendly to me."

I told him I wanted to continue meeting with him under whatever circumstances we could arrange. The American side was also deeply concerned about the stability of South Korea and the cohesiveness of its people and the importance of political tranquility. I was to phone when it was possible to meet, but he reminded me that his telephone was tapped and that without doubt, from now on, mine would be also. I went to my car for the drive back to the embassy and my driver, Choe, a Korean who had worked several years for the U.S. Army, as we rode back through the late afternoon shadows, turned to say over his shoulder that he thought Dr. Chang was a very good man and that many Koreans liked him. I learned as time went on that Choe, a young man himself, had a good sense of political sentiment and an acutely developed perception of popular attitudes and moods.

Checking into my office, I then went to see Ambassador McConaughy as I felt he should be informed of the status of Dr. Chang, the vice-president, emphasizing that no one had been in touch with him for over a year. McConaughy, who was just becoming established in the country, didn't wish to give the impression to the Korean government, to which he was accredited, that he was dealing with the opposition. I offered to maintain the contact as this might be of some value to him; in any event, unless otherwise instructed, I intended to continue seeing Dr. Chang. We met at least weekly thereafter either at his home or at mine and at official functions, as well as in his suite in the Bando Hotel. Marilyn became very fond of this gentle, gracious man and when he came to lunch at our home remembered to include cornmeal muffins, a favorite American dish of Dr. Chang's, in addition to a casserole of fresh, boned trout in a sweet-and-sour sauce. Until the upheaval of April of 1960, I was the only embassy officer who saw the vice-president of the Republic of Korea.

The months of January and February are always the coldest months of the Korean winter and 1960 proved to be no exception. The Han River was a solid mass of ice, water in gutters and open sewers froze over, and the populace in Seoul simply hunkered down to get through another savage winter in the dry cold and biting winds. The numbing weather didn't daunt the students at the college and university levels and political activity and discussion continued feverishly and with increasing audacity. The basic questions about the coming election concerned the fundamental stability of the mass of South Koreans and the integrity and reliability of the Korean military. It was clear that the Republic of South Korea was headed for a political crisis. Plans to control the voting were increasingly apparent, as were repressive actions by the police against the students and the opposition political parties.

The day of the election arrived. Fraud and deceit by the Liberal Party were to be seen everywhere. Students and opposition party members who appointed themselves as poll watchers were systematically harassed, beaten, and arrested. Some polling places controlled by the Liberal Party closed after being open for only half an hour, the reason being given that the ballot box was already full and everyone in the precinct had voted. Many of these ballot boxes had already been stuffed with votes when they had been brought to the polling places early in the morning. The voting day came to an end with a prompt but hardly necessary announcement from Kyung Mu Dai—the presidential "Blue House"—that the Liberal Party and Dr. Rhee had won a resounding victory. I saw Dr. Chang that evening, an exhausted, discouraged, and bitter man. All of his predictions and those of his political colleagues had come true. In terms of public order, while there had been some minor disturbances and arrests at the close of the day, it appeared that the Liberal Party had "won" a well-controlled victory and at the same time had neutralized the opposition. None of us knew that evening the political process in South Korea had only just begun.

The next morning dawned on a glum and morose Seoul. The

newspapers, always a combative and spirited group, reported dutifully on the election results, but went on in many cases to comment on reports of "irregularities" which were only then being reported from the provinces.

By afternoon a train arrived in Seoul from Masan, a port in Kyongsong province on the southeast coast of Korea, carrying a delegation of student leaders who had been involved in the demonstrations and general uproar of the preceding day. Further, they had brought with them stored in the baggage car of the train the body of a student, who allegedly had been killed by the police and whose body had been thrown into the harbor. The body, along with many blood-stained banners and posters, was hidden away by university students in Seoul; the rest of the afternoon and night was dominated by excited meetings and discussion groups from the many university grounds in Seoul. The air was becoming electric. Police patrols and jeeps roamed throughout the city during the night.

The next day groups of students and young people were clustered about on the sidewalks of Seoul. Police patrols constantly cruised by in their jeeps and more and more angry young people crowded into the center of Seoul from outlying schools and districts. Along with my American interpreter, Ken, I went out on the streets to gain firsthand the mood of the crowds that were rapidly forming. Ken told me that many in these crowds were openly discussing marching on the Kyung Mu Dai in protest against the stolen election. For the first time, armed military police in addition to civilian police appeared on the street, afoot and in jeeps. In late morning, I went home briefly to make sure my wife remained there all day. I had forgotten that she was having two tables of friends for a bridge luncheon. By the time I got home the muted roar of the crowds in the streets just below our compound near the old Japanese Diet building was becoming louder.

Back at the embassy I cabled a summary of developments to Washington and then briefly compared notes with the ambassador, whose general view of the situation was the same as mine: explosive, ugly, and bound to get worse. Masses of people were now beginning to surge freely through the streets rather than keeping to the sidewalks. Scores of ROK (Republic of Korea) military police armed with rifles and pistols clustered on each corner of downtown Seoul and especially in front of the Diet building. I called one of my station officers and we drove in a jeep to the front of the Diet building, parking around a corner. As we did so we heard a chanting roar approaching from the avenue. The crowds of people in the streets and on the sidewalks turned to watch as several hundred students, wearing headbands and carrying some of the blood-stained banners and clothing from Masan, were weaving their way up the street to the Diet building. At the sight of this group, an enormous outcry broke from the crowds pressed together outside the Diet as everyone came off the sidewalks and onto the streets to support the demonstrators. This mass of humanity compacted itself and began to move along the avenue and toward the Blue House. At this point the ROK military police leveled their rifles and fired into the midst of the demonstrators. They sent volley after volley crashing into this packed throng before our very eyes; many died, many were wounded, and there was blood spattered everywhere. The cries of the injured arose above the noise of the tumult. The fusillade had broken the throng into two parts, one of which turned and fled back down the street, leaving a crowd of several thousand demonstrators already past this killing ground, running on its way to the Blue House. We managed to get our jeep out of the way and up a back road which skirted the Diet grounds, leading to a small square in front of the main gate of the Blue House compound. We got there just as the leading clumps of running demonstrators, having gotten past the MPs, came thronging up the hill to the gates. Again there were volleys of gunfire from MPs and National Police and the unarmed students fled back down the hill, leaving more dead and wounded. This bloody action broke the back of the demonstration, and we went down the back road to the embassy, where I informed the ambassador of what we had seen. I followed this up with a cable to Headquarters, saying the situation was out of hand and unpredictable. I went back into the streets and found most of the crowd dispersing. There was no more violence that day. It was as though the events in front of the Diet building and the Blue House gate had exhausted the emotions and strength of the demonstrators. More than 125 young people were shot to death in those two encounters.

After getting off cables covering the events of the day and trying to foresee the next developments, I got home after dark. Marilyn was furious at being kept away from the excitement of the day, but was understandably stricken when I related the tragic events that had taken place. A curfew had been declared both by American authorities and the Koreans. The mass killings in front of the Diet building had taken place perhaps three hundred meters from our house, but the crowds were pressed against the walls of the compound as the families locked up inside watched the racing of jeeps and trucks filled with shouting students, many with bloody cloths wound about their heads.

There followed a week of what can only be described as suspended animation. People in Seoul went about their affairs as though in a trance. Traffic moved through the streets, traffic signals operated and were obeyed, and the police moved about in their normal pattern. The recent butchery was only then beginning to be grasped by a shocked populace and, for that matter, by the Liberal Party government itself. Our embassy staff was in a virtual limbo. The ministries of the Korean government were huddled in constant meetings and the routine work of our embassy in dealing with them simply came to a halt. Everyone seemed to sense that the trouble was not over but had just begun. The outrage that had prompted the demonstrations, which themselves resulted in the killing, had been sparked by the crudeness and effrontery with which the election had been stolen by the Liberals. In those succeeding days, there was no attempt made by the Rhee government to redress the situation, to mollify the people, or even to express regret over the dead. As the days wore on without any gesture from the government to the people as a whole, we all felt there would be yet another outburst, one that would likely end in widespread bloodshed.

With this grim prospect in mind, I sought out the minister of the interior, who had jurisdiction over the police. I found him in the Council of Ministers building, in the same walled compound as the Diet building. He was particularly grateful that an American official had come to call on him and expressed his thanks effusively. He told me that the Council of Ministers was meeting around the clock "rearranging things." The more he described their actions, the clearer it became that the government was planning no change of any significance but was simply shuffling the same Liberal Party names and faces from one position to another.

Sitting with this minister in his office, I came to realize that nothing constructive was even contemplated, and I knew the

Rhee government would come to an end within a matter of days. As the minister of interior sat across the coffee table from me, drawing organizational charts on a piece of paper, involving the same old political players, I felt constrained to put out my hand and put it over the paper on which he was sketching how the government would be reorganized.

He looked at me and I asked how he seriously could sit there in a room in which not one pane of glass remained, in which the torn curtains were blowing out of the windows, in which bricks, rocks, bottles, and other debris littered the floor of what had been a sumptuous office and play word games when the Korean people were simply gathering their strength for yet another blow against the Liberal Party which would surely topple the president and scatter the administration.

I told him I thought the senior members of the Liberal Party who had corrupted President Rhee's rule and had enriched themselves and oppressed the people and who had, a few days before, succeeded in killing over a hundred innocent Koreans almost within sight of where we were sitting, should retire from public life if the people would allow them to go in peace. His unhappiness became acute—after all, it was he who had given the order for the police to shoot into the crowd of unarmed students. He said he would have a talk with his colleagues and think the entire matter over yet again. He recognized that the situation was grave and that time was short. At this point, he told me that the entire cabinet was in effect holed up in the Blue House. He said he would telephone me at my home or my office after he had talked with some of the other ministers, and we made our good-byes on that note. He walked with me to the front door of the ministry, where he surprised me by having a ministry photographer take our picture together. My only defense was to put on my graveyard face.

That evening I visited Dr. Chang. With typical compassion he at once expressed great fear for the safety of the ministers and the president himself, hiding as they were in the Blue House. It was his view that the entire government must leave office, but because he was a peaceful man he was revolted by the idea of mob action storming the Blue House and lynching everyone in it.

"That's what will happen—the people will kill them all."

I told him of my conversation with the Interior minister that day and he remarked sadly that the reaction was typical of the Liberal Party leadership, that they were blind to their imminent peril.

Since my earliest days in Seoul, I had struck up a particularly good friendship with the minister of defense, Kim Chong Yol, popularly known as Mike Kim. Mike was a professional military man, and had been chief of the ROK Air Force. He and his charming wife had often been our dinner guests, and we his. I liked and trusted him, for I felt instinctively that he was not one of the inner circle of the Liberal Party responsible for so much of the corruption and the repression. On the morning of the seventh day of this climatic week in April 1960, Mike Kim along with the other members of the Rhee cabinet was in the Blue House on the hill behind the Diet building. During the morning hours dense crowds of people of all ages had gathered on the sidewalks and streets and massed in front of the American Embassy, along the walls of Duksoo Palace gardens, and were jam-packed along the thoroughfare leading up to the Diet building. Here and there strident speakers had climbed up to the top of cars from which they harangued the crowd below in bitter, shrill tones. I told my interpreter to mingle with the crowd and then return and tell me the general burden of the speeches being made and the temper of the people.

In about twenty minutes Ken returned.

"Everywhere they are saying the same thing—go get Rhee and hang him. Go to the Kyung Mu Dai and kill all of the ministers. Kill the government the way they killed our sons. Burn the Blue House. Down with Rhee and his criminals."

Ken had lived in Seoul for a number of years and I respected his judgment of popular mood and emotion.

"They're going to do it this time—I can just tell—they're really going to do it."

I went to the ambassador and told him what Ken had reported to me. He said, "I know, I know, the mood is ugly and there is going to be more violence. I have already cabled the department for advice about what they want us to do."

I went back to my own office, plopped down behind my desk and stared out of my window toward the Diet and Blue House, just visible beyond it on the hillside.

Finally I picked up my phone and dialed the Blue House. The number was a direct line and didn't go through the switchboard at the Kyung Mu Dai and in a moment I heard the soft measured tones of Pak Chan Il, the president's confidential secretary. He spoke excellent English and knew who I was. I told him I wanted to talk with Kim Chong Yol; Pak said he would connect us right away. After a short delay, Mike Kim came to the phone. We exchanged greetings and Mike wanted to know how things were in the center of town. They had no knowledge of what was going on in the streets or what the popular mood was. I gave him a quick appraisal of what was happening near the embassy in the center of Seoul and again what my interpreter had learned. I told him that the crowd outside my window was even then beginning to move down to the broad avenue that led to the Diet building and then to the Blue House. The mood was turbulent and dangerous, and the National Police had disappeared from the streets. I said that in my opinion the throngs would make their own move within the next hour toward the Blue House, storm the fences and gates, and would pillage the building, killing everyone inside.

Mike listened silently and then asked in a subdued voice, "What do you think we should do?"

"I think you and the other ministers must have Pak Chan Il telephone our ambassador and ask that he come to see the president. The president must be prepared to talk with our ambassador about leaving the Blue House and Korea. New elections must be promised, leading to an interim government without membership from the Liberal Party."

"It's that bad?"

"Mike, you'll all be dead within two hours if the government doesn't step down."

Mike was silent for a moment and then said, "Peer, I'll call you back in a few minutes."

I sat in my office nervously drinking coffee for perhaps ten minutes when the ambassador's secretary burst in and said he wanted to see me right away.

In the ambassador's office I was told Pak Chan Il had just telephoned and said that President Rhee wanted him to come to the Blue House, that he had an important statement that he wanted to make to the American government and by radio to the Korean people. The ambassador said he wanted me to go with him and that General Carter Magruder, commanding general of the Eighth Army and United Nations Command, was on his way to join us. Coming through crowded Seoul on a day like this, his drive would take about fifteen minutes. We waited until General Magruder arrived and the three of us got into the ambassador's limousine, which was surrounded by packs of Koreans in front of the embassy. An aide snapped the American flag onto one fender of the limousine and the Department of State flag onto the other and we drew out into the street in front of the Bando Hotel and the embassy itself, turned toward the avenue leading to the Diet and Blue House. As we drove along through the massed throng, they parted magically and we moved slowly but steadily. On all sides there were grim and determined faces; they were not going to be denied this time. The crowds drew aside to make a channel for our car to pass through; within the car was silence. The ambassador mused aloud, "I don't know what the president has to say; Pak Chan Il only said that it was very important and could I come with General Magruder and an aide as soon as possible." I said nothing. General Magruder, a man of few words, muttered something in comment, as we passed on up to the Diet, swung along to the left, and went slowly up the slope to the Blue House gate, the scene of such bloodshed seven days before.

The president's personal bodyguard opened the gates, waved us through, and closed them behind us. We drove up to the portico, passing many nervous armed guards on the way, and were ushered into the entrance hall of the Blue House. Pak Chan Il stepped forward to greet the three of us but he was elbowed aside by Mike Kim, who said, "I'll take care of this." Other government ministers and members of the general staff milled around in the hallways and reception rooms as Mike led us along a broad hallway and into one of the formal reception rooms. There we sat around a table, Ambassador McConaughy, General Magruder, Mike Kim, and me, while Pak took up a chair behind a table in the corner, a notepad ready. In a few moments the French doors of the long, elegant room opened and in came President Rhee on all fours. He had two favorite dogs, corgis, and he was playing with them. As he entered the room from the garden beyond, rolling the dogs around in friendly play, he slowly rose to his feet and joined the party seated around the table. He was smiling, but his expression was confused.

The meeting lasted perhaps fifteen minutes at the outside. President Rhee said that he understood the political and social situation in Seoul and in the country as a whole was so unsteady and unstable that it might be in the interests of the Korean people if he stepped aside, along with his ministers, and allowed an interim government to take charge and guide the country until new elections could be held. He asked Ambassador McConaughy if he generally shared that view. McConaughy replied that President Rhee's statements were indeed statesman-like and appropriate to the situation. President Rhee glanced around at the others at the table, all of whom nodded in assent. Mike Kim offered one additional comment to the effect that the American side might be able to arrange a period of hospital care at the U.S. Army Tripler General Hospital in Honolulu as the president had been undergoing much strain lately and was near exhaustion. President Rhee beamed and nodded brightly at Ambassador McConaughy, who replied that he was sure it could be arranged and that General Magruder would take care of the matter. The meeting was about to end and Pak Chan Il came up to announce that even at that moment an announcement was being made on Radio Korea to the effect that President Rhee and his entire government were stepping down, that there would be an interim government followed by new elections. There was a rather strained shaking of hands all around and the party of four moved back out toward the portico and the limousine. Mike Kim turned to me on the way out and shook my hand warmly and said, "I think this is the right thing to do."

We got into the car, swept down the driveway and through the gate on to the avenue leading back to the embassy. Even as we did, radio loudspeakers attached to telephone poles along the way were announcing the imminent departure of President Rhee and the dissolution of his Liberal Party government. The news of an interim government and the announcement of upcoming elections for a permanent government caused the dense crowds through which we were passing to break into an absolute bedlam of cheering, clapping, and laughing spectators. It had taken our car about fifteen minutes to make the normal ten minute drive from the embassy to the Blue House; on the way back the press of crowds and their insistence on touching its windows, on shouting expressions of joy and pleasure at the three of us inside, slowed the car so that the ride back took almost forty-five minutes.

It was a day of emotion, heavy with sadness. The old man was to go and everyone knew he would never return. Back at the American Embassy, the streets and sidewalks were a mass of cheering and clapping Koreans. On the sidewalk in front of the embassy and on its steps were crowds of American journalists who had been in Seoul for that fateful week. The ambassador and General Magruder went up to the ambassador's office while I peeled off to my office, where I dictated several cables on the events of that morning. I alerted our Headquarters and our office in Honolulu that undoubtedly within a day or two we would need a military aircraft to take Rhee and a couple of aides from Seoul to Honolulu and then to Tripler Hospital. I also cabled that separate and later transportation would be required to take Francesca, Rhee's Austrian wife, to Honolulu as well, for if she stayed in Seoul she would surely be killed. Within an hour, concurring responses came in to my communicators from both Honolulu and CIA Headquarters. I informed the ambassador of the preliminary steps I had taken; he told me to go ahead and make the arrangements with Mike Kim, who had clearly emerged as the leader and organizer of the abdication. I called Mike and told him of these tentative arrangements. He was pleased and we set a time and date when Rhee would be able to travel, accompanied by three aides. Further cables flew and the old warrior's departure from Seoul later went off on schedule and safely.

Within days, an interim government was set up under a respected elder statesman, Huh Chung, who gathered about him an able and politically clean staff, adequate to prepare for new elections. The elections were to be held in ninety days and my good friend John Chang was, of course, the leading contender.

The next months were filled with politicking for the elections. The shattered remains of Rhee's party and his cabinet were quickly disposed of. All of them went to jail except for my friend, the minister of interior, who was hanged. Also, and I believe largely because of my intercession with John Chang, Mike Kim was not jailed but went home in dignity to "rest," as the Koreans refer to any enforced period of political inactivity. The city of Seoul was in a state of complete euphoria. I was vividly reminded of the similar atmosphere that existed in Budapest in 1956 after the Freedom Fighters had thrown out the AVO, the Hungarian Communist Party, and Soviet garrisons. Both revolutions were alike in their purity, their passion, and their spontaneity.

As a footnote to the Rhee regime and minor indications of the extent to which corruption had penetrated that regime, it was learned that the minister of finance, whose home was located on the west slope of Namsam, a hill in the center of Seoul, had bypassed his water-supply line around the water meter, and the electric power-supply line around the electric meter, to avoid paying for these utilities. He also had a secret passageway in which he had his own escape route, entering through a panel at the back of a small closet; this went down a steep slope of three levels, leading to an alleyway straight to a nearby police station. It did him no good—he wound up in jail.

John Chang carried out his political campaign with skill and adroitness and his Democratic Party, to no one's surprise, won the election by a considerable margin. Chang himself became the prime minister; the title "president" had fallen into such bad repute under Rhee that it was not used.

My family and I had long been due to go on home leave in the fall of 1960; we had gone so far as to rent a beach house on Tahiti, at the urging of my brother, a repeated sailor to that island. About six weeks before we were due to leave Seoul for this South Seas holiday, I learned once again that home leave is a privilege and not a right; I received a cable from Headquarters that in light of the new government, headed by John Chang, and my special personal relationship with him, I should defer my leave for a year, but could count on 1961. Much as I personally liked Chang, as did many other Americans in Seoul and in Washington, it became clear in 1960 and 1961 that his gentleness and courtliness would run into hard sledding in Korea, which was by nature neither a gentle nor courteous political environment. He was, one might say, fifty years ahead of his time in Korea. Standing in the wings as the most powerful institution in Korean society was the ROK Army. They had long felt that their time had come and that they were the kind of Koreans who were entitled to run the country. Their reasoning had a certain logic.

17 Coup d'Etat

The history of the Korean people in this century is a history of occupations. In the first half of the century there were the Japanese. After World War II in South Korea, there came the Americans. To be sure, they were benevolent, wealthy, and helpful, but were nonetheless alien to Korean culture and Korean history. In the years since 1945 and then again after the Korean armistice in 1953, the gigantic American presence was felt throughout the entire republic of South Korea. Particularly was this true with regard to the ROK Armed Forces, especially the Army. We had trained them, armed them, and equipped them. We commanded them and in the days of peace after 1953, without ever intending to, we corrupted them. Golf clubs, tennis clubs, bridge parties, cocktail parties—through all of these friendly devices we steadily drew the top echelons away from their Korean heritage, Korean culture, and Korean aspirations. And we did this without really wanting to interfere in their way of life or in their sense of identity as Koreans.

There continued to exist within the Korean military establishments a little-recognized and little-understood body of officers who had never succumbed to the appeal of social dealings with the American high command in Seoul. Without resenting the American presence and without any shred of anti-Americanism, this quiet group of senior Korean military officers were determined that Korean cultural values, Korean history, and Korean social patterns were essential to the life of the nation and must be nourished and allowed to flower again. The military coup of General Pak Chung Hee and his group of senior officers was a manifestation of this spirit. When the coup was sprung in May of 1961, it was clear that Korea was reverting to Koreans for leadership and that the Korean relationship with the Americans, while enduring and close, would never again be the same.

Late in May 1961 General Pak Chung Hee and his fellow

officers staged their armed coup against the Chang Myon government of Korea. We in the station had several days' advance notice through a Korean officer, a member of General Pak's immediate staff, who was friendly with one of my officers in the station. I had informed Ambassador McConaughy, who had no way of measuring this report and took the position that we would simply have to wait. He did authorize me, however, to inform Premier Chang. I did so without naming my source, only telling him that a military coup against him and his government was being planned with a specific action date not yet determined. Premier Chang did not take this report seriously, still relaxing in the euphoria of having won a massive election the year before. He told me he would take "appropriate action" but that he didn't believe anything would come from this report. There had been other rumors of military action over the preceding months.

Because of the fragile situation in Seoul and because of the increasing possibility of military action against Premier Chang, I had installed in my house in the embassy Compound 2 a small two-way radio set, connecting me with my communications shack on the roof of the embassy building. There, we had at all times two communicators on duty, day and night. On the night in question, my radio link beeped me into wakefulness at about two-thirty in the morning. From the roof of our embassy my communicator reported urgently that tracer bullets were arcing over Namsam Hill, coming from the Han River Bridge area and that rifle fire could be heard. Obviously some kind of military action was underway coming into Seoul across the main bridge over the Han River.

I made some phone calls and alerted a few of my colleagues through radios that had been installed in their quarters, got dressed, and prepared to go to the embassy. I had no idea of what I could do but felt any action I might take should originate from there.

Waking my wife, I told her what was happening, to stay at home, and that I would phone her as soon as I could. I drove through the exit gate just before the Korean guard closed the gate and dropped the bar across it as they did at the entry gate some one hundred meters away. They had heard the rifle and machine-gun fire and had apparently heard through their own grapevine that they should take precautions.

The drive to the embassy took me along the main boulevard

that lay between the Diet and Duksoo Palace, at which point our embassy lay to the left a couple of hundred meters. By the time I reached the boulevard, several ROK trucks and jeeps had posted themselves at normally busy intersections and had unveiled thirty- and fifty-caliber machine guns. I turned on the domelight of my sedan and slackened speed; this was no time to be shot by a nervous sentry. Several times on this brief trip I was flagged down by ROK Army soldiers with sub-machine guns, who approached the car to verify my identity and wave me on. Clearly the ROK Army was on the move and a coup was in progress. I wondered about the whereabouts and safety of John Chang.

One of my two communicators was sitting in my office waiting for me. He could only tell me that he had gone to the roof upon hearing the gunfire and saw the lights of an approaching convoy coming over the Han River bridge and on toward the center of Seoul, one column splitting toward the ROK Army headquarters compound which adjoined the U.S. Eighth Army compound, both of which lay along the Han River somewhat south of the city. He had no radio intercepts of any use. I got off a cable to Washington to tell them of the coup and then searched the embassy to see who else was there but could only find the duty officer, a junior officer from the Political Section who had notified his boss, who would in turn inform the ambassador. Contact with the UN Command and U.S. Eighth Army had not yet been made. My secretary had made her way to the embassy and was in her office ready to work. Her first job was to make a pot of hot strong coffee.

The snap and crackle of gunfire in downtown Seoul was audible for the next forty-five minutes, but I could not find out what further was happening. Sitting in my office, sipping coffee and nervously smoking, I suddenly decided to try to reach Prime Minister Chang and I dialed his private number. He kept a suite at the Bando Hotel across the street, as a retreat to which he could repair when he worked late in the city; his own home was some distance away. The phone rang and a quivering voice responded. As I spoke English, I was answered in kind. I gave my name and said I was in the embassy across the street and asked if Premier Chang was there. The voice responded tensely that Premier Chang had been deposed and that he was not there but in flight and that the revolution had begun. I inquired what his name was and he replied, "I am Captain Pak Chung Gyu and

I represent the people's revolution." I told him that I would come to the suite and wanted to see him; I hung up without waiting for a reply.

By this time it was nearly five o'clock in the morning and the darkness had slipped into the grim gray of an oncoming dawn. I went to the ground floor, past the Marine desk, crossed over to the Bando Hotel and into the lobby. There were groups of Westerners, dressed in pajamas and robes, hastily thrown on, having been rousted out of their sleep. The lobby was also filled with ROK Army soldiers—paratroopers. The desk clerk, exceedingly nervous, insisted on knowing my name as I passed him on my way to the elevators. Standing guard before the elevator was a ROK Army major, unusual in that he was quite tall for a Korean. He turned toward me as I was about to enter an elevator and spoke to me in Korean. He glanced at me in a haughty way; I smiled and thanked him in English, which he could not understand. I entered the elevator and pressed the button for the eighth floor where the prime minister's rooms were. Before the major could interfere, the doors slid closed and I was on my way upstairs.

On the eighth floor I turned to the right to Chang's suite. I rapped on the door and it was opened by a good-looking Korean captain, slim with a lean face, obviously nervous and on the verge of exhaustion. He was armed to the teeth. There were a number of other paratroopers standing with weapons, some lounging in chairs, all tense. I asked if I was speaking to Captain Pak Chung Gyu. He nodded and invited me in. He led me into a room in which I had dined several times before with the prime minister and there we had a cup of coffee, hastily prepared by one of the waiting soldiers. Pak established his credentials. He was the commander of General Pak Chung Hee's bodyguard, and a graduate of the parachute schools at Fort Benning and Fort Bragg in the United States, where he had learned English. He had had the mission of capturing Chang in the Bando Hotel. He told me in a choked voice that upon his arrival he found that Chang and several of his immediate aides had already fled and that he was trying to reach General Pak and report to him. We finished our coffee. I took out one of my embassy calling cards, wrote my office telephone number on the back, and told him that if he wanted to talk to me for any reason, just to come to the embassy, or phone me. He was nervous to the point of being physically ill; I stood up and excused myself, telling him I was returning to my office and if there was anything I could do for him or General Pak to call me. He accompanied me to the door and had a lieutenant take me through the lobby and out of the hotel. I returned to my office across the street.

I sent off more cables and asked, among a number of other requests, for full-file data on Pak Chung Hee and Pak Chung Gyu, which were the only names I had at that point. Slopping down more coffee and puffing one cigarette after another, I waited for further developments and dawn to break. What I did not learn until later was that Prime Minister Chang, on first hearing gunfire, had gotten into a jeep and come to our embassy compound in an effort to reach me (I was already on the way to the embassy). He had come to the gate after it had been bolted and was refused admittance because he was bundled up and did not wish to be identified. He went on to the eastern part of Seoul to a Catholic girls' school, where he was given refuge and where he remained for ten days.

As dawn broke and the streets became light, there was no further gunfire. There were machine-gun posts at the corners and army patrols moved through the streets. By seven or eight in the morning, most of the embassy staff were in their offices, getting filled in on the events of the night. I had people in and out of my office during the rest of the morning. Earlier, I had reported my doings to the chargé d'affaires (Ambassador McConaughy had already left Korea for a new assignment, and the incoming ambassador had not yet arrived in Seoul).

At about nine that morning, the Marine guard called from his desk at the embassy entrance to say that a ROK Army captain with my name and card was there and wanted to see me right away. I told the Marine to send him up but was told that the man was armed. I said to tell him to leave his gun and come on up. Two or three minutes later there was a knock on my door. There stood a marine escort and Captain Pak Chung Gyu.

Pak was gaunt and gray with fatigue. He gave me a tired smile and said good morning, coming into the office. The embassy snack bar had opened early that morning and I had already gotten some doughnuts. I offered him coffee and doughnuts and with astonishing speed he disposed of five of them with his coffee, explaining that he had not eaten in twenty-four hours while the coup had been in preparation and in motion toward

Coup d'Etat   177

Seoul. I told him to flop down on the couch while we talked; he gratefully did so. His great preoccupation at that point was: what was the American reaction going to be to General Pak's coup? I said I had no idea but to tell me about General Pak and the people around him. He described them as true Korean patriots, friends of the Americans, strong opponents to the Communist north, but tired of the irresolute and flaccid ways of Prime Minister Chang. There was more to be done in Korea than Chang could accomplish. Silently I agreed with this. Pak said Chang was a good man, but not the man to lead Korea at this time of its history. Pak Chung Hee was the only one with the strength, wisdom, and the military support needed to do so. The ROK Army must supply the leadership of the Korean government and only under General Pak would this be possible.

Again he went back to the theme of American response. What would it be? Would Americans continue to support a South Korean government under military leadership? I said the first need would be to establish contact between the American Embassy and General Pak. I had in mind the stream of conflicting reports in reply to my cables concerning General Pak's political orientation and background. The reports described him as a Communist, as a pro-Communist, and as a loyal anti-Communist Korean. There was no definitive proof of anything. I could say nothing to Captain Pak, but he suggested that I see General Pak right away. He then went on to say urgently that there was someone else I should meet first, a Colonel Kim Chong Pil, whom he described as a relative of General Pak, completely trusted by him, and the chief planner of the coup itself.

We went down to the ground floor of the embassy, retrieved Captain Pak's pistol from the wary Marine guard, and went out to his jeep. Around the corner and up the avenue we stopped in front of the House of Representatives. Captain Pak took me to the fourth floor, along a dim corridor, and into a large barren room in which there were a few tables and chairs and what seemed to be a hundred miles of field telephone wire, and a desk behind which sat Colonel Kim. Kim was of middle height, slender, with a boyish face and a calm, composed manner. Captain Pak introduced me in Korean, and Colonel Kim offered me a chair. Captain Pak stayed on as our interpreter during the ensuing talk.

As matters developed during the next sixteen months of my

tour in Seoul, Kim Chong Pil was, throughout that time, my principal point of contact with the government under General Pak Chung Hee. This relationship became even more plausible when, after only a couple of months in power, the Pak government established the Korean Central Intelligence Agency (KCIA), naming it exactly that way in spite of my earnest and repeated suggestions that they call their intelligence service the intelligence division, the intelligence department, the Korean Girl Guides, or in fact anything else to avoid that set of initials, which became so notorious in the years of the 1970s.

From the beginning of our relationship, Kim Chong Pil showed a keen and continuing interest in my status as a relatively senior CIA officer. He quizzed me courteously but closely concerning the legal status of the CIA within our structure of government. Most of his interests lay in subjects I could discuss freely and fully, taking these opportunities to deliver minilectures of a "basic civics" nature, coming down heavily on the many restrictions placed on CIA by the Congressional legislation of 1947, with particular regard to its limited role within the United States and in dealing with United States citizens at home or abroad. More recent history would indicate that at least as far as this area of teaching was concerned, I had failed miserably as a tutor. The recent imbroglio in which the KCIA's obvious efforts to win friends and influence people, particularly members of the U.S. Congress, shows an intelligence service on a rampage, being used as a covert arm of Korean diplomacy intended to influence American appropriations and legislation. Inexcusable and despicable yes, but nevertheless understandable when viewed from the Korean stance. The U.S. role as the single great power ally of the South Korean government, as well as being the source of its military well-being and, perhaps, its guarantee to national independence, has certainly led the Korean government to acts designed to please key and friendly members of the U.S. Congress, which controls the purse strings. The modern history of Korea, viewed objectively, certainly cannot give the present leaders of that troubled country a feeling of firm confidence in their viability as a nation.

Most Americans have difficulty in remembering Korean names in their entirety. This confusion is heightened by the unusual, by American standards, repetition of three surnames: Pak, Kim, and Lee. The profusion of these three names had literally forced the American military during the Korean War to fashion American nicknames for their Korean comrades-in-arms. Thus there was a Rocky Lee, a Whitey Pak, and Mike Kim. For a Korean to be given an American nickname signified the Korean officer had "arrived." Kim Chong Pil, being of the new breed of Korean without long-standing ties with Americans, had no such nickname; we quickly fell into the habit of referring to him simply as KCP, and I understand this sobriquet has been shortened to CP.

The conversational ball was clearly in KCP's court and he began deliberately and in detail to explain to me, with Pak's assistance, why General Pak had staged his coup, why it was necessary, and in general what the plans were for the foreseeable future. For the first time I heard a Korean relate the view that Koreans had to establish their own national identity once again; that they wanted close ties and the friendship of the Americans, but that these ties had to be on the basis of mutual respect and equality. Korean customs, culture, and family traditions had to become, once again, the basic fabric of Korean society. KCP was a clear thinker who articulated his thoughts well and in depth. At one point he stopped and asked me my opinion of what he had been telling me.

Everything he had said made eminently great sense; the Korean identity and personality must come to the fore, and he would find no opposition on the American side. I stressed strongly that now that they had taken over responsibility for governing the Republic of Korea, they must take the initiative to reestablish good working relations with both the American Embassy and the American military command. It would be tragic, I told him, if the Koreans and Americans, who had shed so much blood together during the war, were to find themselves in hostile postures; too many lives had been lost on both sides to allow self-pride to dominate our joint conduct during the unsettled weeks which lay ahead. We talked on in this vein for several hours. Kim listened well and from time to time gestured to Pak Chung Gyu to take a written note of something I had said. As our first session wound to a natural close, Kim said that he wanted to relate everything I had said, as well as the general nature of our talk together, to General Pak that evening, and asked if I would be willing to meet General Pak at his command post the next morning. I assured him that I would and it was agreed that Captain

Pak Chung Gyu would pick me up at the entrance to the American Embassy the next morning at nine o'clock. It was already dark and Captain Pak, accompanied by a soldier armed with a sub-machine gun, drove me in a jeep to the entrance of Compound 2.

After sending off a long cable to Headquarters relating the events of the day, my conversations with Captain Pak and Kim Chong Pil and what would be happening the next day, I found the chargé still at the embassy with several members of his staff and I informed them of basically what I had been doing during the day and what I had sent off to Washington. They were all weary and disheveled after a long and active day. The chargé sighed, stood up, and walked slowly back and forth, saying that the United States really faced some problems now, noting that General Magruder not only commanded the U.S. Eighth Army, but was the United Nations commander. He had spoken with the general on the phone several times during the day and General Magruder had taken the position that the ROK Army, as an integral part of the UN Military Command and therefore under Magruder's personal command, had by staging a coup committed mutiny. Under these circumstances, the chargé went on, General Magruder would not meet or deal with General Pak. The chargé smiled bleakly and went on to say that General Magruder's intelligence staff also had information to the effect that Pak Chung Hee had a Communist background.

My own office had been busy with cable traffic during the day and I already knew that it was Pak Chung Hee's brother who had been a Communist supporter, had fought on the North Korean side during the war, and had been killed in battle. Our knowledge of Pak Chung Hee himself brought us to the firm conclusion that he was not a Communist nor did he have personal Communist connections or sympathies. I related all of this to the chargé, who said I would have to arrange a meeting with General Magruder and bring him around. Meanwhile, the word from the Department of State, with advice from the Pentagon, was that the embassy was not to deal with Pak Chung Hee until instructed. The chargé wanted me to continue the contact with Kim Chong Pil and to keep in touch with both Kim and Pak until this delicate matter of political background was resolved one way or the other. I was to keep the chargé informed of every session I had with either Kim or Pak.

The next morning, promptly at nine, the Marine guard phoned my office, saying there was a Captain Pak at the entrance. I went down and found Pak standing by his jeep. On the rear jumpseat were two soldiers, each brandishing a Thompson sub-machine gun. Pak offered me the right-hand seat of the jeep and said I was expected at the ROK Army compound in Yongsan. I was not happy at the prospect of riding in an open jeep through the teeming streets of Seoul, obviously an American, with two machine guns behind me, and I said as much to Pak. He grinned self-consciously and spoke rapidly to the two soldiers, who placed their guns on the floor as we roared off to Yongsan, scattering Korean pedestrians on both sides.

Machine guns studded the barbed-wire perimeter of the ROK Army compound and every gate was barred and patrolled. Pak had to show his credentials before we were allowed to enter. In the compound we drove past ROK Army tanks, personnel carriers, and trucks, pulling up in front of the headquarters building, which I had visited previously on several occasions when it was under different occupancy. Military field telephone wire was connected to every telephone pole in sight and clumped together in a bundle as thick as my arm where it disappeared into a window on the second floor. We entered and Pak's credentials were again checked at several guard posts. The office on the second floor was filled with officers and enlisted men who were constantly coming and going, writing messages, and answering telephones—all the activity of a military command post, which it was. Captain Pak rapped on a door, went inside, and reappeared a moment later, waving me in. He was again to be interpreter, this time at my first meeting with General Pak.

This office was spacious, unpretentious, and very busy. At the far end of the room was a large table, rather than a desk, and on it sat half a dozen telephones. There were papers piled up on the desk and in the back wall were two doors from which junior officers from time to time slipped in, placed papers on the desk, and moved quietly out again. While I was with Pak for the next two hours, not one of the phones rang, and I assumed that incoming calls were being intercepted elsewhere.

Pak was seated in an easy chair behind a round tea table, around which were several cushioned chairs. As I approached him, he stood up and extended his hand, his face impassive. He was short, compactly built, smooth-skinned, and his eyes were very intent. He said nothing but Captain Pak presumed to say to me that General Pak was glad to meet me and have the opportunity of talking together. We exchanged murmured greetings, seated ourselves, and an orderly made an immediate appearance with a tray bearing a teapot and cups, together with bottles of Coca-Cola and glasses. He placed this in the middle of the table and another aide brought in a plate of Korean cookies. General Pak spoke little English and preferred to work through an interpreter, probably for the usual reason—to allow himself time to digest a comment in English before phrasing his reply. He understood a fair amount of English and would interrupt Captain Pak to insert an English word to give a more precise expression of his thought. He looked bone weary and I could imagine that he, along with his staff, had been many hours in the saddle.

It was quickly apparent that Captain Pak and Kim Chong Pil had spent considerable time with General Pak relating our respective conversations together. He frequently referred to matters I had brought up with both Pak and Kim, as well as new points and opinions I expressed later in our talks. He launched into an expression of why he felt a coup against Prime Minister Chang had been necessary. His peroration covered all the major points that had been brought up the previous evening by Kim Chong Pil. All of this was done calmly and with deliberation.

After a while General Pak referred to a theme I had emphasized: the mutual need for contact, friendship, and a constructive relationship between the Koreans and Americans, both diplomatically and militarily. He endorsed this attitude and went on to complain that he had already tried to reach General Magruder but had been rebuffed and told the general was too busy. General Pak smiled thinly as Captain Pak translated these words for my benefit; I myself felt embarrassed to learn that the U.S. commanding general, the day after the military coup against the Korean government, had declared himself too busy to talk with the new leader of the country. There was nothing for me to say. Pak went on to state that he was prepared at any time to meet with General Magruder and of course with the chargé and suggested that I might make his views known. He asked if I might see him again in the next day or two and advise him of the reactions to his offers of cooperation. Captain Pak interrupted to say that I could call him at any time and make an appointment with the general.

This talk went back and forth with Oriental deliberation and precision; after about two hours it finally came to a logical and agreeable end. General Pak reiterated that he would like me to keep in touch with Colonel Kim and that any message I might give Kim would get to him. He added that if anything urgent occurred, Kim Chong Pil would arrange for an immediate meeting between us.

The next day General Pak declared a state of national emergency, having in mind the possibility of an opportunistic incursion from North Korea. He also formed a revolutionary council, of which he was chairman, to rule the nation. This revolutionary council consisted of senior military officers chosen by Pak, each of whom was to serve as Pak's personal point of contact with the normal civilian ministries. During the first eight days after the coup, there was a strange and tense confrontation between the American Embassy, the military command, and the new military junta. General Magruder, backed by the usual uncritical support of the Pentagon for a field commander, continued to take the attitude that Pak was part of his command and had actually mutinied by staging a coup; he would not meet with Pak.

I met several times with Kim Chong Pil and even more often with Pak Chung Gyu. One day Captain Pak and I were sitting in the Duksoo Palace gardens musing about the strange situation that found the Koreans and Americans out of touch with each other. Captain Pak, who was by nature excitable and intense, said he was going to recommend to General Pak that a Korean Army battalion surround the American Embassy to prevent anyone from leaving or entering until, as he put it, "the American side comes to their senses," and recognized General Pak. My God, I thought, we are going to wind up with bloodshed if this goes on much longer, I finally succeeded in talking Pak out of this scheme. This outburst was reported to the chargé and to General Magruder and by this time both the American military and the embassy were coming to the realization that a continuation of this impasse could lead to grave trouble. Luckily, at this time, Pak's background and that of his dead brother were finally clarified. The chargé, much relieved, asked that I make an appointment for him to see General Pak; General Magruder used his own extensive military contacts with the Koreans to arrange a meeting with General Pak, who immediately came to call upon him. A potentially serious crisis was averted, the American side moved quickly on the military and diplomatic fronts to establish connections with Pak and his group of advisers in the revolutionary council. Soon thereafter we had a new American ambassador, Samuel Berger, who proved to be an outstanding man, wise, perceptive and honest.

Sam Berger and his delightful wife, Margie, remained in Seoul during the rest of our tour until we were transferred to Hong Kong in July 1962. It was during Sam Berger's time as ambassador that his wise guidance and counseling to Chairman Pak and his cabinet were instrumental in bringing about the miraculous growth of the Korean economy, and for the first time in its history bringing that nation and its population into the modern industrial world. The fundamental credit for this phenomenal growth, beginning in 1961, belongs to the Koreans themselves; the presence of Ambassador Berger was certainly a major contributing factor in this welcome development.

For the remainder of my time in Korea, Chairman Pak ran the country with a firm and, some might say, a repressive hand. I did not see it that way. In the years following World War II, South Korea had become an American client state benefiting greatly militarily and economically in that status, but without developing a sense of national identity or purpose. The excesses of the aging Syngman Rhee regime further debilitated the Korean spirit and sense of self-esteem. The gentle and mild leadership of John Chang, while admirable on every moral ground, was unable to keep a controlling rein on the fractious political horses that made up the Korean political scene. While Chairman Pak's handling of the South Korean government was certainly not a model of Jeffersonian democracy, it was nevertheless progressive, innovative, constructive, and certainly appropriate to the time. It was in the nature of the Korean people to contend with each other, to vie with each other and to be violently critical of each other. Chairman Pak's style of government offended those contending political forces who wished to replace him, and also offended American observers who were watching the situation with typical American supermorality from the outside and who were determined to prove that Pak's regime was oppressive, corrupt, and undemocratic. Over the years, the astounding Korean economic progress has continued, political opposition within Korea has been curbed and frustrated, and Pak's critics at home and abroad, particularly in the United States, have been loud, articulate, and relentless. Whatever reservations I may have about the style of Pak's government or of the functioning of its ministries, I felt then and feel today the style was appropriate to the time, necessary to the conditions of Korean history and not nearly so fearsome or savage as Pak's critics would have one believe. And American critics should recognize in themselves the uncontrollable urge, once beyond the three-mile limit, to impute perfection to themselves while professing horror at the faults and shortcomings of their allies. It is sad but true that we seem incapable of liking people who are not like us, or not like what we earnestly desire to picture ourselves as being.

A notable visit to Korea was that of President Eisenhower in 1960. As the facts of Korean political life would have it, Eisenhower's scheduled visit happened to take place in the ninety-day period between the fall of President Rhee and the holding of new elections. The interim government of Huh Chung presided and Huh himself was host to President Eisenhower and his party. The Eisenhower visit to Seoul had originally been scheduled to last from the late morning until the early evening of one day. The Koreans welcomed "Ike" in such a tumultuous fashion all the way from Kimpo Airport into Seoul and during his visits to various governmental offices, that Eisenhower decided to extend his stay overnight and until noon the following day. The Koreans were ecstatic. The weather was warm and pleasant and Seoul had been freshly painted and decorated by the enthusiastic Koreans. Eisenhower was entertained at a formal state dinner by Huh, and the center of Seoul was a mass of good-humored, cheering Koreans who took the occasion to shake every American hand they could find. The chief of the Secret Service detail dropped exhausted into a chair in my office at one stage of the afternoon, drank some coffee, and exclaimed that in all of his travels with the President, he had never met such a mass of enthusiastic humanity as they had encountered in Seoul.

President Eisenhower, together with his son and daughter-in-law, stayed overnight in the guest house of the residence. Ambassador McConaughy hastily organized a stag breakfast the following morning, to which I was invited. Because this was a period of intense political activity in Korea, preliminary to the new elections, he invited some of the principal contenders for the premiership, of course including Chang Myon, with representatives from Korean universities, newspaper publishers, missionaries, the president of the Chamber of Commerce, and student leaders. Breakfast began at eight in the morning and ended only after eleven A.M. when aides informed the President that his aircraft was ready for departure to Japan. The President was animated, active, and clearly interested in his conversations with the Korean guests, who in turn were articulate, candid, and informative. After the Koreans left and before leaving for the airport, Eisenhower told McConaughy that finally he had his own satisfactory sensing of what the Korean situation was about, and what their immediate problems—and by inference what our immediate problems—would be. It was altogether a highly successful visit, both from the American standpoint and from that of the Koreans. It was the high point of their year.

A less enjoyable visit took place in the summer of 1962. During that spring the Communist-oriented and supplied Pathet Lao had been campaigning actively in the central highlands of Laos, to establish Communist military supremacy in the country as a whole. The King of Laos sat quietly in his palace at Luang Prabang, while the rightist forces under General Phoumi Nosavan, widely supported but badly equipped, were being systematically chopped up by the Communists. Diplomatic talks in Geneva convened to settle the Lao problem and had been haltingly underway for some time. President Kennedy had sent W. Averell Harriman to promote an accord which would in effect create a Laotian government consisting of leftist, conservative, and "neutral" components; thus the entry of the Communist Pathet Lao into the central government of Laos was accomplished, much to the dismay of both the king and General Phoumi. General Phoumi at once announced his intention of touring the capitals of non-Communist Asia, seeking moral and any other support which would help oppose the growing strength of the Communists in Laos. His announced itinerary was to take him to Bangkok, Singapore, Manila, Taiwan, Tokyo, and Seoul—in these capitals he hoped to gain enough tangible support to reorganize Laotian opposition to the Pathet Lao and to carry on the fight.

In a weird display of aggressive diplomacy and power politics, Averell Harriman undertook a parallel trip in which he preceded General Phoumi to these particular Asian capitals, to make the American position clear: support the Geneva accords and do not support General Phoumi. Ambassador Berger was instructed to arrange a meeting between Harriman and the leadership of the Korean government in order that Harriman could present the American position with regard to the Geneva accords and the anticipated supplications of General Phoumi. Berger did so only to find out that Chairman Pak did not wish to see Harriman, considering him inclined to accommodate the Communist Pathet Lao, and had instructed his prime minister, General Song, to see him. General Song, popularly known as "Tiger" Song, was widely known and liked in South Korea, having been the Korean general to capture Pyongyang, the capital of North Korea, during the drive north to the Yalu River in 1950.

Ambassador Berger asked me to accompany him, along with several other embassy officers, to the meeting between Mr. Harriman and Tiger Song. It took place in the prime minister's office in the Diet compound in the same room in which I had sat with President Rhee's minister of interior, following the riots of 1960. Tiger Song spoke good English and the conference proceeded smoothly without interruptions for translations. Unknown to me, Harriman was already in a short-tempered, combative mood; he rapidly spelled out the American position in regard to General Phoumi's trip to Tiger Song in a clipped, terse fashion. In effect, if the Korean government was inclined to be sympathetic to General Phoumi upon his arrival in Seoul, the Koreans could expect a change in relations between the United States and South Korea. This would reflect upon the economic and military aid they had been receiving. Harriman's presentation was direct and brusque. On the other side of the room the Korean group, headed by General Song, smiled politely. I knew behind this facade of courtesy and equanimity they were both discouraged at this turn of events and furious at this display of arrogance by their American friends.

The meeting ended in a correct but cool manner. Sam Berger

and I exchanged glances as we were waiting to take our leave and Sam rolled his eyes and shook his head slightly. The American group filed out and went to their cars, returning to the embassy. Sam took me aside in the hallway to tell me that he had been privately informed that Harriman carried President Kennedy's authority with him. There was nothing to be done. The Harriman visit ended with a stiffly formal stag dinner, which I did not attend, and Governor Harriman left for Tokyo the next day.

General Phoumi was to reach Seoul two days later. In the interim I called Pak Chung Gyu to ask about General Pak Chung Hee's general reaction after General Song's report of the meeting, and was told that Pak was furious but helpless. American assistance was critical to South Korea's growth and even survival, and though General Pak was sympathetic to General Phoumi's plight and objective, he could not offer the assistance General Phoumi would seek. General Phoumi came and went on schedule and that was the treatment he received. There was a distinct chill in the air between Pak, his Revolutionary Council, and the embassy for some time thereafter. Sam Berger opined to me that the effect of the Harriman visit would probably require half a year to reverse.

Marilyn and I finally had our long-deferred home leave in the States. We had rented a house on the island of Maui in the Hawaiian islands, located on a small quiet beach, where we spent the month of July. Our visits to San Francisco and Washington were kept to a minimum as we were anxious to reach the restful change of sun and sand.

Prior to leaving Seoul, there was one more obligation I had to perform. Before General Pak had taken over, a good friend on his staff had informed us of the details of Pak's planned coup. With approval from my superiors, I had warned John Chang of the impending development but, to his ultimate sorrow, he discredited what I had told him. Following the successful coup, our military friend and informant developed a serious case of nerves as to what might happen to him if General Pak learned of our prior knowledge and the source of it. He insisted upon an immediate flight to the United States and sanctuary there. We could only agree to help him in the light of what he had done for us and we spirited him out of Korea by military aircraft to a holding area in Okinawa. From there, he and his family were relocated in the United States, where he remained even after I had left Seoul for Hong Kong. Eventually, homesick for the aroma of the rice paddies and the garlic blasts of kimchi, he approached an emissary of Pak, had been given a guarantee of immunity, and returned with his family to Seoul. To General Pak's credit, the man was not punished and still lives peacefully in Korea.

On our way back to Honolulu for our flight to Maui, we spent a few days in San Francisco with my brother. During this visit I received a call from the chief of our Far Eastern division, Desmond Fitzgerald. Des, a long-time friend, told me the assignment board in Washington had just adjourned and my next assignment, following three years in Korea, would be as chief-of-station in Hong Kong.

Following the Harriman visit to Seoul in 1962, there was little for me to do but meet my successor and, as chief-of-station, arrange an orderly turnover of the job, to introduce him to his contacts in the Korean government and the diplomatic and military community, and to prepare for my own move to Hong Kong. This we did in a welter of farewell parties. We left for Hong Kong on a Cathay Pacific flight after a profusion of sentimental farewells, collapsed on the plane, and were asleep before it left the ground, late in July 1962.

18 Hong Kong R and R

Our flight from Seoul took us down the Yellow Sea, across the East China Sea, past Formosa, and into Hong Kong. The flight was mainly in the dark of a moonless night and the many bottles of champagne we had shared with friends while sitting out several flight delays in Seoul encouraged sleep. Later, a pleasant Chinese stewardess gently shook us awake to say we were about thirty minutes out of Hong Kong in case we wished to freshen up and have some coffee. Sipping coffee, we watched the sky in the east lose its blackness and become a thin gray. Soon we could distinguish islands beneath us, and while sunrise was still to come, the thin predawn light gave us good visibility as we approached Hong Kong, flying low over the water between Victoria Island and Kowloon, settling on the runway at the east end of Kai Tak airport. We taxied up to the large, modern terminal, disembarked and were taken in mini-buses to the customs area. Once through customs, my new CIA station administrative officer, Jerry, met us after having waited hours because of our numerous delays in leaving Seoul. His driver had a large carryall van which took us through the already teeming streets of Kowloon to the wharf, where we boarded a walla-walla, a water taxi, for the trip across Hong Kong harbor, as the driver took the longer route by ferry with our baggage. The sun was not yet visible, but the rosy light of dawn dappled the clouds above us as the water taxi bounced across to Queen's Wharf on Victoria Island. Midway across, the sunlight came through behind us and lighted the terraced hills of Victoria. Tall office buildings, imposing apartment houses, and individual homes perched on the cliffsides and the peak took shape in the light of the rising sun. The walla-walla plunged along as we drank in the beauty of Hong Kong—Korea seemed very far away.

Another carryall was waiting for us on the Hong Kong side. We drove up to and through the Gap, and down the winding

Hong Kong—R and R

roads of the seaward side of the island to Repulse Bay. Our apartment, which we had inherited from the departing chief-of-station, was set in a small park of its own. The house, although quite large, contained only two flats; ours was on the ground floor, although the balcony overlooking Repulse Bay rose about fifty feet from the cement driveway below. The second-floor flat was used occasionally by the landlord on a weekend or for some sort of celebration when the house would be invaded by the endless numbers of relatives and friends. We could hear the click of Mah-jongg tiles at one part of the house and at the other the younger group playing American records until the early hours of the morning. (There was neglible security risk, as nothing confidential was discussed at home.) They were always very friendly and we found that Orientals enjoy nothing more than large family gatherings. The top quarters of the house were occupied by a housekeeper, who kept a number of chickens running loose on the back stairs and eating well from one of my good Korean bowls.

There was a large courtyard at the entrance to the house and a black, official sedan had been left for my use. We had also inherited a Chinese couple, who lived in the back rooms, and everything was ready for occupancy. We just collapsed into bed to catch up on lost sleep, after telling Jerry I would check into the office later that morning.

Marilyn and I agreed that Hong Kong was really our "rest and recreation" post after Korea. We were there for only seventeen months of our anticipated three-year stay. During these months, while I worked very hard at a difficult assignment, we also enjoyed ourselves to the hilt—so much so that at the time we left Hong Kong in December 1963, we were surfeited with the life of permanent tourists and bored with confined life on a small island. Upon our arrival, however, we were enchanted with the land of the lotus eaters.

Jerry had thoughtfully arranged for me to have luncheon with five of the senior espionage officers (known as case officers) in the station. Although I had spent three years in Asia, this luncheon was my first exposure to members of that group in the CIA who were looked upon as the old China hands. Most of them spoke Cantonese or Mandarin and had served repeated tours in the Far East or in the Far East Division at headquarters. I was very much an unknown quantity to them, except for the fact

I had spent many years in Europe, spoke Russian, and had concentrated on Soviet matters. We spent time during lunch getting acquainted, exchanging war stories, and in general talking about our respective backgrounds. Professionally speaking, we were walking stiff-legged around each other, sniffing like strange dogs. I quickly saw that my three years in Korea had really not prepared me to run a so-called China show, and that I would have to rely heavily on those case officers in the station who were experienced in China affairs.

By early August we were well settled-in. The move was made easier by the fact that our senior diplomatic officer had been the deputy chief of mission at our embassy in Seoul; Marshall Green and I knew each other well and his wife Lisa and Marilyn were good friends. He introduced me to the principal officers of the Hong Kong government, most of whom had had long experience in and about China and who knew that I did not share this background. Each of them, in his own way, tactfully cautioned me about the rules of the game in intelligence work in Hong Kong.

The main point was that HMG (Her Majesty's Government) really couldn't afford to be flagrant or tactless regarding the authorities on the Communist Chinese mainland. We had to be mindful of the fact that the Communist Chinese government had a variety of commercial and quasi-official officers in the British crown colony of Hong Kong and that all of us were routinely under scrutiny. Some of these mainland offices were the Bank of China, the China Travel Agency, and certain commercial outlets that sold goods produced on the mainland and marketed in the colony. There was also a quasi-illicit but notorious gold trade between Hong Kong and Macao, a neighboring Portuguese colony, by means of which the Communist Chinese government reaped large amounts of hard currencies which they used in buying essential goods and commodities throughout the world.

Then again, Hong Kong received much of its drinking water from Communist China and there had been in the past veiled threats by the authorities in Canton that drinking water to the British colony could be easily curtailed. There had been occasions in the past when disturbed relations between the United Kingdom and Chinese Communist authorities had resulted in "difficulties" with the water supplies from the mainland. It was impressed upon me that the political situation in Hong Kong, vis-à-vis the Chinese in Kwangtung province, was always delicate and one of the most potentially troublesome areas was the matter of intelligence collection. This did not mean that the British themselves were inactive in acquiring information on and about the mainland or that the mainland Chinese were unrealistic; it meant that over the years the British had learned to go about their work with a certain finesse and sense of balance, which they wanted me to appreciate.

The British were a sincere and impressive group and I assured them, while they need not expect me to give them details on any operations we ran to the mainland, they could be certain I would be guided by their advice and their policies and would seek their counsel when and if I felt myself to be on uncertain ground. During the year and a half I worked in Hong Kong this policy seemed to be adequate to the maintenance of good relations with our British colleagues, which were of course essential to our accomplishing any work at all in Hong Kong. Certain British intelligence and security organs maintained representatives in Hong Kong and I had routine and frequent liaison with each of them.

The month of August 1962 was spent getting my heels down in the stirrups, acquainting myself with my own case officers, our own diplomatic mission, and in forming friendships with our British colleagues. August drew to a close with a bang. On 1 September, at five in the morning, after many storm warnings, typhoon Wanda screamed across the colony and later moved to the mainland of China. Wanda was, at that time, the worst typhoon in the recorded history of Hong Kong; it left many dead and much destruction of property. We rode out this howling terror in the safety of our strongly built flat at Repulse Bay, but many less fortunate lost their homes, cars, and personal belongings. A modern high-rise apartment overlooking Repulse Bay was devastated as the incredible wind broke every window in the building, sucking out clothes, rugs, mattresses, and furniture, spreading them over the hillsides. It took several days before any order was restored to the island and we ourselves were completely marooned for two days until large, fallen trees could be cleared from the roadways. The shipping wreckage in Hong Kong harbor was visible for months afterwards.

I find it hard to write about our intelligence work based in

Hong Kong against mainland China because there was very little successful intelligence work done, in fact. Much was attempted and much failed. We had two main intelligence targets: the uranium gaseous-diffusion plant under construction at Lanchow and the plutonium plant at Pao Tou, both in north-central China. We wanted to learn the state of construction of these two important scientific enterprises, to determine when they went into full production and the amount of purity of their nuclear products. We accomplished neither, nor had my predecessors, and, as I understand it, neither did my successors. The advent of photographic satellites later in the 1960s, however, changed that bleak picture markedly, but that all took place after my tour in Hong Kong.

It was small solace later to learn that this high-expectation, low-yield experience was not mine alone. Mainland China was simply a difficult target for intelligence penetration on the ground with human agents. We had some minor successes but "minor" was the word.

We had problems, though, and problems are also part of the intelligence business. The Kuomintang Party of the Nationalist Chinese in Taipei were active in running agents through Hong Kong where, being ethnic Chinese, they could mingle with their countrymen and from time to time slip into the meager legal Chinese traffic into and out of Kwangtung province to Canton and perhaps from there up the coast to Shanghai and Peking. As often as not, these agents from Formosa were uncovered, not by the Communist Chinese authorities, but by the Special Branch of the Hong Kong police. Invariably, the captured KMT (Kuomintang) agents would be incarcerated for a week or so and then unceremoniously shipped back to Taiwan. Because the British in charge of the Special Branch of the Hong Kong police knew that the CIA was in direct contact with the Nationalist Chinese intelligence organizations in Taiwan, they came to me to complain about the actions of such KMT agents, which was simply an unproductive embarrassment to Her Majesty's Government. As such they were an embarrassment to the CIA and certainly to me personally. When the Chinese people found themselves in two divided political camps (as with the Germans, Koreans, and Vietnamese), double agents abounded. Unscrambling these intelligence omelets was really more than human patience could endure. The simplest solution for the British was to send the suspected KMT agent back to Taiwan and push the suspected Chinese Communist agent back across the border at Sumchun into Kwangtung province and hope for the best. Altogether it was a never-ending burlesque, except that people did die performing it.

There was a constant flow of Chinese from the mainland into Hong Kong. They arrived along deserted beaches or in crowded ports, buried in cargoes of freshly caught fish, working as deck hands on fishing junks, and of course swimming across the straits between Chinese-held islands and those of the British colony or the New Territories. As could only happen in a British-run colony, there were unwritten but strictly observed rules of the game. An escapee from mainland China, if caught by the British police, would be sent straight back. If the escapee could find his way first to a British colonial police station, report his presence, and ask for an identity card, he would be given the card and could thereafter legally remain in the colony. It was a game, although a rather dangerous one, and the losers very often were repeaters and, not infrequently, made it to the police station just in front of the gendarmes. Then there were others who died attempting to swim the straits; Communist Chinese border guards shot and killed many hiding on fishing boats bound for Hong Kong and we learned that many Chinese families left behind were arrested and taken to prison or worse.

The British police routinely interrogated all Chinese seeking asylum in the crown colony, and through this process gained a great deal of information regarding rations, the Chinese economy, morale among the population and other sociological intelligence which, while not critical, continued to add to the obscure picture of mankind on the mainland of China.

All during the year 1963 a place called Vietnam was making its way ever further into the headlines of the English-language press of Hong Kong, and on radio and television. There was little direct involvement for us in Hong Kong except through the media, although a long-time friend of mine was chief-of-station in Saigon. From time to time a Saigon cable would ask us to surveil a South Vietnamese personality transiting Hong Kong— more exercise for our indigenous surveillance team. In August, Henry Cabot Lodge succeeded Frederick Nolting as ambassador in Saigon, and in October our station chief there was abruptly relieved of duty and sent back to CIA headquarters. In November we received word that Far East Division Chief William Colby was visiting Vietnam, and I wondered what American upheaval was underway there, in the wake of President Diem's ouster and murder. One morning in November I received a cable from Colby in Saigon, asking me to come there to have talks with him.

Political events in Saigon had come to a critical point on 1 November. There had been a coup by the Vietnamese military against President Diem and his brother, Nhu. The coup had become bloody and after two days of battling in the center of Saigon the bodies of Diem and his brother were found heaped in the back of a weapons carrier. The overthrow of the Diem regime had taken place, as had been often predicted in the press and, I might add, in official American cable traffic. I packed a bag and flew at once to Saigon, where I met Colby. An interim junta of Vietnamese generals had established a shaky government after the death of Diem, but this was clearly not the main matter on Colby's mind. In October our new ambassador in Vietnam, Henry Cabot Lodge, had peremptorily fired the station chief, John Richardson, who at once returned to the States. The station was in the hands of a deputy and Colby was there to see what should be done.

Bill Colby, though a relatively young man, had a broad and varied career in intelligence. During World War II, as a member of the OSS (Office of Strategic Services), he parachuted behind German lines in France where he lived and fought with the French Maquis resistance movement, and later parachuted into occupied Norway. After the war, he left the Army and took a law degree, although he did not go into the practice of law. He joined the CIA at its inception and served in a number of assignments at Headquarters and various stations in Europe. He gravitated toward Far Eastern (FE) affairs and was chief-of-station in Saigon, then succeeded Desmond Fitzgerald as chief of FE, the position he held when I saw him in Saigon in 1963. We did not know each other.

On this my first visit to Saigon, I stayed at the Caravelle Hotel. It faced out on the old Saigon opera house, beyond which lay the fabled Continental Hotel, full of French colonial history. Along the left side of the Caravelle ran the stylish Tudo Street, known in French days as Rue Catinat. Colby had been put up in an apartment rented and controlled by the Saigon station, but we generally took our meals together, usually at the home of officers in the station. At his invitation I went along with him as he met station personnel and inspected some of our outlying facilities away from the city centers, such as our air section and parachute parking shed at Tan Son Nhut airport. One evening at dinner he told me that he wanted me to go with him on a circuit of Vietnam, leaving at dawn the next day from Tan Son Nhut. He told me what kind of clothing to bring and the next morning his driver picked me up at the Caravelle Hotel en route to the airfield, just before sunup.

During the next few days we visited Dalat, Nha Trang, Danang, and Hue. There were official calls to be made at each of these stops and I went along as Bill carried on his fact-finding tour. From Hue we flew south to Kon Tum in the highlands where Bill inspected an interrogation center and talked with Vietnamese province officials. Thanks to the French colonial presence, almost all senior Vietnamese officials, civilian or military, spoke French, in which Bill was fluent and I barely intelligible. From Kon Tum we flew to Dok To, where a Huey helicopter awaited us. On the Huey we flew northwest to the border junction between Vietnam and Laos and Cambodia over heavily forested, mountainous terrain. There on the Vietnam side of the border, we circled over a camp, Ban Het, perched on the top of a mountain, built by a CIDG (Civilian Irregular Defense Group) element, whose mission was to patrol the border to intercept Vietcong elements infiltrating South Vietnam through Laos, along the so-called Ho Chi Minh trail. We circled Ban Het several times, communicating by radio, and then turned and headed southeast toward Pleiku, where our own station aircraft awaited us. The flight from Ban Het to Pleiku gave me a glimpse of the nature of the war in Vietnam. The Huey flew at its maximum speed and at treetop height, following the contours of the valleys and hills, as closely as safety permitted. The purpose was to avoid giving any Vietcong elements on the ground time to shoot us down. The flight, at or below treetop height, was exhilarating and turned out to be the first of many such hair-raising trips.

There was a sizable group of American military advisers assigned to ARVN (Army of the Republic of Vietnam) units based in Pleiku. The chief of these advisers met our chopper and Bill gave him a brief rundown on where we had been, asking him what success (not much) the CIDG element at Ban Het was having in interdicting Vietcong elements crossing into Vietnam by means of the Ho Chi Minh trail. It was from this colonel that I first heard the Ho Chi Minh trail described as the "Averell Harriman Memorial Highway," with derisive reference to the accord Harriman had negotiated the year before, giving the Pathet Lao *de facto* control over those portions of Laos of strategic interest to North Vietnam, such as the eastern half of the Laos panhandle, where the "Harriman Highway" was located.

We stayed overnight in Pleiku at the U.S. Army compound there, a stopover point that came vividly to mind some two years later as the location of a savage Vietcong attack that was instrumental in sharply escalating American intervention into the Vietnam war. After dinner at the Officers Club, Bill and I sat by ourselves in the lounge while he detailed the purpose behind his asking me on this tour. Bill said I should prepare to move from Hong Kong to Saigon the next summer, perhaps in the month of June, to take over the Vietnam station. The deputy was doing a very good job and Colby would like to see him finish his two-year tour, which ended in June. We flew back to Saigon the following morning and I caught a Cathay Pacific flight back to Hong Kong, while Bill took off on the rest of his Asian inspection tour.

At home again in Hong Kong, I told Marilyn what had happened, described Saigon and the life American families led there and what she should expect. We both agreed that Hong Kong, even after only a year and a half, was too much of a good thing; we were ready to move on and especially ready for Vietnam.

Marilyn was again pregnant, but we had at least six months to prepare ourselves, and the new baby would be a couple of months old by the time we moved to Saigon in June 1964.

Naturally enough, we enjoyed Hong Kong in spite of the absence of any real professional satisfaction to me. It was a city of contradictions, ever changing and always exciting. There were then over three million Chinese in Hong Kong, most of them escapees and refugees from Communist China, to which were added about thirty thousand Europeans, a catch-phrase for British, Americans, French, or anyone from a non-Oriental country. This latter group consisted mainly of civil servants representing HMG in governing the colony itself, even though it was almost completely autonomous and functionally independent of London—the diplomatic group included members of the various consulates represented there, many Western business firms and officials of these firms, a sprinkling of journalists, newsmen, educators, and students of China. Besides shopping, there were excellent restaurants, tennis clubs, and beaches.

During our first week in Hong Kong, I gave Marilyn an ultimatum, saying I was going to buy a car, a boat, and a dog, and she could pick the breed. Our first boat was a hand-built Cape Cod catboat, which we soon found too small when we wanted to take out friends and visitors. This was replaced by a grand and imposing forty-foot junk, which seldom rolled more than an inch out of the horizontal and which could accommodate three or four families and any dogs that liked the water. We also ended up with a German shepherd dog, which although lovable was nothing but trouble. He did not like the Chinese, he contracted hepatitis, and then in sheer gratitude gave us a houseful of fleas. When we were finally decontaminated, we decided that Tarpley (named after a friend of our son in Korea) would be better off chasing Communists at the border and he was initiated into the ranks of the British police.

The summer of 1963 brought a "dry monsoon" to Hong Kong. The summer months are very rainy, usually with rain falling every day as the monsoon sweeps up the China coast. At great intervals there would be a summer with no rainfall and this was such a summer. Hong Kong depended upon water caught in catchments and reservoirs, in addition to the water piped in from Communist China under a contract between the crown colony and the administration of Kwantung province. This was a summer in which there had been difficulties with the Chinese and the deliberate restriction of water from the mainland made a truly acute fresh-water shortage in the colony.

For about four months during the summer, water was severely rationed. The colony and its attendant New Territories was divided into water districts and each district was allocated three hours of water every fourth day. The district in which our house was located had water from six to nine in the morning every fourth day; our house was cluttered with pails, barrels, and every kind of container we could obtain; in addition, the bathtubs and sinks were filled while the ration was on. Inconvenient though it was, it was incredibly more so for the Chinese population, and especially the water people—the families who lived aboard junks or sampans. Directly below our house in the Wanchai district was a typhoon shelter in Hong Kong harbor, almost completely carpeted by them. During this miserably hot summer, long lines of Chinese would queue up every fourth day with their pails in front of them in the broiling sun, squatting on the pavement until the police unlocked the water tap on the hydrants. The Chinese policeman, with true British precision, would time his watch to the second and release the water to the waiting Chinese. Slowly the line would move forward as each person filled his containers, and then moved on. I marveled at the stoicism and orderliness of these poor and thirsty Chinese, who waited with infinite patience for their meager ration. Never any unrest. Never any disturbance.

One of my British friends in the Special Branch of the Hong Kong police, actually a Scot by birth, sponsored us for membership in a British military club which had a swimming beach on the ocean side of the island, in the village of Stanley, which was distinguished by the presence of Stanley prison. With our Scottish friends, we would picnic there from time to time, especially on the days when the tides and winds kept garbage off the beaches. Incoming freighters had a habit of unloading their trash at sea before entering Hong Kong, where to do so was forbidden. One day while lying in the sun with the walls of Stanley prison looming above us, I asked what the inside of the prison was like. With a smile, Lundy answered that he could tell me the size and shape of every stone and brick in the prison; when the Japanese had taken Hong Kong in December of 1941, as a member of the Hong Kong police he was taken prisoner and had spent the entire war within its walls. Reticent by nature, he had little to say about his imprisonment, but documented stories about Stanley which I had read revealed that a man was lucky indeed to have survived the war there.

Early one morning in November, I was awakened at about five o'clock in the morning by the jangling of my phone. On the other end was one of my communicators, who told me that I had better come in to read a message. I dressed and drove to the consulate, where I was handed a cable. It was a "book" message (going to all CIA stations around the world) announcing that President Kennedy had been assassinated that day in Dallas. A few days later a memorial service was held at an Episcopal church on Garden Road, close to our consulate. Senior British officials were present, as were senior officers of the diplomatic corps and other prominent residents of the colony. It was a

Hong Kong—R and R

touching and moving service; the sincere sorrow and sympathy of all the non-Americans was apparent.

During December the days were sunny and bright, the nights cool and clear. My older son and I slept outside on our bedroom balcony on cots, waking up to the harbor below us, astir with activity. One of the first station chiefs at Hong Kong had previously been assigned to Matsu Island in the Formosa Straits between Taiwan and the mainland of China, and before leaving Matsu he had liberated from the U.S. Navy a pair of bridge binoculars, a deck-mounted high-powered pair of glasses. This had been passed on from one station chief to another and now rested on the balcony leading from our living room, where we could watch people moving below us and the landings and departures of ships and planes; our older boy soon became adept at identifying the markings of each plane as it circled over our house, lowering for a landing at Kai Tak.

Early one Sunday morning in December, the phone rang. I thought about the call with the news of President Kennedy and wondered, my God, what now? This time was quite different, but again my communicator was telling me there was a message I should see at once. I normally checked in to the consulate on Sunday to read cables and Marilyn often went with me. We dressed and went to the commo shack, where I was handed a cable.

A paraphrase of the cable would be: To de Silva from McCone (the Director of Central Intelligence): Upon receipt of this message, you are relieved as COS (chief-of-station) in Hong Kong and as of this date are COS in Saigon. Please report to my office no later than (I had forty-eight hours) for instructions and five days of consultations. You will then accompany me to Saigon for a meeting with U.S. government officials. Following that, return to Hong Kong for your family and personal effects, for transfer to Saigon, arriving no later than the end of December.

I turned to my communicator and asked how long the cable had been in and he replied that he phoned me as soon as it had come in. He went on to ask: "Can I come with you?" I had to smile. The CIA communications people were always dependable, hardworking, and steady under pressure. I told him, "I'll see what I can do." My reply to the director read: Your message number —— received. Will report as directed.

Driving home I looked down at the beautiful harbor and the

nine hills. My life and the life of my family had been unalterably changed in ways in which I could not imagine. There were many things to be done, and after plane reservations had been made, we took a walla-walla to Kowloon for a round of last-minute shopping and to arrange for all the things that must be done while I was away. As we waited for a boat, the 100-foot schooner, *Wan Fu*, owned by the Hong Kong Hilton hotel, docked and the manager and his wife, whom we knew well, came over to say hello, after having found a rickshaw for Greer Garson and her husband whom they had taken on a tour of the islands. They were as startled as we were by the news of my leaving.

We managed to find a few gifts that I could take to friends at home and then we made hurried plans and a list of things to be done in my absence. There was the car and boat to be sold, arrangements made for packing, more summer clothing had to be bought, good-byes had to be made, and the house decorated for Christmas with presents for the children and servants, in addition to making sure the latter had new jobs. The earliest I could return would be a day or two before Christmas. I had a brief meeting with my station officers to explain what had happened, that my deputy would be acting in my place until he was confirmed as my successor or a replacement sent out. All of this took place on a normally quiet Sunday.

Along with my older son, Perry, my wife drove me the next morning to Kai Tak for a Pan Am flight to San Francisco. The car ferry from Victoria to Kowloon seemed especially brisk and invigorating and the chop of the harbor splashed spray up on the foredeck; we stood just inside and watched the Kowloon shore approach. An exciting place, Hong Kong, I thought, already forgetting how tired we had become of the mindless pleasures of life there. During the drive we again covered all the things that must be done, including getting medical records for an obstetrician in Saigon. There was scarcely a moment for good-byes before I found myself in the aircraft, taxiing to the head of the long runway that jutted out into the harbor. The plane accelerated and took off over the water and on through Shau Ki Wan pass, climbing over the South China Sea.

19 Into War

In Washington, I went to the Dupont Plaza Hotel, called the duty officer at the CIA director's office, reporting my arrival. I also phoned my old friend George, who was at that time stationed in Washington. Nothing would do but that he come to the hotel and take me to his home in McLean, Virginia. I checked out, told the CIA duty officer where I could be reached, and caught a good night's sleep.

The next morning my first call was to Bill Colby, telling him where I was. He said to check in at once and we would see the director, who was expecting me. I drove to the agency and parked in the visitors' lot, where I was greeted by my old friend, the front-lot guard, Sergeant Dave. Sergeant Dave was (and is) a retired Marine sergeant who has taken care of the visitors' parking lot at the CIA building at Langley for as long as I can remember. Like so many of the long-time employees of the agency from the days of my first employment there, Sergeant Dave was efficient and always friendly and helpful.

My building pass was waiting and I went directly to Colby's office where he explained why the schedule had been changed. After our talk in Saigon in November, Bill had gone on to Bangkok and had cabled back to John McCone, proposing that I be named Saigon COS, effective the following June. McCone had agreed and Colby continued his trip. McCone had not counted on President Johnson's irascibility concerning Vietnam at that moment. Ambassador Lodge, a card-carrying Republican, had just fired and thrown out the CIA representative and was not to be further irritated. President Johnson wanted the post filled at once by the best-qualified man the agency could offer. Not only was he interested in doing the best job possible, but he also had his eye on the upcoming presidential-election year of 1964.

McCone visited President Johnson every morning at nine A.M.

to give him the overnight intelligence briefing and during such a briefing, early in December, he added as an aside that the agency had selected a successor to John Richardson and had mentioned my name, saying I would be transferred to Saigon in June 1964. As I heard the story later, President Johnson, raging, said that if the best man you have for Saigon is in Hong Kong, of all places, I want him in Saigon now. McCone went back to Langley and wrote the cable I received that Sunday morning.

Bill and I drank coffee and waited for the prearranged appointment with the director, when we went up to the seventh floor and were ushered at once into the director's inner office. I had met John McCone once before in 1961 when he had just become director-designate of CIA, following the sacking of Allen Dulles by President Kennedy after the Bay of Pigs. We had met at a Far Eastern meeting of COSs in the Philippine Islands and had dined together there but in no way could I say I knew him well. He remembered me and greeted me as warmly as John McCone could greet anyone. He was a small man, compact, white-haired, with icy blue eyes, framed by steel-rimmed spectacles. We had a quick cup of coffee and McCone told me to continue working with Bill Colby, to follow his instructions, but to be ready to accompany him to meet President Johnson at the White House. As we walked toward the door, McCone said to me, "For God's sake, remember what's been happening here recently—President Kennedy has been assassinated, President Johnson is new in the White House, and the Vietnam problem is getting worse every day. Lodge is becoming more and more obstreperous and Johnson wants no more problems out there as there were between Lodge and John Richardson; remember all of these things when we go to the President's office tomorrow."

December 1963. As was the entire American nation, Washington was still numb in the wake of President Kennedy's assassination. Along with the public, the government had been more badly shaken than I had anticipated. However, by the time I came to Washington early in December, the processes of government were clearly returning to something approaching normal. The Presidential election of 1964 was beginning to loom large in the minds of possible political contenders and the media, always concerned with the present and immediate future, were beginning to work over the crop of emerging potential candidates.

The problem of Vietnam lay on the policymakers' tables, increasingly unwanted, already beginning to carry a stench. President Diem and his brother, Nhu, had been murdered. The "dragon lady," Madame Nhu, was in Europe inveighing against the dead American president and his administration because of the fate of her husband and his brother. Other considerations aside, much of official Washington had to concentrate on the declining fortunes of the post-Diem South Vietnam government. The cabal of coup generals of Saigon already showed signs of strain and the euphoria of the anti-Diem partisans had begun to evaporate; unease and a sense of foreboding had begun to take its place, in an atmosphere of self-consciousness and guilt.

A fateful cable had been sent from the Department of State to Ambassador Lodge in Saigon, late in October 1963, over a weekend at a time when top policymakers, including President Kennedy and Secretary of State Dean Rusk, were out of town. This cable had been prepared and dispatched by Assistant Secretary of State for the Far East Roger Hilsman and Ambassador-at-Large Averell Harriman. Later in Saigon, I saw the cable itself in the embassy file room and, in brief, the cable instructed Ambassador Lodge not to stand in the way of a military coup against President Diem, if in fact such was being planned, and to make known that, in the event of a successful military overthrow, the United States government could be relied upon to give continuous support to a successor government, dedicated to continuing the war against the Communists.

These stunning instructions told Ambassador Lodge to bring pressure on Diem to fire his brother, Nhu, and to persuade Diem to end the martial law then in effect. It went on to say that if Diem declined to cooperate, the embassy was to make its position known to the Vietnamese generals who were planning the coup. Ambassador Lodge had reached Saigon only four days before this cable arrived and although he apparently felt its instructions were clear, Lodge, being a prudent and responsible man, felt constrained once again to have his American contacts with the Vietnamese generals take the temperature of the revolutionary waters: were the generals in fact prepared to move? An interesting and surprising finding emerged. Faced with immediate action, the generals hesitated, to the dismay and annoyance of the anti-Diem elements in Washington. It was not until the end of October that the coup-minded generals were able to steel themselves sufficiently to make the actual attempt. Once underway, it was successful, with the tragic and unwanted aberrations that both Diem and his brother were slain.

The few days of my briefing visit to Washington raced by like a fast-motion film. Old Vietnam hands in the agency, beginning with Bill Colby, force-fed me from morning until night with background information in much too great detail for me ever to remember. There were several sessions with officers in the Department of State, notably with the assistant secretary of state for Far East affairs, Roger Hilsman, whose sole, rambling advice to me was to remember his days during World War II when he led a group of armed irregulars in the jungles of Burma. I couldn't find the connection and said as much to my escort as we left the State Department building, who simply responded, "That's Roger for you."

During these days at CIA headquarters at Langley, I got to my temporary office in the Far East Division by seven A.M. to read all accumulated cable traffic to and from Saigon. One morning at about eight o'clock a secretary called to say the director wanted me in his office at once. There I was told I would accompany John McCone to his nine o'clock meeting with President Johnson, who wanted to have a look at the new Saigon station chief before he was fed to Ambassador Lodge in Saigon. There was time, as I sat in McCone's anteroom, for a cup of coffee with his attractive secretary. The director came out of his office and we took his private elevator to the basement garage from which his chauffeur drove through the morning rush-hour traffic to the guarded street between the White House and the Executive Office building. The director's car was at once recognized, the gates opened, and we pulled up to the west entrance of the White House.

Inside there was an atmosphere of quiet but constant purposeful action. Young men in dark suits strolled through the corridors—secret-service men. They nodded courteously to McCone as we walked down the hall to a waiting room outside the office of the President's secretary. Sitting there for a brief moment, the director, a long-standing Republican, reminded me of the President's concern about keeping Ambassador

Lodge, a potential Presidential contender in his own right in 1964, satisfied and happy.

A buzzer sounded, the secretary beckoned and we were ushered into the Oval Office. Behind the famous desk bulked President Johnson, absorbed in a paper he was reading. The President punched a button on his desk, a young man entered, was given the paper and a few words of instructions, and President Johnson turned to us.

Without waiting for Director McCone to say anything, the President stood and shook my hand with both of his and motioned to a group of sofas and easy chairs across the Oval Office from his desk. As we moved to the sofas, McCone introduced me as the new station chief in Saigon. We seated ourselves, a waiter entered quietly with a tray of coffee. The pouring done and the waiter gone, the President turned to me and said that he had read the file Mr. McCone had given him about me and assured me that I would have his full support. But at the same time one of my fundamental missions was to get along peacefully and amicably with Ambassador Lodge, whom he described as not the easiest man in the world with whom to deal. I murmured appropriately, as the President took a sip of his coffee, leaned back and looked to John McCone for the morning intelligence briefing.

The director read from a group of short, clipped sheets, which were prepared for him to present to the President each morning of the week. As McCone read, the President nodded, sipped coffee, and said nothing. As apparently was the custom with visitors to the Oval Office, a man came in with cameras slung around his neck, prepared to take pictures. As he began to focus his lens, McCone held his hand up at once and, pointing to me, told the photographer, "Don't take any of him." The President emphasized these instructions and the photographer took a half-dozen photos of the meeting from behind me, cleverly catching my bald spot, and then disappeared through a side door. John McCone had apparently covered all the ground necessary with the President; it only remained for President Johnson to repeat once again his admonition that I cooperate fully with Ambassador Lodge. I smiled and said that I would, as we shook hands and were steered toward the exit door.

On the drive back to Langley, McCone said that from his experience, the meeting had gone well, remarking that President Johnson was a quick-tempered man, but had seemed quite amiable that morning.

The next day I was driven to Andrews Air Force Base, on the outskirts of Washington, in ample time for a cup of coffee before Director McCone's arrival. Including myself, there were perhaps six or eight in his party going to Saigon. In addition to Bill Colby, there was Karl Kaysen, a Harvard economics professor who was on one of the many government advisory boards concerned with our Vietnam problems. After the usual mild confusion at the foot of the stairs, we found our way inside, the door was shut, and the aircraft moved to the end of the runway. It was early and I had not had breakfast. The past week had been somewhat jumbled, and I looked forward to a few hours in which I could relax. The 707 turned off the taxiway to the takeoff strip, tuned up to a thunderous roar, rumbled down the runway and up into the Maryland skies, on our way to Anchorage, Alaska. The crew chief passed through the aircraft announcing that breakfast would be served in about an hour. The 707 was a tanker aircraft with only a few windows, modified for passenger occupancy. The forward compartment had bolted-down tables and chairs and the after-compartment was made up of sleeping bunks, well screened and comfortable. The first flight leg went straight to Anchorage where we landed about midnight. The base commander served us a late dinner of fresh Alaskan crab legs, a large steak, and a good, cold salad. Once more aloft, everyone went to his bunk and to sleep. We were then on our way direct to Saigon.

Dawn found all of the passengers up and dressed, strolling about the cavernous interior of the aircraft or having breakfast. McCone, Colby, and I had our breakfast together at one of the tables. McCone, his wire-rimmed spectacles giving sharp emphasis to his piercing blue eyes, filled me in on the events that had led to the abrupt departure of my predecessor from Saigon. Ambassador Lodge, he related, had arrived in 1963, giving the clear impression that he was under instructions from President Kennedy and that unless Diem got rid of his brother, Nhu, and made a complete reversal in the way the government was being run, Lodge should use his influence to bring about a change in the top leadership. He had found our station chief to be a courageous and intelligent person, but a strong supporter of Diem; as in Washington, people concerned with the Vietnam problem in those days were either pro-Diem or violently anti-Diem. Lodge himself was neither but was under instructions from the President of the United States who, along with his brother, Robert Kennedy, was anti-Diem. By October our station chief, John Richardson, and Ambassador Lodge were obviously standing on two very different sides of t e issue and Lodge, while respecting John personally, concluded that his continued presence in Saigon would be obstructive; Richardson was recalled to Washington forthwith. The moral of all this was, McCone went on, don't get on the wrong side of Lodge. He can be abrupt and ruthless. McCone didn't want any further difficulty between his station chief and the ambassador; the war was quite enough trouble as it was.

At thirty thousand feet we flew over the Vietnam coastline just north of Nha Trang and began our descent to Tan Son Nhut air base. Because a commercial airliner, not long before, had taken some Vietcong small-arms fire while making a low-level approach to the landing strip, all 707s came in at a steep circling dive over the landing strip, but soon we were easing into a gentle landing at Tan Son Nhut. I'd been told this visit of the CIA director was to be secret and was astounded at seeing the scores of American and other Western reporters and journalists waiting for us in the terminal as we fought our way through the crowd to the waiting cars for the drive to the American Embassy. A number of American Embassy staff people had met us on landing and took over the chore of rescuing our baggage and delivering it to our respective billets.

Later that morning Secretary McNamara and his party, also flying in a White House jet, arrived from Paris to join the conference and I soon had my first taste of a full-scale Military Assistance Command, Vietnam (MACV) briefing dominated by the secretary of defense. The briefings were presented in the Combat Operations Center (COC) at MACV headquarters on Rue Pasteur. Basically a conference room, it contained a large, long table, rimmed with chairs, at the end of which stood a lectern for the briefing officers. The remainder of the room was filled with row after row of chairs to be occupied by those being briefed and the MACV briefers, of whom there were many. Less than thirty minutes after McCone's plane touched down at Tan Son Nhut, we were all jammed into the Combat Operations Center awaiting McNamara's arrival. In a few moments, accompanied by a couple of staff aides, and after a brief round of handshaking, McNamara took the seat at the head of the briefing table. At once he began scribbling on a pad of yellow paper in a crabbed, left-handed scrawl.

General Paul Harkins, the commanding general of MACV, gestured to the first briefing officer, who took his place at the lectern and began to present his part of the briefing. The numerous MACV briefers each covered a piece of the action: new strategic hamlets, acts of terror, numbers and locations of ambushes, Vietcong losses, friendly losses, weapons lost, weapons captured, and all the other bits and pieces that made up a statistical analysis of the war in the countryside. During these earnest presentations, which were accompanied by charts, maps, and photographs, McNamara continued filling up his yellow pad with notes concerning whatever was running through his head. Only infrequently would he pause and listen to a given briefing officer, perhaps to ask a question and then resume his note-taking. The briefing concluded, McNamara dropped his pencil, pushed his chair back from the table, and began to bombard at large the MACV senior staff, present in the room. How many more strategic hamlets have been constructed since I was here last year? How many more yards of barbed wire for these new hamlets have been issued since my last visit? What are the newest POL (petroleum, oil, and lubrication) requirements for ARVN (Army of the Republic of Vietnam)? Tire requirements? I sat there amazed, and thought to myself, what in the world is this man thinking about? This is not a problem of logistics and, in any event, there are plenty of people here at MACV fully competent to handle the matériel side of the war. This is a war that needs discussion of strategic purpose and of strategy itself. What is he talking about?

The next day Secretary McNamara choppered upcountry with General Harkins to get the usual "feel of the situation." Thus, meetings at MACV came to a halt and McCone, Colby, and I were able to concentrate on the activities of the station. Ambassador Lodge invited us to lunch at t e residence and also invited the acting station chief, who had been filling that post since John Richardson had departed two months before.

During an otherwise pleasant luncheon and without ever looking directly at me, Lodge went out of his way to emphasize to John McCone that he neither wanted or needed a new CIA station chief, gesturing in my direction, but was in every way content to have Dave continue acting as chief until the summer of 1964. Dave and I were both dismayed as we were talked over like competitors at a dog show. Lodge's main theme was that he knew and liked Dave and was accustomed to working with him; on the other hand I was a new and unknown quantity and could only be a bother. Wearing a tight little smile, McCone, who had no great affection for Lodge, mused that unless the ambassador really had cause for refusing my assignment, he, as director, felt he must insist on my assuming the position as chief-of-station. These exchanges had Bill Colby, Dave, and myself repeatedly gazing at the ceiling as the meal finally came to an end, and we rose, retreated to our cars and to our respective offices.

This luncheon took place at the Residence, which was acquired in an unusual manner. When John Richardson and his family arrived in Saigon in the winter of 1961-62, they set about house hunting for accommodations more suitable for entertaining than the house occupied by the outgoing chief. The director of the Vietnamese National Police, hearing of John's quest, threw his considerable influence into the search. The police came up with a spacious home, not far from the center of Saigon. While not outright ostentatious, it was indeed luxurious. There was, however, one serious drawback. The house had been used as an interrogation center for Vietcong suspects and it was common knowledge among the Vietnamese that a number of them had gone to their reward under interrogation in the house. Although it had been completely renovated inside and out, no servant would work or live there because of the spirits which inhabited it. Before the Richardsons could move in, a group of Buddhist monks had to be called in to exorcize the demons who were present, following which a household staff could be employed.

Cabot Lodge had lived in the official residence, a very large but exceedingly unattractive structure not far from the Cercle Sportif (a sports and social club, built during the French colonial days). He was not happy with this house and as soon as Richardson departed, he had John's house redecorated and promptly moved in himself. The deputy chief-of-mission in turn moved from his house into the former Residence, leaving his old house empty; it was here that we were to live.

The day after Ambassador Lodge's luncheon was departure

day for McCone and the entire group which had accompanied him from Washington. I saw them all off at the airport and with a feeling of some relief watched them lift off the runway, wheels tucking up beneath the aircraft. When I was sure they were airborne, I returned to the Embassy for my first close look at the station and its staff. A group of my senior officers were prepared to give me a less formal and more detailed picture of the activities and operations of their own sections and my first afternoon in the station after the departure of the Washington group was passed in that way. Toward the end of the afternoon, my secretary buzzed to tell me that Ambassador Lodge wanted to see me at once. In his office on the top floor, he saw me without delay. He motioned me to a chair and stood up to pace slowly back and forth before a window. "I'm sure you remember our luncheon yesterday at my house and I want you to understand I have nothing against you personally. I simply do not want a new station chief, but that's now beyond arguing. There are, however, two things I want you to do without delay, although I know you're about to return to Hong Kong to collect your family. First, you will have noticed that on the door of your office there is a large brass plaque bearing the title 'Special Assistant to the Ambassador.' I don't want to see that plaque on your door when you get back from Hong Kong. Second, you have inherited from your predecessor a very large and long black Chevrolet sedan. That car is newer and longer than my official car. Get rid of it." With these cheery words of greeting, I returned to my office more than a little curious as to how this assignment would turn out. That evening I telephoned Marilyn in Hong Kong and told her when I would be back, sent off a cable to my deputy in Hong Kong, informing him of my plans and giving him time to prepare for a takeover of that station. Four days before Christmas, Marilyn met me at Kai Tak and, on the way back to Hong Kong island on the ferry, told me of what she had done in preparation for our move. The packers were due early on Wednesday, Christmas morning, and reservations were made for an eight A.M. flight for Saigon on Friday. Our last few days in Hong Kong were frantic as we tried to tie up all the loose ends. Marilyn, by now obviously pregnant and down with the flu, struggled through it all cheerfully, although I'll never understand how. Early Friday morning, with the help of two amahs, our cook and driver, and friends from the office, we barely got to Kai Tak on time. In checking out at the ticket counter, it developed that the medical inoculations for one of our children were incomplete, lacking a signature. Our British friends, who had come to say good-bye, took over the burden of making the necessary phone calls to gain an exception and amid a great deal of confusion we made a dash for the aircraft, which had delayed its departure for us. A moment later, we taxied out to the runway, sailed out over the harbor, and turned south toward Saigon.

Good-bye, Hong Kong. Hello, war.

20 The Vietcong Challenge

Flying in from the South China Sea, we passed over Saigon and began the steep, spiralling descent to Tan Son Nhut, coming to a halt before the terminal building. After going through customs, Marilyn and I with our two sons were driven off by my deputy Dave and his wife, Jean, to have lunch at their home. They were an extremely relaxed and friendly couple and our two young children were soon surrounded and being taken care of by their brood of eight. After a delicious French lunch of *coq au vin*, Dave and I retired to another room while Jean filled Marilyn in on some of the first things she should know about the station and life in Saigon. Later that afternoon my family went to our new home on Nguyen Dinh Chieu street, while Dave and I continued on to the embassy. It was dark when I reached home and from that time until I was wounded in March 1965, I spent six long days a week in my office or traveling about the countryside and invariably at least two hours at the embassy every Sunday. My duties were endlessly demanding, but never dull; during our time in Vietnam, Marilyn and I had three weekends away from Saigon, spent at a beach house in Nha Trang. That was the extent of our junketing about the Riviera of the Far East.

Our house on Nguyen Dinh Chieu was furnished with all we needed for the moment, and a staff of servants was already installed. The houseboy, Duc, was in charge, the number one boy (he later lost his life to a Vietcong land mine, which destroyed the bus on which he was riding). Our cook, Ba, was a Montagnard tribesman, who had miraculously learned to cook all the classic French dishes for which he personally had no taste at all. There was an amah for our second boy, and later another amah when our third child was born in 1964. A boyesse took care of the laundry and cleaning of the house. In addition to my driver, there was a part-time gardener, and four gate guards, each of whom was on duty for a six-hour shift. The kitchen,

The Vietcong Challenge 215

servants' quarters, bath, and laundry were behind the main house and separate from it; there lived Duc, his wife, and four-year-old son, and the two amahs.

Our arrival in Saigon in 1963 coincided with an all-time low in the fortunes of the Vietnamese government in their struggle with the Vietcong. The overthrow of President Diem on 1 November 1963 had ushered in a period of governmental confusion and political instability that was to endure during all of 1964. The war had taken a marked turn for the worse; after the events of November, the Vietcong had moved quickly and powerfully to take advantage of the disarray of the government in Saigon. Acts of terror, both in Saigon and in the countryside, multiplied.

On the American side, there were already recriminations being voiced between the pro-Diem and anti-Diem factions; with an eye toward the future, I personally searched through the State Department files and spoke with many of the station officers to uncover any evidence that might indicate CIA involvement in the planning or conduct of the coup, or in the tragic deaths of the Nhu brothers. There was no evidence of any involvement. A station officer, having a Vietnamese wife and many friends among the senior officers corps of the ARVN, personally knew those ARVN general officers who themselves engaged in planning the coup and who, on 1 November, set it in motion. Ambassador Lodge, possibly in furtherance of verbal instructions given him by President Kennedy before going to Saigon in August and certainly in implementing the actions called for in the notorious State Department cable of 24 August 1963, to inform the Vietnamese generals, known to be planning a coup, that the United States government would not stand in their way, had used this station officer as a relay point in making Washington policy known to this group. That was the extent of American involvement. The murder of Diem and his brother burst tragically on the embassy and on Washington; no one had planned for that. The murders, by an unidentified member of the coup group, were not altogether illogical consequences of actions set in motion by our own positions and policies as made known in Washington.

I was present at several meetings between Ambassador Lodge and the troika—the generals who had led the coup—as efforts were made to patch together a government able to deal with the savage, ever-increasing pressure of the Vietcong. This clique of generals fell to bickering among themselves. They increasingly displayed vague and indecisive leadership and their conduct in their war against the Vietcong was uncertain and irresolute. In this atmosphere of confusion, it was no surprise that in January 1964 they were in turn overthrown by General Nguyen Khanh, who launched his coup from his base in the Second Corps area in the Vietnam highlands. Khanh was to remain in power slightly more than a year, during which time he put down one coup attempt and neutralized several others before he, in his turn, was sent into exile in France by the leadership of the army, who installed a civilian premier, Phan Huy Quat. General Khanh's year in power showed him to be, while highly intelligent, quite erratic, moody, and in general unpredictable.

Thus the political and sociological stage was set in favor of the Vietcong to make massive and lasting inroads in their quest to achieve domination of the rural population in South Vietnam.

The beginning of 1964 found the CIA station numbering about four hundred people, most of them located in Saigon, but a few were spotted around the country in such cities as Danang, Hue, Nha Trang, My Tho, and Bien Hoa. Our intelligence work covered every aspect of the profession. We had a number of well-placed and well-informed sources at the top levels of the Vietnam military establishment.

The Agency for International Development (AID) Mission had an extensive program devoted to the upgrading and modernizing of the Vietnamese National Police in terms of training, equipment, and modern investigative techniques. Quite on their own, the Vietnamese government had established a Central Intelligence Organization (CIO). Our relationship with the National Police and the CIO quite naturally worked to our advantage in dealing with individual senior National Police officers who wished to cooperate with us. The divided condition of Vietnam between the north and south made counterespionage and counterintelligence functions of high importance and sensitivity—even as they had been in Germany and Korea.

As we had in Korea with the Republic of Korea CIA, we worked in Saigon with the Vietnamese CIO in helping them to establish a National Interrogation Center (NIC), fronting on the Sagion River. There we shared a compound and a number of our instructors worked with the Vietnamese National Police

The Vietcong Challenge

interrogators in guiding them toward modern and humane interrogation methods. There had been a long tradition in Vietnam, as there had been in Korea, of dealing with a Communist agent or defector by simply beating the soles of his feet until he was forced into saying whatever he thought his tormentors wanted to hear. Leaving morality aside, this kind of interrogation was historically known mainly to produce fabrication and hysterical lies to gain relief from pain. The information was invariably worthless and very often dangerous to use. Other techniques of interrogation, though severe and stern, produced an increasing flow of voluntary information, accurate and eminently usable. These techniques amounted to nothing sinister or mysterious. We had long ago learned that information gained by physical duress or fear would be, more often than not, false and unreliable. On the other hand, a person undergoing interrogation soon came to the conclusion that his own well-being was best served by responding truthfully under questioning. This soft approach did not work in every case, of course, but was so consistently productive that it became our standard operating procedure. The Vietnamese (as the Koreans before them) were astounded to learn that these modern techniques actually worked and the primitive and inhuman methods of interrogation were seldom of any value, and merely provided a sad commentary on their French mentors during their colonial past.

The station had a number of paramilitary and cross-border operations intended to plant agents along the Ho Chi Minh trail in Laos and in North Vietnam. Their mission was to radio back to a center in Saigon the makeup and armament of VC units, or to an increasing degree, North Vietnamese army units sent into combat in South Vietnam. This had all the effect of putting a Band-Aid on a compound fracture, but it was all we had the authority to do. Parachuting agents into North Vietnam, ever popular whether in Europe or Asia, was a dwindling program and ended shortly after my arrival. Agents radio links from the north to the south were still in operation, but analysis of the traffic only showed enemy control. One by one they fell silent.

We had noted that many links from the Ho Chi Minh trail in Laos (actually a complex of trails and small roads, never a single thoroughfare) turned eastward into South Vietnam across the spiny, mountainous highland regions of the republic, passing through the uplands, heavily populated by the Montagnard tribes. The highland tribals were made up of the Rade, the Jarai, the Nnong, and numerous other lesser tribes. Historically, these tribals were held in contempt by the Vietnamese; there was an instinctive and automatic antipathy between the Montagnards and Vietnamese, who lived in the lowlands along the sea. The French had been well aware of this division and had taken every opportunity to exploit it; the Montagnards were in general loyal to the French. Because the tribals living in the uplands were generally astride the infiltration routes from Laos and North Vietnam, the CIA organized some of the tribes into teams to observe infiltration points into South Vietnam and harass and attack cadres coming from the north. This attempt had been formalized into a program which produced CIDG (Civilian Irregular Defense Groups), working on their own, but responsible to us.

In December 1963, the CIDGs were transferred to the control of the U.S. Army Special Forces—the Green Berets—the decision being made at the Washington level that anything of this magnitude should be handled by the MACV (Military Assistance Command, Vietnam). It was a wise move and the Special Forces were ideally equipped for the rough-and-tumble needed to deal with these primitive tribes in the highlands.

Visiting a Rade tribal village, not far from Bhan Me Thuot, I talked through an interpreter to the tribal chief, a short sinewy man of indeterminate age, barefoot, clothed only in a breech clout, with a canvas sack slung over his shoulder. Besides his tribal dialect, he spoke a kind of pidgin-French, which I could not understand. He thanked me for the supplies and equipment we had been sending and as we sat and tried to communicate in this ungainly fashion he reached into the sack and drew out a small, struggling green frog, snapped its neck, took a bite out of one leg and offered the still-twitching frog to me. I can't remember how I got out of that one.

Another clandestine CIA venture was the slipping of high-speed patrol boats from Danang up the coast to North Vietnam, depositing agents ashore for further communications by radio and to sabotage radar installations and North Vietnam patrol boats. We divided our patrol boats into two categories, calling them the Swifts and Nasties. The Swifts, contracted for in Norway, were fast, lightly armed, and built to move quickly and quietly to a target area and return. The Nasties were slower and

The Vietcong Challenge 219

noisier but heavily armed and could defend themselves against opposing North Vietnam patrol boats. Our maritime base in Danang was in the charge of Tucker Gougelman, a former Marine officer who had lost a foot during the Korean War. A true soldier of fortune, Tucker was a bear of a man, bluff, hearty and courageous in the extreme. A bachelor, he had spent many years in Vietnam and upon retirement chose to live in Bangkok. In the spring of 1975 with the fall of Vietnam and Saigon imminent, he returned to Saigon for the sole purpose of helping Vietnamese friends to escape during the last frightening days. He didn't make it out—he was seen to be led away by the Vietcong. His remains were turned over to the Americans in 1977. One of the heroes.

Saigon was the largest station I had ever headed and at the time was the largest in the agency. It was made up of clerical help, communicators, administrative personnel, finance officers, supply officers, a full medical staff, parachute riggers and warehousemen, research analyists and report writers, a host of case officers of different backgrounds and specialities, psychological warfare experts, interrogation specialists, paramilitary personnel and training specialists. At Tan Son Nhut, we were alloted our own parking hardstand and supply enclave, where there were something more than a dozen aircraft of different capabilities manned by American civilian pilots and crew chiefs. At one end of the parking area bulked three C-123 cargo aircraft, menacing and ominous in their black paint, ready for clandestine flights over North Vietnam to drop agents.

I flew upcountry to outlying bases in the first month to meet province chiefs, MACV sector advisers and especially our people assigned there. There were endless briefings. I read scores of organizational charts and wound up the month with the firm conviction that I knew nothing of the nature of the war being fought in Vietnam, and my first task was to make up my own appraisal of the war, and how the station should be organized, aimed, and usefully directed.

General William C. Westmoreland arrived early in 1964 to become deputy to General Paul Harkins, and as such, deputy commander to MACV. It was generally known that General Harkins would end his tour in the early summer and General Westmoreland would take over MACV. General Westmoreland had been personally chosen for this assignment by the then chairman of the Joint Chiefs of Staff, General Maxwell Taylor. What was not known was that Ambassador Lodge, eyeing the Presidential conventions of 1964, would ask President Johnson to be relieved, so that he might return to play an active part in Republican activities that year. Johnson had no choice but to agree. General Maxwell Taylor was appointed as the next ambassador and, as a result, General Westmoreland became Taylor's subordinate upon his arrival in Saigon as ambassador in July. Robert McNamara remained as secretary of defense. Thus these three, as heavenly stars, were to be perfectly aligned to dominate the American government's policy and strategy in Vietnam in the crucial decision-making years of 1964 and 1965, a power alignment which I believe proved most unfortunate. Individually courageous, strong and forceful, in 1964 they came to the wrong war.

Meanwhile, the early months of 1964 saw endless discussions within the CIA station. Were our programs of any value? Were they directed at worthwhile goals? If they were, could they really achieve these goals? Did we really understand what the Vietcong were trying to do, could we counter their efforts effectively? How were they able to accomplish their growing successes in the Vietnam countryside?

Two basic strategies of the Vietcong were quite apparent and I will never comprehend our slowness in recognizing them. One was their successful ambush tactic against military units and police patrols. The other was the unceasing application of violence and terror against segments of the rural population: schoolteachers, medical technicians, village chiefs, and individuals performing any administrative services for the Saigon government. Terror—simple and effective. Torture and murder. In retrospect, it is difficult to understand how we in Vietnam and Americans in general were so slow in coming to the bottom line on this problem: acts of terror did terrorize the population, and once terrorized and intimidated, the rural population, in the absence of any protection or other motivation, would thereafter be responsive to the Vietcong. They would feed them, recruit for them, conceal them, and provide them with all the intelligence the Vietcong needed to maintain their control over the rural areas. This simple reasoning eluded us for a long while—though we were by no means alone in our blindness.

Once enlightenment had come, the next level was to seek a

The Vietcong Challenge 221

solution: how to break the stranglehold of the Vietcong over the peasantry. Armed battalions of ARVN (Army of the Republics of Vietnam) in the vicinity? That could work as long as they remained in the district. Once the battalion moved on, the people were again at the mercy of the Vietcong. Every now and then a Vietcong unit would take a beating from an ARVN group, but events such as these were few and far between. ARVN units usually confined themselves to armed reconnaissance patrols during the day but were frequently ambushed by the Vietcong. When darkness fell, the ARVN usually bivouacked, sending out sentries and perimeter guards for security through the night. The Vietcong would often watch and stalk them in the daylight hours, only to trap them at night with mortar fire or grenades thrown while they slept. Village chiefs and Saigon functionaries seldom dared to spend hours after dark in villages or hamlets, but would prudently withdraw to a district or provincial capital where they could expect police or military protection.

We in the station worried about the problem, sweated over it, and hacked out the principles, one bit at a time. The cure was finally found and parts of the puzzle began to fall into place. But by then it was too late—the American military had decided to apply a different solution. The military solution proved tragically wrong.

Cabot Lodge left in June, as did General Harkins, and in July 1964, a new team of senior officials arrived. General Maxwell Taylor, now ambassador, was accompanied by Ural Alexis Johnson, who also carried the title of ambassador and who became Maxwell Taylor's immediate deputy. Ambassador Taylor pinned a fourth star on Westmoreland as he took command of MACV. James Killen came to Saigon as the new Agency for International Development chief (AID); he and I renewed our acquaintance from our days in Korea where he also served as head of AID. Barry Zorthian took over the U.S. Information Service (USIS) and William Sullivan, the rapidly rising star of the Foreign Service, accompanied General Taylor as executive officer for the Diplomatic Mission and the Mission Council. A panel of senior American officials, named by Ambassador Taylor, made up this council to meet with him each week. As the senior CIA officer in the country, I was automatically included as a member of the Mission Council. Other members were Alexis Johnson, William Sullivan, James Killen, Barry Zorthian, Melvin

Manfull (Political counselor), and a senior Foreign Service officer, Jack Herfurt, who became secretary of the council.

Before there had been any hint that General Taylor would be descending on the Saigon scene as ambassador, General Westmoreland had held a series of meetings with the most senior MACV officers, at which he set out his methods for operating and the goals he expected to accomplish. A general officer on his staff whom I had known from my days in Europe attended these restricted meetings and told me in confidence at least part of what Westmoreland described as to the instructions he had received prior to leaving Washington. The orders were from General Taylor, with whom Westmoreland enjoyed a senior/-junior relationship of many years, and were essentially as follows: "Westy, you get out there and take charge. Get the military command and the ARVN organized and then fight the war right, the way we did in France. It's a big war and we'll fight it like one. We must bring enough firepower and bombs down on the Vietcong to make them realize they're finished; only then will they toss in the sponge." Westmoreland may well have received other advice before coming to Saigon, but if my friend's account of the substance of General Westmoreland's meetings with General Taylor was accurate, he could not have received any that were less useful. But the principle of fighting the big war, the big action in Vietnam, had thus been established. This doctrine, and the decisions later issuing from it, led inescapably to April 1975 and American defeat.

Bill Colby made another of his arduous swings through southeast Asia and spent several days in Saigon where we had time to discuss local problems firsthand. The agency inspector-general, Lyman Kirkpatrick, also visited Saigon for a firsthand look at our problems and the action in South Vietnam. Kirk, a polio victim, was confined to a wheelchair, but his infirmity had only limited his ability to walk; his brilliant mind was unimpaired. He traveled widely and actively, was tough-minded and sharp, and destined to rise to the number three position in the agency before retiring in 1966 to a professorship at Brown University.

Kirk expressed a desire to visit our maritime base at Danang before we turned it and our patrol boats over to MACV. Getting to Danang and back required some planning because of his wheelchair, which we could not fit into most aircraft. We had just taken delivery of a new DeHaviland Caribou aircraft, distinguished by a high tail with a clamshell door which let down to allow jeeps and similar vehicles to be rolled into the boxlike interior, a natural for a wheelchair. We scheduled a flight to inspect the base at Danang and Tucker Gougelman laid on a lobster lunch at the beach, to return to Saigon by evening.

As we taxied down the flight strip, Kirk asked to have the clamshell door left down, to get a complete view of Tan Son Nhut and Saigon as we climbed away from the field. We hurriedly had his wheelchair tied down to eliminate the frightening prospect of a sudden lurch sending it rolling out the rear end as we nosed upward at takeoff. With the door in its lowered position, we took off in the characteristically steep climb of the Caribou, curving away from the field with all of Saigon visible beneath us. I prayed the ropes would hold, as Kirk watched as we flew over green fields and arms of the river, completely unconcerned, while I sweated profusely, but the flight went off without incident.

Among those on the Caribou was one Colonel Gilbert Strickler, a station officer who deserves special mention. "Strick," a much-decorated combat officer from World War II, held the reserve rank of colonel and had been called back to active, uniformed service, while conduting the duties of his station assignment as liaison officer, working with the staff of MACV. We had become good friends in Saigon and later on became neighbors in suburban Virginia.

I had never met Strick before but Desmond Fitzgerald gave me a brief rundown about him as we were leaving Langley in December 1963, to accompany John McCone to Saigon. Walking toward the main entrance of the CIA, Des asked me, "By the way, do you know Gil Strickler?" I told him I didn't and Des hurried on: "There's not time to tell you all about Strick, but I'll say one thing. He's a great person, but there's an important point to remember: if you ever ask Strick for an elephant, you'd better have the hay ready." Nothing was more applicable than Des's comment. Strick could lay hands on anything in the Vietnamese or American military structure. I learned never to ask how he operated; I simply stood back in awe as every request and task was promptly fulfilled.

What was the Vietnam war? It was generally characterized as a "guerrilla war," without further elucidation. Also, as a psychological war, again without elaboration. It was also described as a political war, fought with guns, but I could never really determine what this description implied. An American adviser to ARVN, a member of MACV, and a colonel in the U.S. Infantry, once described it to me in these terms: "It's just another goddamn war. There's nothing mysterious about it. The only thing to do is to get American troops and firepower in here, some aircover and artillery, and we'll lay these rubber-sandaled bastards out so fast that Uncle Ho won't be able to get his people out quick enough, except for those we've killed." This last definition turned out to conform most closely to the strategies used by the American side as the crippling war wore on. But the enigma remained. What kind of a war was it really?

The true nature of the war continued to be elusive, but even more elusive were the strategies and tactics that could successfully contain the Vietcong thrust and turn the war around, as a then-current expression had it. The Republic of Vietnam armed-forces' one-half million men consisted of experienced infantry and artillery, a rapidly improving air force, and river patrols manning light naval craft; yet the countryside was being rapidly lost to the enemy. A relative handful of Vietcong "rice burners," some from the north and some indigenous to the south, with inadequate equipment and still largely armed with captured weapons (although the A-47 assault rifle and heavy rocket launchers, supplied by the Soviet Union and Communist China, were beginning to make their appearance) soaked ominously throughout the population of South Vietnam. They were dominating more and more hamlets, more and more villages, more and more valleys and populated areas, and inflicting ever greater losses on the Republic of Vietnam Air Force (RVNAF).

Spring of 1964 found the Vietcong still using their two main techniques: small-unit combat and ambush tactics, and the ever-increasing use of terror. The ARVN and the rest of the RVNAF fought with courage and determination, but were repeatedly humiliated by their inability to protect the population from the Vietcong. Nor did the answer seem to lie in the numbers of American military advisers sent to Vietnam to work and fight with the Vietnamese. These advisers had first been introduced during President Kennedy's administration when he and his brother Robert came to the conclusion that the "insurgency" in South Vietnam could best be fought by "counterinsurgency" tactics. The idea of "counterinsurgency" had become an instant cult that promised victory if the Americans would simply understand the Vietcong phenomenon, devise a strategy to counter it, and advise ("lead") the South Vietnamese in dealing with their adversaries. The United States Special Forces (Green Berets) were created in this atmosphere.

As I sat in Hong Kong in 1962 and 1963, it was even then clear that the main thrust of both doctrine and strategy issuing from Washington was that the American military would advise and direct the South Vietnam military as they fought their strange war. Even then many of us were becoming convinced that, considering the varied factors that had to be considered, a guerilla movement such as the Vietcong could not be contained let alone defeated by orthodox American strategy and tactics. Given the difference in language and appearance between Vietnamese and Americans, our total lack of experience in jungle and tropical warfare amid rural populations, and our tendency toward impatience and irritation toward our Vietnamese allies when they didn't perform as Americans, success was bound to be elusive.

By 1964, it had become chillingly apparent that the heavy and indelible stamp of American Army tactical and strategic doctrines, born in World War II on the plains of France and later ratified in Korea, had been irrevocably imposed on the Vietnam military establishment. Under American military training and philosophy, South Vietnam was divided into corps areas with formalized armies and their attendant staff. The Vietnamese had been trained to think in terms of military divisions with their panoply of staffs, all amounting to a form of military organization which the American advisers understood and with which they felt comfortable. Considering the U.S. Army to be their patron and main source of supplies and support, the top elements of the South Vietnam armed forces were only too willing to adopt U.S. military strategies and forms of organization which were to be proved irrelevant to the kind of war being fought in their own country. In 1963 and 1964, the road-bound, top-heavy ARVN forces valiantly strove to pin down the small and highly mobile Vietcong formations, but they were continually frustrated and bloodied. The Vietcong grew stronger. The American side seemed constantly to feel that pouring in more artillery, more airpower, and more infantry would provide the answer, while the Vietcong managed steadily to elude major confrontations, and using terror with relentless precision, they continued to demonstrate that the night and the people really belonged to the Vietcong.

Clearly the Vietcong had constant access to excellent intelligence concerning the location, movement, and armament of ARVN elements and police units. The conventional wisdom was that there were many Vietcong agents buried in the ranks and staffs of the ARVN itself and in the police leadership. That there were such agents I did not doubt, but from my experience in the intelligence business found it beyond belief that the Vietcong could organize and communicate with as many agents as would be needed to pass on the volume of precise intelligence necessary to carry out their attacks as quickly and effectively as they did. We concluded that, on the contrary, the Vietcong were getting the great bulk of their intelligence needs from the farmers, the peasants, the fishermen, and other ordinary folk who inhabited the countryside. One of the characteristics of the Vietnamese rural population was that they seldom traveled away from their homes. Farmers habitually stayed on or near their paddies, rarely going even to the district towns, remaining on their farms near food supplies and the tombs of their ancestors. An occasional need for simple tools and clothing and perhaps some foodstuffs, available only in the nearest district town, would draw them away from their huts. Many rural families were likely to pass their entire lives without going to the capital city of Saigon.

This made the rural population the natural target of the Vietcong. This population provided them with their food, their willing or unwilling recruits, "taxes," and, of most importance, their intelligence on the location and movement of ARVN elements or GVN (Government of Vietnam) civilian functionaries. The peasants, rooted in the land, were easy prey for the highly mobile attack squads, tax collectors, and terrorists who moved among them with impunity, at the same time learning from them everything they needed to know about hostile forces.

The Vietcong had only one inducement to offer the peasantry to make them cooperative; the use or threat of terror. The peasants were defenseless. Armed government formations were normally located only in the larger towns and cities and when they moved into the countryside on patrol, they moved among people who were continually under the pervasive influence of

The Vietcong Challenge

terror and who knew that, once an ARVN armed force had passed through their vicinity, they were likely to be visited by Vietcong agents and terrorists. The Vietcong were indistinguishable from any peasant in the field; they could move about as freely throughout the population areas of South Vietnam as a fish could swim in the sea.

The CIA station had, over recent years, experimented with a number of different programs in an effort to counter Vietcong successes in the countryside. Basic to these programs was the operational principle that only the Vietnamese, under Vietnamese leadership, could bring about a secure countryside in which the peasants, the holders of intelligence concerning the Vietcong, could be persuaded to cooperate with government forces. Propaganda teams, psychological-warfare teams, and counter-terror teams had been tried without lasting or significant success. The fundamental problem remained: how to make the rural population (the water) hostile or poisonous to the Vietcong (the fish)?

The key to the problem was the farmer and his family. Between them they knew who the Vietcong sympathizers and collaborators were. The farmer knew where their armed units were located and where they moved. He knew the tax collectors, the recruiters, and the terrorists. How could we induce the farmer and his family to cooperate with GVN units? If one likened the entire intelligence problem to a table top, one could see that this table was tilted toward the Vietcong and that everything on it was sliding toward them. If the key factor was the flow of intelligence, how could the Vietnamese tip the table in their direction so that the desperately needed flow of intelligence would come to them? If the intelligence war could indeed be turned around, the Vietcong infrastructure and armed teams could slowly be rooted out, dispersed or eliminated.

About forty miles east of Saigon lay a peninsula fronting on the South China Sea on one side and on the other facing the Rung Sat, a mangrove swamp area through which the Saigon River twisted its way from Saigon to the sea. The French had named this peninsula Cap St. Jacques; after their departure, the Vietnamese renamed it Vung Tau, but it remained a popular seaside resort, as in the French colonial period. Being a peninsula, Vung Tau was relatively safe from Vietcong pressure, and the

GVN had established a small transit airport and training area for the Regional Forces. The coastline was dotted with a collection of seaside villas for high-ranking government officials. As the American U.S. Army advisory presence had grown, the airfield had been expanded to accommodate a helicopter repair base. Other small American and Vietnamese installations were located at Vung Tau, taking advantage of its proximity to Saigon and its relative security from Vietcong attack.

The CIA station had long maintained a small camp at Vung Tau, with a few Vietnamese instructors, paid and supplied by us, providing rudimentary arms training and instruction in strengthening the political motivation to the small indigenous team who made up our propaganda and census-grievance programs. This camp could accommodate about eighty students and the Vietnamese who passed through it for training remained there for perhaps three or four weeks at a time before returning to their home provinces and districts for work. The corps of instructors at this camp had over the years shown themselves to be strongly motivated and dedicated to their work and as impatient with the meager successes to date as we were. The camp commander and chief instructor, who had been lent to us by the Ministry of Interior, was a Vietnamese Army captain named Mai, and it was largely through his initiative and imagination that we jointly began to evolve a doctrine and set of tactics that proved to have the potential of tilting the intelligence table in the direction of the GVN and against the Vietcong.

No station officers were permanently assigned to Vung Tau; my case officer, Tom, in charge of the programs there, would frequently visit it and as frequently Captain Mai would come to Saigon for discussions with the minister of interior and with us.

A novel experiment Captain Mai had been running in the province of Quang Ngai on the north coast of South Vietnam was brought to my attention by Tom, described as "completely new, sophisticated, and very successful" in smoking out the Vietcong in the countryside.

Quang Ngai was an important but violent province, riddled with Vietcong. Using it as the site for many savage ambushes, the Vietcong would debauch onto the coastal plain and into the populated areas of the province from the piedmont and upland country of the province's western portion, where the terrain rose in rough broken country to the jagged wilds of South Vietnam's central spine. The provincial capital, Quang Ngai City, ranked with Danang and Hue as one of the major urban centers of South Vietnam. I was told that it was well worth my spending a day at the Vung Tau training camp to hear the details of the experiment firsthand from an exuberant Captain Mai, who was not given to excesses of exuberance. A day or two later Tom and I flew to Vung Tau, where we were met by Captain Mai. He enthusiastically described in detail what had been happening in Quang Ngai.

A long-standing personal friend of Captain Mai's, a police official in Quang Ngai City, had called on him at his home in Vung Tau, during an official visit to Saigon. His police friend had mentioned that a number of local citizens had come to him for advice as to how they, as individuals, could fight against the Vietcong. These volunteers had only one thing in common; each of them had suffered in one way or another at the hands of the Vietcong. One had had his hut burned to the ground by a guerrilla group; another was an ARVN veteran who had come home to find his wife had been murdered, still another had been a village chief near Quang Ngai City who had been tortured and had watched the death of his two children at the hands of the Vietcong. Mai went on that as he listened to his friend, the idea emerged that perhaps these volunteers could be formed as a group, be given weapons and training, and sent back to their home district, just outside Quang Ngai City, there to fight as they thought best against the Vietcong squads and cadres moving throughout the district.

These squads had long moved at will through the countryside impressing young men into their ranks by forcibly taking them back to their foothill hideouts, threatening them or their families with assassination, and thus coercing the kidnapped youth into fighting for them. The pattern was invariably the same: these young men were given illegal acts to perform; the individual would then be told he was now a criminal and subject to punishment by the central government authorities if he returned to his home. Thus were many young terrified boys "recruited" into the ranks of the Vietcong irregulars.

The policeman knew that Captain Mai was working with the Americans and he asked if there were any way he could be supplied with weapons to arm his volunteers and give them a chance to protect themselves against the Vietcong when they returned to their homes. Captain Mai asked our case officer, Tom, for permission to issue a few weapons from the small weapons room at the school. The case officer arranged for a flight to take Captain Mai and the weapons to Quang Ngai City, where he spent several days with his policeman friend, discussing how these volunteers could be trained, what their instructions should be, and how they would be paid and in general supervised. Mai continued by saying he had just returned from Quang Ngai a few days before, where he had seen his friend and had asked about the team which had gone back to its district. What he had learned of this team upon their return to their village, he said, was startling enough to cause him to ask for this meeting at Vung Tau so that he could pass on his findings.

As we talked, a number of disparate factors fell into place concerning our analysis of Vietcong tactics and our attempts to counter them. That night in Saigon, I met with a number of case officers concerned with the Vietcong problem in the countryside and we spent several hours discussing the Quang Ngai development. Thus was born the most effective counterinsurgency tool devised during the period of our American involvement in Vietnam. The beginnings of this program, the doctrines governing it, its accomplishments, and its ultimate fate will be discussed later.

The first half of 1964 saw several visits to Saigon by Secretary of Defense McNamara, CIA Director McCone, and my immediate boss, Bill Colby. Bill and I always enjoyed seeing each other and John McCone's visits proved valuable to the station and to Ambassador Lodge, although it was apparent that the two of them tended to be stiff with each other. McNamara's visits invariably left me with a feeling of gloom and foreboding. The man simply had no comprehension of the nature of the conflict in Vietnam, let alone any idea of how it should be handled. As time wore on, he demonstrated that he believed only in the application of military force. A rational man himself, he tended to view the world as being populated by rational people; surely once the Vietcong perceived the fact that an overwhelming American military force could not be stopped, McNamara logically believed, then they would, as rational men, cease their violence. How wrong he was.

The Vietcong Challenge

I have mentioned that Ambassador Lodge was a prudent and private person. While he could be charming, friendly, and gregarious, there was a healthy streak of secretiveness and suspicion of others, as befits a good political leader, in his makeup. In the late spring of 1964, Ambassador Lodge had made up his mind to ask President Johnson to replace him as ambassador; he wanted to return to the United States to become part of the Republican political process of that election year. Not that he was running for the Republican candidacy, but who could tell? Lightning could always strike. To preserve the secrecy of his intentions, Lodge declined to use the embassy communications channels to Washington in negotiating his return to the United States and instead would send his trusted executive assistant, Colonel Michael Dunn, a sharp, able Army officer, to Manila to cable "back-channel" messages to President Johnson. Thus was his transfer arranged.

By the time of his departure in June, Ambassador Lodge and I were on quite good terms. I had removed the offensive "Special Assistant" sign from my office door, the monstrous Chevrolet was gone, and I had become a person in whom, from time to time, Ambassador Lodge could confide. While not everyone in the embassy could make this statement, I sincerely regretted his departure, along with his charming and intelligent wife, Emily. Paul Harkins and his wife left the same month; Harkins, a dedicated career Army officer, was just one more victim caught up in the political gears of American military involvement in Vietnam. The new embassy team, headed by General Maxwell Taylor, arrived in July. By mid-July the number of U.S. military advisers in Veitnam had grown steadily to approximately fifteen thousand personnel.

The American Embassy building in Saigon had originally been a French commercial house and was of typically aberrant French design. My office was on the second floor—by European custom the first floor. My large commo section was on the fifth floor, beneath the top floor containing the offices of the ambassador, deputy ambassador, and their various executive assistants and secretaries.

The building was on a corner, one side fronting a principal thoroughfare of Saigon and the other on a narrower street along which ran a railway spur line, leading to the commercial docks on the Saigon River. My office overlooked this side street and the railroad tracks and faced into another narrow street leading away from the embassy. The station had offices elsewhere in the embassy and in other buildings scattered throughout the city, but the key offices were in the embasssy. My own office was a long, comfortable room, large enough to include a conference area to receive guests and carry on meetings. The office of my deputy, Gordon, adjoined mine, as did that of my secretary, Thody, a most efficient and personable woman, who worked with me later in Washington and again when I was sent to Bangkok.

Throughout my many years abroad, I was invariably known as a CIA official and I was intrigued by the remarkable way the CIA was regarded by foreigners. Whether in Europe or in Asia, the local chieftains in government, the military establishments, the trade-union hierarchy, and the so-called intellectuals, in dealing with me, clearly felt they were in touch with the really direct and significant route to the American decision makers in Washington. To say this in no way is meant to lessen the importance and respect accorded to the ambassador and the embassy proper. The CIA connection was looked upon as a less formal, more confidential, and more rapid means of dealing with the U.S. government. This fact was recognized, perhaps ruefully, by every ambassador with whom I ever served. The same fact was also recognized, sometimes resentfully, by other embassy officers, who were directly responsible for the execution of American political and diplomatic policy in the country concerned. This unwanted but very real prestige automatically imposed upon a station chief the need for care and circumspection in carrying on his personal relationships with prominent officials or individuals in the country of his assignment. Wise ambassadors used this relationship effectively in the American interest; less secure ones dealt with it warily.

An example of this role-playing in Vietnam can be cited with regard to the An Quang, the Buddhist political activist sect, headed by the Machiavellian Buddhist bonze, or monk, Trich Tri Quang. During one of the many divisive and antiviolent demonstrations inspired by Trich Tri Quang, he caused one of his aides to telephone my "Buddhist case officer" asking that he immediately come to a prearranged meeting place. A wild, surging demonstration was in progress in downtown Saigon and my officer had to exercise considerable caution in getting through the nighttime streets jammed with demonstrators and torchlight parades to the meeting site. This activist bonze wanted to pass on information to us to force-feed his point of view and his objectives for the current demonstration to the American government. The case officer returned from the meeting, hot, disheveled, and irritated and related the subject of the meeting and then went to the Embassy Political Section with his report for them to use as they saw fit, but not before he passed on to me a vignette of his meeting with Trich Tri Quang.

In the back-alley courtyard in which they met, he found Trich Tri Quang and a bonze concealed in a doorway. My case officer was astounded to note that Trich Tri Quang, the head of the Buddhist movement in Vietnam, was attired in the black cassock of a Catholic priest, buttoned from his throat to the ground, all of this topped by a Catholic priest's cap. His aide was similarly dressed, but for reasons best known to himself, high white tennis shoes protruded from the folds of his cassock, and on his head perched a baseball cap. Both wore dark glasses although it was night, and displayed very white, toothy grins. Inscrutable Buddhists.

21 The Key to Counterinsurgency

By late spring of 1964 Captain Mai, his instructors, and my own case officers had become solidly enthusiastic about the Quang Ngai pacification experiment. I agreed when they collectively recommended that three additional teams be recruited in Quang Ngai province, brought to our small camp in Vung Tau for training, and then returned to their home districts for deployment. As it happened, the Quang Ngai province chief had also been impressed with the teams and had independently informed Minister of Interior Vien of the remarkable successes being enjoyed there. I had business every few days with Minister Vien about National Police intelligence matters throughout the country, and at one of these routine meetings we turned to the phenomenal success of the teams in Quang Ngai. We agreed we should expand this program and Vien enthusiastically agreed we should deploy three additional teams in Quang Ngai. He volunteered to give them full ministerial support. We discussed the need to expand the program without delay, and when I mentioned that expansion would require more land for suitable accommodations, mess halls, rifle ranges, classrooms, and warehouses, Minister Vien said he would look into the matter of additional land at Vung Tau.

That night Gordon and I examined the problems involved in a sizable expansion. Headquarters had already cabled its assent to our building a 5,000-man camp, and I mused aloud that we should find a name for these teams. After a few moments thought, Gordon said, "How about calling them "People's Action Teams?" Why not, I thought. That's exactly what they are and the name has a strong connotation of action and local responsibility. "That's it," I said. And the PAT teams were born.

Three additional teams were recruited from three separate districts to the west of Quang Ngai City, at the base of the foothills leading to the mountainous spine of Vietnam. Captain

The Key to Counterinsurgency

Mai and his instructors had organized a course of study and training which bore down heavily on political motivation for the team members, stressing the importance of rejecting the appeal of the Vietcong and the need to take up arms against them. The destructive philosophy of the Communist movement was set out in detail in the course of instruction: the ultimate domination of the Vietnamese people by the alien Communist philosophy, the corrosive effects of Communism on the cohesiveness and unity of the traditional Vietnamese family, the destructive effect of Communist collectivists on the farmer, and its shredding effect on the fabric of Vietnamese traditions and culture. The instructors had also cobbled together training courses on simple handicrafts and skills which team members could use to help the farming families in their home districts on their return to these villages, thus to provide one more lever in gaining their confidence and ultimately the information they possessed.

Experience in Quang Ngai province had shown that, in addition to the heavy motivational training, the teams had not only to help the peasants, but also defend them. A series of meetings among ourselves, Captain Mai, and the perceptive policeman from Quang Ngai City led us to the adoption of an assortment of weaponry with which to equip the next three teams. We had arbitrarily agreed on the figure of forty as the number of men in each team and that every man should be armed. The weapons mix consisted of an old reliable weapon, the Browning Automatic Rifle, standard U.S. Army M-1 rifles with grenade launchers, sub-machine guns and pistols. Each team would also be issued a PRC-10 radio to maintain a link with the radio-base station at district headquarters which Minister Vien in Saigon promised would be set up in each district where teams would be deployed. Earlier we had learned in Quang Ngai that the local farmers, willing to be friendly and cooperative once convinced that the teams were not a threat, were helpful, honest, and cooperative and stood in friendly awe of these heavily armed government teams which were prepared to use these weapons to defend the villagers.

The combination of selfless helpfulness and armed security practically guaranteed the villagers' cooperation in providing information about the Vietcong infrastructure and the marauding bands of guerrillas. Not only did the teams provide protection, the protection was permanent. The teams never left the district and were not far away when they were needed—not too far for a child to run to for help. As the Vietcong grew and occasionally would appear in larger numbers than the PATs were able to handle, the PRC-10 radio was used to call in a larger ARVN unit to trap the Vietcong force or to bring a GVN air strike to bear on a Vietcong formation large enough to provide a target.

There had earlier been a number of attempts by the South Vietnam minister of defense, under the general tutelage of MACV, to create local militia units which were intended to provide security to the local countryside. Most notable among these attempts was the Popular Force, recruited locally in the provinces and assigned the duties of guarding bridges, warehouses, and entrances to hamlets. Of all the echelons in the military establishment of Vietnam, the Popular Forces was the lowest rung on the ladder and as such received a minimum of arms, training, with very little attention and poor leadership. They were ineffectual, and often turned out to be a conduit for passing weapons from the ARVN warehouses to the Vietcong, because of the rapidity with which these pitiful units would throw down their arms and flee in the face of an attack.

The PATs, from the beginning, never doubted their strength or their spirit as patriotic Vietnamese, well-trained, well-armed, and fighting in a worthy cause. Together with Captain Mai and his instructors and provincial officials, we had insured that each of the PATs was made up of men from their home district. They knew the terrain, had friends and relatives throughout the district, and were known to the farmers among whom they lived. This heavily armed group, once returned to their homes from Vung Tau, never left their district, but constantly roamed and scouted through it. They had no barracks to return to, no compound in which to sleep; each team kept its own schedule of leave for individual team members. When his turn came, he would go home to spend time with his family and then rejoin his team, which would not be far away in the district. This insured permanent integrity and the knowledge that the PAT was always within call in time of need.

In the event of the death of a team member, a district or provincial representative, in keeping with Minister Vien's promise of support, would at once visit the widow or the parents and tender the death benefits in cash, customary in Vietnam.

The Key to Counterinsurgency

The unique feature of this supportive gesture was that the death benefit was *in fact* paid to the widow or the parents, and within a week's time. Theoretically, the same kind of payment was paid to the survivors of deceased members of ARVN, the Regional Forces, and the Popular Forces; in practice, many months would pass before the survivor would get the death benefit and even then there would have been many along the line who had taken a piece of it.

Vietnamese province representatives made it a practice to call from time to time on the families of PAT members to check on their welfare, to see if there was illness or if the local officials could help with some unforeseen problem while the member was out on duty. This kind of care and attention was unknown in Vietnam; among the PATs it inspired abiding loyalty and dependable performance.

Quickly it became understood that the effectiveness and success of each team depended entirely upon their closeness to the people whom they defended and among whom they lived. They in turn received intelligence, food, and concealment when needed. No uniform or any insignia was worn; no armband, badge or anything to distinguish them from the other villagers. They constantly circulated through their district, sleeping at night on the floors of village huts, or by the dooryard outside, buying and paying for their food (they carried no rations), and during the days they would use their skills (and motivation) to assist farmers and their families in small but valued ways. They would repair a dike, give rudimentary first aid, clean out a well, until their repeated returns to a given village were warmly anticipated and welcomed.

One team member himself had thought up a useful idea which spread rapidly back to the training course at Vung Tau; I found myself putting in an order for hundreds of hair clippers from Hong Kong. This imaginative PAT member had come by a set of clippers and in the evening twilight in a cluster of farmers huts would line up the young children and cut their hair, as the approving elders sat in the dusk smoking and talking. In these relaxed hours, the farmers would talk about the Vietcong who moved about in the district and their patterns of movement—the tax collector and his armed escort came at routine intervals from the direction of the dikes, would collect "tax" money and disappear into a particular copse of wood. With this information, an ambush could be set. Statistics on dead and wounded always make grisly reading, but in the case of the PAT teams, some of the remembered statistics will give the bottom line on the PAT concept. Over a five-month period, three teams killed over 150 armed Vietcong and retrieved their weapons, and more than 200 of the enemy were captured *with their weapons*—a significant point. Our teams' losses were 6 men dead and perhaps 20 wounded, and there were no desertions. Desertions from the ARVN, the Regional Forces, and the Popular Forces were always discouragingly high. The PATs seemed immune to them.

Minister Vien telephoned one morning and asked me to drop by his office, where I found him poring over a map of the Vung Tau peninsula. Outlined in red was a sizable area astride the single main road from Saigon to the tip of the peninsula. This parcel of land constituted several hundred acres owned by the Vietnamese Catholic Church. Most of the land was vacant, but there were several buildings in one corner, used as a seminary. The seminary was being transferred to Saigon and Minister Viet said the entire area could be made available to us at a nominal rent. With a couple of assistants, we flew together to Vung Tau and spent a day inspecting the site—it was ideal. Set off by itself, it was well-isolated but at the same time easily defensible, both from the water and the roadway leading back to Saigon, the forty-mile stretch being quite often under attack by the Vietcong roaming the hills, and dominating the road. The site would have to be supplied by armed convoy or from the sea; neither solution posed any problem. The CIA had already approved enlargement of the program and made available money for the acquisition and construction of a training site. Vietnamese engineers, together with others supplied by the CIA, projected a camp capable of holding five thousand students at one time with suitable but simple sleeping accommodations, mess halls, warehouses and supply buildings, and instruction and administrative areas.

While construction was going on, Minister Vien and Captain Mai sent representatives to the province chief in Quang Ngai to set the recruitment wheels in motion for additional PATs. Similar advance teams were sent to other strategic provinces in the north and plans were made to send teams, as soon as they could be formed, into the delta. The new training center at Vung Tau

The Key to Counterinsurgency

was completed in August of 1964 and the first new teams began to stream in for the thirteen-week training course.

In Saigon we organized our joint effort to send to the provinces one of my station officers who would accompany a Vietnamese official from the Ministry of Interior to check on the performance of the Vietnamese support structure in each province and district. Were the local teams being paid on time? Did they have all of their equipment? Were there any unusual problems that could not be solved at the province level? Always these inspectors would check in with these local MACV field offices, located at the provincial capital near the offices of the province chief. Consisting of a couple of U.S. Army officers and supporting administrative staff, these elements were known as the sector advisers. They lived very close to the Vietcong problem. Their views and responses were less contrived and much closer to the ground than the responses one got at MACV Headquarters on the Rue Pasteur in Saigon.

Queried about the performance of the PAT teams in Quang Ngai province, the sector adviser and his assistants were solidly enthusiastic. "We don't know what you're doing with these people, but they're the only local Vietnamese force of any value at all, and they're damned valuable at that. When can we expect more of these teams up here?" Invariably the sector advisers praised the program, and quite often during his periodic visits to MACV headquarters in Saigon, a sector adviser whom I had met on one of my field trips would drop by the American Embassy for a cup of coffee and a chat about the PATs. It was distressing, quite often, that these pleasant visits would close with the request by the visiting sector officer that I not mention his visit at MACV as, "it would not be understood." One of them said to me, "You know, we're not supposed to report much about the successes of the teams, but you really should know that they're going great."

After a Mission Council meeting in the ambassador's conference room one Wednesday, Ambassador Taylor motioned me over to the far side of the room as the council members filed out. Since his arrival in July, he had asked me to give him, in his office and privately, a weekly briefing on CIA activities in Vietnam of all categories: agent work, training of police interrogators, liaison work with the Vietnamese Central Intelligence Organization (CIO), and pacification progress. The last category of course included the PAT program and in my detailed references to the PATs I had written a summation of the 5,000-man training center at Vung Tau. As the conference room emptied, Ambassador Taylor, in his level courteous voice, said the time had come for him to have a look at the Vung Tau camp, and would I arrange for a visit to the site the following Monday? He would devote the entire day to the briefing and wanted to hear, not only about the construction of the camp, but about the content of the program.

I spoke with Minister Vien, who was only too eager to go with us, and between his office and mine we sent word to Captain Mai and his staff to lay on a complete briefing, to include a walking visit to all the major facilities of the new camp, just completed but already partially filled with new recruits in training.

The following Monday, Ambassador Taylor, Minister Vien, and I, almost filling the interior of a so-called "thunderbird" passenger jet, flew to Vung Tau, having been preceded by a propeller-driven station aircraft, carrying ten personnel, divided between staff aides of Ambassador Taylor and Minister Vien and one officer of mine. We entered waiting cars and streamed out of the Vung Tau airfield, until we came to the spanking-new camp gates. The entire camp had been fully alerted and, in spite of my earnest request for a low-key visit to Captain Mai and my own officers stationed at Vung Tau, there were lines of trainees and instructors drawn up to welcome the party in front of the camp administration building. Ritualistically, we all sat for a moment in wicker easy chairs and sipped a glass of Coke before moving into an assembly room where chairs were lined up before a lectern, behind which were arrayed a series of charts, graphs, and maps. I knew the content of this initial briefing and positioned myself to be able to watch Ambassador Taylor, to gauge his reaction as the briefing went along. Captain Mai spoke excellent English as did most of his instructor staff, a very impressive group. They made their presentations with dignity and authority; knowing Ambassador Taylor, I was greatly pleased to note the intentness and concentration with which he listened to the individual speakers. From time to time, he would gesture to his staff aide, Joe Luman, to make a note on a particular point, a habit of Taylor's which I had learned would prompt later questions to me on that subject. The case officer traveling

The Key to Counterinsurgency

with me watched Luman and made his own notes accordingly.

The day at Vung Tau was jam-packed with surprises for Ambassador Taylor. Although every week I had told him in considerable detail of the progress in construction of the camp, seeing the camp in actuality impressed him noticeably. The mess halls, sleeping quarters, classrooms, warehouses and administrative offices were sparkling clean and well-organized. The students undergoing training were bright, strongly built, and obviously in good spirits. All of them, as well as the instructors, wore the black cotton pants and tops of the Vietnamese farmer, also the garb of the Vietcong irregulars and infrastructure.

Most of the morning was spent on briefings, followed by a light lunch; then Captain Mai took us on a long tour of the facilities of the camp. The cleanliness of the camp, its completeness and variety made a visible impact on Ambassador Taylor whom I watched attentively as we went from one part of the camp to another. The long day drew to a close, and as Minister Vien planned to remain in Vung Tau overnight, Ambassador Taylor and I flew back to Tan Son Nhut alone in the T-bird. Never an overly talkative man, Taylor was thoughtfully silent all the way back to Saigon until we approached the landing strip; he leaned over and suggested that I arrange with Westy that he and his entire senior staff be given a thorough briefing on the PAT program, to include photographs and descriptions of the camp and its functions. He also wryly suggested that I not tell Westy that the camp at Vung Tau had been built in two months, from nothing. "That would break his heart." But Taylor wound up telling him himself.

After the next Mission Council meeting, General Westmoreland followed me back to my office in the embassy. I told my secretary to turn off visitors and the phones and we seated ourselves in easy chairs around the coffee table. Westy said he had been talking with the ambassador over the weekend and Taylor had given him a detailed account of his visit to Vung Tau the preceding week. Taylor had been astounded that our 5,000-man camp could have been built from nothing in less than two months; Westy asked if his engineers could get together with mine to find out how this had been accomplished and at the same time visit the site. I told him to go ahead and have his people contact mine; let them make their own schedule. He went on to say that Taylor in particular had been deeply stirred by the philosophy that lay behind the PAT program which had seemed entirely new to him, but he sensed great promise in its application and he wanted Westmoreland to get the same briefing.

Over the next two hours, I reviewed the origins of the program, the nature of the problem it was meant to solve, what was going on at Vung Tau, and what our projections were for the future. Westy listened intently, asking a question now and then, and at the end of my exposition leaned back, gazed steadily at me, and said in his clipped, military voice, "Well, I can see we're going to have some problems. In particular, your projections for expanding the program show that it will be absorbing many tens of thousands of Vietnamese as it grows. This means that we will have to slice up the Vietnamese manpower pie all over again before too long." I agreed that problem would arise and we should address ourselves to it before the expanding PAT program moved much further along. He agreed and said that, first, he would appreciate my giving to the top members of his staff the same explanation and briefing I had just given him. He suggested two briefings, one on a Saturday and one on the following day, so that he could divide his staff into two groups, in order to have "someone minding the store."

Briefing dates having been set, I put my station staff to work on the substance and form the presentation to the MACV staff should take.

As the military tempo of the fight with the Vietcong increased, General Westmoreland had in turn increased the size of the MACV staff. There were now several more general officers and, additionally, clouds of colonels. I knew most of them personally and knew that while many of them understood the PAT program and supported it, there was a significant number of generals and senior colonels who saw in the PAT program a kind of threat to the principle that MACV should lead a unified American command in the field of pacification.

The two briefings took place on schedule, each lasting about two hours. My station officers had broken the entire topic into an individual number of presentations which they set out clearly and with obvious authority. Each session gave a clear and complete picture of the theory behind the program, the way in which PAT members were recruited, trained, equipped, deployed, and used. Most of this briefing was new and the doctrine and techniques used in training and utilizing the teams were new and

The Key to Counterinsurgency 243

in many ways unsettling to this military audience. Eyes opened wide as the armament of each team was described and wider still when the listeners were informed that we already had on hand the total arsenal of weapons for three hundred teams and would have no trouble getting more when needed. The CIA's ability to move quickly, effectively, and with a minimum of fuss never failed to amaze the MACV staff. Murmurs of anguish could be heard in the conference room when the staff was informed that each PAT group, on completion of their training at Vung Tau, elected its own leaders. There was further stirring in the audience when they were told that team members wore no uniforms of any kind, but only simple farmers' clothing, indistinguishable from that of anyone else working in the paddies. When the listeners were informed that the teams had no home base, no barracks, no flagpole and no military compound to return to, heads wagged negatively and the room sounded like a barnyard of chickens, while hands shot in the air.

The questions were interesting. "If they don't wear uniforms, how can you tell your own men from the farmers?" The answer was easy: "You can't, but neither can the Vietcong." "Don't you think that a special cap or an armband or some kind of emblem would be good for unit morale?" They were told that there was no problem of morale and were further given statistics such as: there had been no desertions to date and there had been only four weapons lost in action, while the teams had captured over four hundred Vietcong weapons. Sounds of disbelief passed through the room as these facts were absorbed. After each of the two briefings, there was a great deal of give-and-take concerning the functioning of the program, the manner in which it was supported with money and weapons, and detailed questions concerning the training given at Vung Tau, all of which was dealt with factually and completely.

When the embassy conference room finally emptied on the second day, two staff generals well known to me stayed behind to raise problems that troubled them. I must realize, they said, that an armed program of this scope must be beyond the CIA's capability to administer and control and that the MACV would, before long, have to step in and take it over. I didn't agree and replied that the Vietnamese Ministry of Interior was the proper agency to control it and the CIA would simply provide supplies, expenses, and encouragement, which we would funnel through the Ministry of Interior through the embassy Agency for International Development (AID), in order to maintain the civilian coloration of the entire activity; the Vietnamese were to carry on the brunt of the program and perform all of the work. One of the generals then exploded with some heat to inform me that people armed in the way I had described and performing the combat tasks about which they had been told had to be recognized for what they were: soldiers. He went on: "And they've got to be made to look like soldiers and act like soldiers." I thought to myself, "Well, the day's briefing was lost on that one."

After the two generals had left, I noticed a major lagging behind, obviously waiting for a moment to talk with me. I recognized him as the sector adviser I had spoken with in Quang Ngai province, who had told me the first PAT team working outside Quang Ngai City was the only effective force in the province. I asked him what he was doing in Saigon and he replied, "The old man called me to Saigon to tell me of your briefing of him last week and to learn at firsthand my opinion of the PAT program." The major cocked a sidelong glance at me: "I told him just what I had told you, except they're even better than the last time you were in Quang Ngai. I don't think he liked this, but I told him the truth . . ."

The fundamental importance of separating the Vietcong infrastructure from the peasantry can perhaps be illustrated by drawing upon an incident that took place in Quang Ngai. The Vietcong, particularly in "hot" provinces, usually organized their cadre leadership to correspond with the different boundaries recognized within the province, even if these boundaries had been established by "puppet" officials. In Tu Nghia district to the west of Nghia Han district, the local Vietcong committee chief used the party name of Phat. We had, from a number of sources, identified Comrade Phat as the chief of that district and had also established that Phat was in frequent communication with Comrade Nguyen, the committee chief in the adjoining district of Nghia Han. We learned that Comrade Phat had dispatched a letter to Comrade Nguyen by courier, a letter which said substantially the following: "We have found in our district that the puppet government, with the assistance of the Imperialist Americans, has organized some politically unstable elements into groups which are heavily armed and which move through

The Key to Counterinsurgency 245

the district harming our interests and killing our brothers. I write to warn you of this new and dangerous effort by the puppet government to bring confusion and discouragement to our loyal cadres. Dear brother, Nguyen, be vigilant and protect yourself against the crimes of these imperialist lackeys." Signed, "Phat."

It was an interesting letter, referring to the local PAT unit as it did. Apparently Phat had already had some unfortunate experiences with the team in his district and wanted to alert Comrade Nguyen to expect similar difficulties. The letter, however, arrived a bit late for Nguyen as the PAT team retrieved Comrade Phat's letter from the body of Nguyen, who had been killed in an ambush by the PATs, along with several other members of the district Vietcong committee, an ambush prepared on the basis of information provided by the farming families of the district among whom the PAT group had been working.

In addition to the PAT program, we had developed a radically different form of activity, particularly active in the delta. Our Vietnamese colleagues had insisted on this activity, and we had perhaps reluctantly agreed to support them with money and weapons and other supplies. It could be described as a counter-terror program, consisting of small teams of four to six men, dressed in the usual black farmers' garb, armed with folding stock carbines which could be hidden under their black tunics, and with grenades carried in the pockets of their loose-fitting shorts.

In one instance, a counter-terror team had been trailing a Vietcong command unit for several days and finally found it coming to rest when the Vietcong made bivouac in a copse of wood standing by itself in a spread of open, uncultivated flat land. When operating this way in the flat land of the delta, a Vietcong unit would hide out for a few days of rest in such a patch of forest, digging foxholes in the open fields adjacent as a precaution against surprise attack. In this case the counter-terror team pinpointed the Vietcong position on an artillery fire control map, went into the town of My To, and arranged for an ARVN artillery battalion to shell the coordinate of the Vietcong bivouac at an agreed hour, a few nights later. They returned to the vicinity of the bivouac and one night silently approached the six foxholes that had been dug and booby-trapped each of them with hand grenades. Moving away to a safe distance, they awaited the night of the bombardment. On schedule, dozens of artillery rounds poured into the forest, scattering the Vietcong bivouac. The next day the counter-terror team moved back to inspect the results of their work. The six foxholes had been used by the Vietcong; the six grenades had exploded and each foxhole contained a body.

22 Vietcong Terror

It must be remembered that the Vietcong's use of terror in its most frightful forms was one of its main techniques of aggression against the people of South Vietnam. The Vietcong were monstrous in their application of torture and murder to achieve the political and psychological impact they wanted. There was little the rural population of South Vietnam could do to defend itself (although as time wore on the PATs began to have an impact on Vietcong assassins and terror squads). This implacable use of terror in its own way served an intelligence purpose for the Vietcong. A bloody act of terror in a populated area would immobilize the population nearby, make the local inhabitants responsive to the Vietcong and, in return, unresponsive to the government element requests for cooperation.

The Vietcong use of terror was purposeful, precise, and frightful to behold. Because I frequently visited the PATs in Quang Ngai during our early days there, I had occasion to see the results of some terrorist acts. Once outside the district and provisional capitals, one encountered village after village obviously under Vietcong influence and domination; the steady unsmiling eyes of young farmers of military age at work in the paddies signaled one's entrance into Vietcong country. During a routine visit to the MACV sector adviser's office in Quang Ngai City, the sector adviser rushed up to me and said that the Vietcong terror squad had been active in the village of Duc Pho on the seacoast not far away the night before. Would I like to go with him to have a look? In his chopper, we flew low and fast to the southeast, perhaps twenty feet above the foliage to upset the aim of any gunner who might be concealed there. At this altitude the onrushing Huey made a very difficult target and as we flew out over the sea, we went up a bit before coming back to the village from the relative safety of the sea and the beach, slowed, and clattered to a landing in a patch of brown earth in the center of the village. There was another chopper on the pad, bearing the markings of the Vietnamese Air Force, which turned out to be assigned to the local ARVN headquarters in Quang Ngai City. An officer from that staff had also flown out to take a look at the damage of the night before. The pilot told us where we could find the scene of the incident and went on reading his newspaper.

We threaded our way through the village to the remains of the village chief's house, a thatched hut still smoldering. There in an open space before the ashes of the hut was a grisly sight.

A village committee man told us what had happened the previous night. A Vietcong squad of heavily armed men had come into the village about midnight crossing the rice paddies from the west. A Popular Force team of ten lightly armed, ill-trained, and thoroughly scared young men, aroused from their sleep by other villagers, had exchanged a few shots with the raiding group, had thrown down their weapons and fled. The Vietcong then set about their work. They went directly to the village chief's house, where they found him, his wife, and their five-year-old son awake and alarmed at the commotion. The Vietcong chief had one of his men circulate among the nearby huts, where the inhabitants were up and standing apprehensively in their doorways. They were herded to the open area in front of the village chief's hut, where the Vietcong leader harangued them about the crimes of their chief. First, he shrilled that the chief worked for the puppet regime in Saigon, that he had not provided a stock of rice which he had been ordered to do by an earlier team visit, and he had given information to a Regional Forces unit "harmful to the people's cause." Having detailed these crimes, the leader sentenced the chief and his family to death.

Using their cane-chopping knives, they took the three heavy bamboo poles they had brought with them and placed each onto the ground and with a single stroke of a machete cut diagonally through the pole. The cutting slice of the machete left one end of each pole tapered to a sharp, fine point. Under the direction of the Vietcong, other villagers were forced to dig small pits in the ground in front of the house, where they buried and weighed down the blunt end of each sharpened stake. As the chief, his wife, and their neighbors watched in horror, two of the cadre seized the young boy, raised his squirming body above the sharp pole, and brought it abruptly down onto the pole, which protruded through his abdomen, spattering blood everywhere, with the boy still screaming. Impaled on the bamboo pole, the boy finally died and the body hung there grotesquely. The next seized was the wife, who was far gone in pregnancy and fainting with fear. She was raised overhead and also impaled before the horrified eyes of her husband. To make sure this horrible sight would remain with the villagers, one of the terror squad used his machete to disembowel the woman, spilling the fetus onto the ground. The husband's turn was next and it took four men to raise the convulsively struggling man above the bamboo and drive him down upon it. The leader then lectured the frozen villagers about their loyalty to the Vietcong; after setting fire to the hut, the murder squad moved on and vanished into the darkness.

And there I saw them, the three impaled bodies and the unborn child lying in the dirt. The villagers had been warned not to move the bodies for twenty-four hours, but upon our arrival a group of villagers began to approach the bodies for burial. A Catholic member of the village was making the sign of the cross over each body, murmuring a prayer in Vietnamese.

The sector adviser and I slowly turned away from the sight and moved back to the chopper. "Well, that's one more village the Vietcong own. Three people dead and the village is theirs." Bitterly he went on: "Unless we can protect villagers like this, or give them the means to protect themselves—and these pitiful Popular Force kids can't hack it—they will never be able to support the government even if they wanted to. They can't fight the Vietcong alone."

Back at the pad in Quang Ngai City, the sector adviser and I murmured our good-byes and the major drove off in his jeep to his office, presumably to put another red pin on his wall map, signifying one more village where friendly forces should use extreme caution. My own light aircraft was waiting and I flew on to Danang, changing there for a larger plane for the flight back to Saigon.

On another occasion, I was visiting the sector adviser in the delta town of My Tho, when he was interrupted by a phone call. He hung up, put on his cap, buckled on his sidearm, and asked if I'd go with him to the village of Ba Tri, where another "incident" had taken place the night before. This time it was the wife of the village chief who had been impaled. Her husband had been forced to watch this, and when the murder squad left they took him along, his hands tied behind him. The sector adviser, an army colonel in his second tour in Vietnam, stolidly told me that the Vietcong would take the chief with them, force him to tell everything he knew about government personnel in My Tho province; then he said, "they'll chop his head off. That village is dead for us for a long time to come."

The Vietcong use of terror within the city of Saigon itself was frequent, sometimes random, and sometimes carefully planned and executed. The targets in almost every case were the Americans. They were the hated imperialists. They could be individuals or gatherings of people. The plans of terrorists almost always reflected excellent intelligence on the comings and goings of their American targets; we had to assume that the Vietcong had agents inside American offices in Saigon or working elsewhere for the Americans as drivers, gardeners, cooks, or messengers. One Saturday morning during an American softball game, adjacent to the front entrance of Tan Son Nhut air base, a large mortar shell was detonated under the bleachers. Miraculously, only two Americans were killed and a few others wounded, although the bleachers were crowded with American families, including children, watching the game. An examination of the explosion site disclosed a wire leading from the crater under the bleachers across an adjoining field and, hidden by shrubbery, through a window into a washroom and toilet area, used by Vietnamese employed on the air base.

On a scheduled visit of Secretary McNamara to Saigon, only the alertness of an elderly Vietnamese, idly fishing along a small canal over which the main road from Tan Son Nhut passed on its way downtown, probably saved his life and that of Ambassador Lodge. The fisherman, early in the morning of the day McNamara was to arrive, saw two men standing in a rowboat under the low single-arch bridge spanning the canal, adjusting something overhead. After watching them for a few moments, the fisherman saw them sit down in the boat and drift off down the canal. Suspicious, the fisherman looked for the local policeman, whose duty was to guard the bridge, and told him what he had seen. Extra police were called and the underside of the bridge was inspected. A bundle of dynamite sticks was found, disconnected, and removed. A wire connected to the dynamite had been spooled out in the water of the canal, leading to an old car parked on the bank about three hundred yards further up the canal. The detonator and plunger were found under the front seat. McNamara and Lodge, on their way from Tan Son Nhut into town, passed over the bridge about an hour and a half after the explosives had been defused. Apparently police activity under the bridge and at the abandoned car was observed by the Vietcong terrorists; there was no effort made to get back to the car or to destroy the bridge.

Driving to work each day, I had my driver go by a different route, directing him daily in a random manner. One morning we were driving along the avenue which fronted on the old French sports club, the Cercle Sportif, when we encountered a small crowd along the sidewalk, clustered around a number of both Vietnamese police cars and American MP jeeps. We drew over to the side and I pressed through the crowd to find a gory scene; a man had been blown apart and the police were gingerly picking up parts of the remains and putting them in cardboard boxes in a van parked nearby. American MPs were taking notes and another MP told me what had happened. Early that morning an American soldier was driving his jeep along the avenue when he had a flat tire. Stopping, he found he had no tools in the jeep and radioed back to the motor pool. He was told to stay with the jeep until help could be sent. This occurred before the morning rush hour, but there was still a fair amount of traffic. Among the traffic was a Vietnamese on a bicycle, pulling a lightweight two-wheel cart, a common sight on any street in Saigon. The American soldier was standing by his jeep, smoking a cigarette, as this bicycle passed by. The Vietnamese had reached under his shirt, drew out a grenade and pulled the pin, and tossed it into the front seat of the jeep, peddling away quickly. The soldier, with amazing reflexes, reached into the jeep, picked up the armed grenade, and lobbed it into the cargo carrier behind the bike. He dived under his jeep as the grenade exploded, and later I watched as they picked up chunks of the Vietcong.

MACV ran a busline for American military personnel and Vietnamese employees which touched at the various offices and military compounds around Saigon, a convenience for the soldiers and others authorized to use the circuit. In the hot, humid climate, the bus windows were habitually left open, until one day at a scheduled stop, a Vietcong terrorist, prepared for the occasion, tossed a grenade through a rear window into the half-filled bus, killing several passengers instantly and wounding many more. Thereafter the transportation unit covered the windows with a heavy wire mesh but this didn't deter the Vietcong, who would attach a grenade to a tangle of fishhooks, hanging the grenade against the mesh-covered window; bus windows thereafter were no longer left open.

One Sunday evening my wife and I had decided to go to an early movie at the Kindo, the army theater, a mile or so from our house. Just before leaving, some friends, John and Nan Riordan, dropped by. Although Marilyn and I wanted to see the film—the name I well remember, *The List of Adrian Messenger*—we preferred to spend the evening with the Riordans. As we were sitting enjoying a drink, we were jolted by the unmistakable thud of a bomb detonating not far away. John and I got into my car and drove in the direction from which the explosion had come and, nearing the Kindo, we could see masses of people and sidewalks filled with rubble. Medics were working over a body of an MP lying on the sidewalk who was already dead and about to be carried away in an ambulance. Talking with American bystanders, we learned that a Vietcong had run behind the MP guard and into the lobby where he threw an airline bag containing a bomb into the theater and had then run out into the street. An alert American major seated in the rear of the theater grabbed the bag and threw it into the street where it exploded, killing him and the MP on duty.

Late one morning in the summer of 1964, my wife and son had gone shopping in a large arts-and-crafts store on Tu Do Street, a few doors from the front entrance of the Caravelle Hotel. As Marilyn was browsing through some items in the shop, there was a loud blast, the unmistakable sound of a bomb. The next sound was the predictable one following an explosion: the rumble and clang of iron shutters as they were slammed down in front of the doors along all the shops lining Tu Do. After waiting for the always-possible second bomb, the doors were opened and Marilyn and Perry were able to get out and find their way back to our car, passing the front of the Caravelle, picking their way through the dirt, rubble, and heaps of stones. A bomb in a suitcase had been placed under a bed in a room on the fifth floor of the hotel by a "Chinese businessman." Part of the wall of the fifth floor had been blown into the street below, and a large hole had been blasted through the ceiling of the room below. The Chinese was never seen again.

Terrified people were trapped in stalled elevators, but miraculously, no one inside or outside the hotel had been injured. Had the bomb gone off a scant twenty minutes later, the hotel lobby and corridors would have been filled with people returning for lunch.

The Cercle Sportif, a holdover from the French colonial days, featured a large high-ceilinged clubhouse and restaurant, with fans lazily revolving overhead. It was surrounded on every side by gardens filled with high trees, and a grass courtyard lined with tennis courts. A large swimming pavilion, built above-ground because of the high water table in Saigon, was composed of a long pool for adults and a shallow pool for children, surrounded on three sides by a tiled area for sunbathing. The fourth side was a covered open-air restaurant and beneath were dressing rooms and showers.

About twice a week I went to the Cercle Sportif for a swim and late lunch, and on those occasions would send the car home for my older son. We would spend about an hour and a half having a swim and light lunch and I would then return to the embassy, after which my driver took my son home. Cabot Lodge was a regular at the Cercle Sportif, going there almost every day at noon to swim for a few laps, relax in the sun, and have lunch before returning to the embassy. His pattern of movement was so predictable that I chided him, remarking that while I was not a target to a Vietcong terrorist, he was. He always shrugged it off, but this situation worried me. I became even more concerned when police intelligence uncovered a plot for a Vietcong assault on the swimming and dining area at the sports club. Their agent, a member of a Vietcong attack group, had disclosed that a sack of explosives was hidden near the wall of the swimming pool. A search of the grounds by the National Police, accompanied by one of my case officers, turned up a bag of hand grenades. The Saigon police, probably after a prolonged period of beating on the feet of the agent, came up with other names and arrests were made. The attack plan was to be implemented during the noontime lunch period when the grenades were to be thrown into the pool and dining area. Had this occurred, the carnage would have been truly terrible. Returning from the police, I went to

Lodge's office and told him what we had learned. He leaned forward, placed his elbows on his desk, pressing his fingertips together, wrinkling his brow, and looked at me steadily, saying nothing. I left the room, but was pleased to note that thereafter his visits to the swimming pool were timed in a rambling way.

Across the street from the Caravelle and behind the old opera house was the ugly mass called the Brinks Hotel, used as bachelor officers' quarters for the U.S. Army. It was six stories high and arranged so that drivers could park cars underneath it and passengers could walk up a flight of stairs to the lobby above. On the afternoon of Christmas eve, a panel truck, loaded with explosives, was driven into a parking place under the hotel, a timing device was set, and the driver disappeared. Bob Hope and his troupe arrived that afternoon for his annual Christmas tour. As Bob Hope and his party were loading up in cars at the airport for the ride into town, the van blew up, killing two Americans and damaging the underside of the buildings extensively. The first sight that greeted Hope's troupe, looking across the street from their own hotel, was the wreckage of the Brinks Hotel.

The next day, as we sat under the hot Saigon sun with thousands of servicemen at Hope's Christmas-day performance at Tan Son Nhut, he brought the house down with his opening remark: "I've gone from many airports to my hotel, but this is the first time I've found the hotel on its way out to meet me."

Looking back, Marilyn and I can find no reason for our confidence and complacency that somehow acts of terror would not involve us. We were not alarmed until a Vietcong courier coming into Saigon from the province surrounding the city was captured and found to be carrying detailed drawings of the Army dependents' school to which all of our children went. U.S. Army guard posts were marked, and there was a detailed written analysis of the school and its surrounding play yard, with notes concerning the workings of the school, guard schedules, where school buses were parked, and other unnerving details that could only add up to one chilling conclusion: the Vietcong were planning to attack the American elementary school.

Detailed plans had already been made for the evacuation of wives and children from Saigon and elsewhere in Vietnam, should developments warrant such a move. There was a reluctance to evacuate all American dependents because of the effect that the move would have on the Vietnamese populace. At the same time, the families came first.

While Ambassador Taylor already had the authority to order an evacuation at his own discretion, the obvious plan to blow up the children's school took the decision out of embassy hands entirely. President Johnson in February 1965 himself decided that the situation in Saigon and the countryside had become so dangerous that the families must leave. The State Department had the task of relocating civilian families and the Defense Department had the same obligation toward military families. All families had a number of choices: they could return to their homes in the States or could elect to find temporary quarters in Hong Kong, Bangkok, Singapore, the Philippines or Honolulu in the hope of having the husbands join them from time to time. My wife and I decided upon Baguio in the Philippines, as it was close to Saigon, there was a good private school for our son, and there were frequent military flights to Clark Field.

The CIA station rented an apartment for Marilyn, and toward the end of February I took leave to take my family, one of the last to leave, to Baguio, actually a resort town north of Manila situated over six thousand feet in the mountains, away from the sweltering heat of sea-level Manila. In one day they were settled in the apartment and I hired a sixteen-year-old Filipino girl, Consolacion Felipe, to help my wife and care for the children. She was one of ten children living in a barrio just outside the American Air Force encampment at Baguio, in which there were, conveniently enough, a post exchange, a commissary, an officers' club, and the usual amenities found on a small U.S. military base.

The family settled, I caught a courier flight from Clark Air Force Base back to Vietnam, making the usual secure but gut-wrenching dive down to the landing strip at Tan Son Nhut.

Meanwhile, the war in the countryside rumbled on. The Vietcong gained success after success and Vietnamese morale sagged further. Coup talk was rampant and no longer concealed. In the Gulf of Tonkin, North Vietnamese patrol boats launched two attacks on American destroyers late in August 1964. The response was prompt and effective: American carrier aircraft on patrol in the Gulf of Tonkin launched several punishing strikes against the port facilities supporting these North Vietnamese torpedo boats. These air raids were one-time affairs; there were no further torpedo boat attacks. The raids themselves gave heart to South Vietnamese forces at all levels, including General Khanh, the prime minister. This boost did not last long, and the bickering started anew among the generals. Reports of coups and coup plans could be heard in every coffeehouse and the Buddhists, led by Trich Tri Quang, used every device they could to humble General Khanh and his government.

Our station continued to invest much time, money, and effort in its field programs, among which was the PAT program. Reports from Quang Nai were always heartening, but knowing the predilection of field commanders in Vietnam, whether American or Vietnamese, to tell Saigon what they thought it wanted to hear, I sent observers and often went myself to verify personally the heartening stories being reported back about the conduct and achievements of the PATs.

There was another CIA station program about which little has been said. The counter-terror program was born early in 1964, the idea being to bring danger and death to the Vietcong functionaries themselves, especially in the areas in which they felt secure. They had several redoubts: the Umin Forest, Udong Hai, and Zone D, as well as others. The rest areas and rehabilitation zones, across the border into Cambodia and Laos, were well known and well beyond our reach.

The purpose of the counter-terror teams was simple. On the basis of information provided through our intelligence work and the knowledge of movements of Vietcong in and among the population of South Vietnam, we had obtained descriptions and photographs of known cadres, who were functioning as committee chiefs, recruiters, province representatives, and heads of the raiding parties. Based on these photographs and their known areas of operation, we had recruited really tough groups of individuals, organized in teams of three or four, who were willing and able by virtue of prior residence to go into the areas in which we knew the Vietcong senior cadres were active and to see what could be done to eliminate them.

In Tay Ninh province I once choppered out to learn the progress of one of our local team efforts to regain control of the Black Virgin mountain, a physical promontory of religious significance to the Cao Dai, a closely knit religious sect of value to the Vietnamese government. While in Tai Ninh, my resident case officer hurriedly asked me to go with him to a nearby hamlet. There I was shown the bodies of the hamlet chief, his wife and two children, each under the age of ten, floating face down in a pond of water. The Vietcong had killed them all the previous evening, and the hamlet inhabitants were in such a state of shock they had not been able to bring themselves to remove the bodies from the pond. I despaired of ever being able to counteract this kind of influence on the population of the rural families of Vietnam, but thought about the work going on in Quang Ngai as our only hope for the future.

My God, I thought, we are finally finding the right solutions. In implementing them would our adversaries be the Vietcong or our own military establishment? It turned out to be both.

As the People's Actions Teams continued to roll out of Vung Tau and be deployed to Quang Ngai and to a couple of neighboring provinces as experiments, the good news continued to come back; their kill-ratio, to use an expression anathema to Americans today, was exceedingly high; their casualty record and loss of weapons was minute. Vietnamese province chiefs and MACV sector advisers were enthusiastic beyond our expectations.

The reaction in Saigon was not what I had anticipated. When I say the reaction in Saigon, I really mean to say the reaction at MACV. There the word was generally confused. "All right, that's all very well, but we can do better." That seemed to be the general response as the CIA station reported the results of its work to the embassy and to MACV, the information being simultaneously reported to Washington.

A great difficulty was developing, one which I and my colleagues could easily discern. I am now talking about the early winter of 1964, the time when the first serious plans were being drawn up to introduce American combat troops into Vietnam. The Presidential election was over, President Johnson had been elected, and political problems had receded. No longer did one have to say that the war was being contained, the Vietcong being defeated, and that there was light at the end of the tunnel.

One of the principal and ominous developments of 1964 was the growing ability of the Vietcong to fight battalion-size ARVN units. By midsummer 1964, several such confrontations had taken place, and while the ARVN forces were not driven from the field, they nevertheless suffered heavy losses. Of greater importance and significance was the wiliness of the Vietcong, really units of the regular North Vietnamese army. Infiltration of both men and equipment from North Vietnam had accelerated and NVA (North Vietnamese Army) cadres were increasingly to be found in Vietcong guerrilla units. Further, a few units, lifted directly out of the NVA, had come down the Ho Chi Minh trail in Laos and were positioning themselves in the rugged and generally uninhabited mountains of the Vietnamese central highlands. From these mountain redoubts, they would debouch to the east out of the mountains, down onto the piedmont, and from there drop down to the populated and cultivated flatlands in the east, all the way to the South China Sea. In the flatlands, they would engage ARVN units at will, and would relieve the farm population of money, food, and manpower. Once on the lowlands, and in touch with local Vietcong elements, they would also absorb the intelligence needed to strike at local Vietnamese Army or security forces.

The winter of 1964 saw the birth of more than a score of new People's Action Teams. All had been recruited in various districts of Quang Ngai province and, in what was becoming established doctrine, had been returned to their home districts for work. Their successes continued. They were increasingly respected and relied upon by the province chief. Their accomplishments were having a real impact on the Ministry of Interior in Saigon and were increasingly a topic of conversation in the embassy and at MACV headquarters. The Vung Tau camp functioned smoothly and attracted a stream of visitors (probably including some Vietcong), so many in fact that Major Mai (we had finally gotten him promoted) established a small office of his own that did nothing but escort visitors and give briefings on the PAT program. Mai had grown enormously in initiative and authority. His corps of instructors were completely dedicated to him and to the goals of the program. More than one of them said to me that, for a change, the Americans were finally giving the Vietnamese authority and responsibility, as well as providing financial and material support, and were not forever looking over their shoulders and telling them what to do. The 5,000-man camp was filling, though far from full, with team recruits to be trained and indoctrinated. I stationed three officers in Vung

Tau to give Major Mai and the entire training program strong and prompt U.S. support and to relay to our office in Saigon their needs when outside help was needed.

One day in Saigon I got a phone call from the number-two man in the Australian Embassy, whose office happened to be in the Caravelle Hotel. He had an Aussie major general with him who wanted to see me. At my office, this impressive and intelligent person said his government had heard of the PAT program and wanted to offer six army officers to the CIA station to assist in the program, both at Vung Tau and in the provinces. They felt the experience might later be valuable when their country disengaged from Papua, New Guinea. We had a long conversation about the complexities of such an arrangement. We devised ways around them and six junior officers selected by the general were to be sent at once from Australia, attached to the Australian Embassy in Saigon, and detailed to my office. This was accomplished in the late fall and winter of 1964. The officers were impressive, alert, and highly perceptive regarding the doctrines that governed the PAT program. I assigned four of them to our group at Vung Tau; the other two went to our base in Quang Ngai province. Before I left Vietnam, the Australians had become so enthusiastic about the experience they were getting they requested permission to detail six additional officers to our station. They were all top-flight officers and made outstanding contributions to our efforts, which I warmly remembered when we were posted to Canberra in 1971.

While the PAT program had become our major endeavor in the provinces, our other activities continued. Our counterterror teams grew slightly in number, but were modified in combat use so as to reinforce the PAT program. Our censusgrievance teams constituted a program that was unobtrusive but of considerable value. There were small teams of Vietnamese trained at Vung Tau who then circulated in the hamlets and villages on the outskirts of Vietcong-dominated territory, calling on the families, inquiring as to the composition of each household, asking about problems or grievances villagers had with regard to local administration and local authority, and reporting their findings to district and province authorities. What was of greater importance, however, was the increasingly evident fact that a grievance or injustice reported to these teams resulted in corrective action being taken *by Vietnamese*, a rare experience for most Vietnamese, whose usual contact with the authorities was limited to the tax collector and the policeman.

We saw this, as did a growing number of local authorities along with Interior Ministry officials, as the beginnings of a real rural revolution in Vietnam, which would affect, as time passed, the entire structure of Vietnamese society. These activities constituted the beginning of a fundamental social change. They started with the lowest unit—the family—and worked up through a cluster of families to the hamlet, then to the village and on up to the district. I often wondered at the fact that I, a CIA officer, had become so deeply involved. I thought of the relatively simple days of espionage and counterespionage in Central Europe, only to remind myself that everything we were doing in Vietnam was occasioned by one basic need: access to the information in the mind of practically every peasant in the countryside of Vietnam, plus his willingness to cooperate actively with his Vietnamese authority.

The peasant was both the problem and the solution, and the continuing successes of the PAT program repeatedly demonstrated how right we were in this appraisal. More and more frequently, sector advisers (military officers detailed to the provinces to MACV) dropped by our offices in the embassy to tell us how well the teams were working, how valuable their efforts were, and inquiring as to what they themselves could do to help further. There was one disturbing note: many of these sector advisers would close our meeting with the remark that they would prefer that no one at MACV knew they had come to see me, as some people did not think too well of the PATs because they were run by the CIA.

During the summer of 1964, there had been a strategy and high policy meeting at Camp Smith just outside Honolulu. I had attended most of the sessions, accompanying Ambassador Taylor in the aircraft President Johnson had sent for him. Secretary McNamara and an extensive party had come from Washington to attend the conference. Bill Colby was there from our Headquarters and we had the opportunity to review our own activities. The PAT program was really just getting underway, but Bill saw its significance at once and assured me the fullest support in money, matériel, and manpower.

As 1964 came to an end, Westy and I found an occasion when

we could sit quietly and review the events of the year, especially since his assumption of command during the previous summer. The war had been going badly, a fact which Westy reluctantly admitted—although with the Presidential elections behind us, the way stood open for a massive infusion of American combat power into the Vietnam fight.

I noted a general sensitivity and wariness on the part of some of his senior staff when now and then our conversations touched on the PAT program. I asked him if he had also noted this and, if he had, what was the reason for it. He thought for a moment and chose his response with care: "Let me emphasize one point. Your PAT program is fine and I think CIA deserves a lot of credit for originating it and finding the right Vietnamese to adopt and support it." He shifted around a bit and went on. "The program is so good that it should be expanded many times over, but that leads us into a problem. As you know, I and my staff deal with the matter of Vietnamese manpower acquisition in the form of the draft and the allocation of this manpower into the ARVN, Vietnamese Air Force, Navy units, and the Regional and Popular Forces. We also deal with the Interior Ministry concerning the amount of manpower needed to keep the National Police up to strength and, in some cases, to enlarge it. Now, here comes the PAT. Most of us at MACV agree that although it is new, it is increasingly successful and effective and may provide the key to a Vietnamese problem we haven't been able to lick. But the PAT team needs manpower and that has already been apportioned out to the elements I have named. Two questions come out of this: manpower for the PAT program must be carved out of somebody else's hip. O.K., whose? Then, and this may be the toughest question of all, which American element is best suited to support the Vietnamese in their development of the PAT program? CIA or MACV? These are the problems bothering us and I'm sure they're bothering you as well."

We both fell silent for a moment, although I was glad General Westmoreland had finally come to the understanding his remarks indicated. I told him I would like to think this over for a few days, commune with my Headquarters about this conversation, and arrange for another talk with him. We agreed to meet soon; he left my office and I fell to writing a detailed cable to Headquarters concerning our conversation.

* * *

I should have mentioned before that on 21 April 1964 Marilyn gave birth to our only daughter, Catherine. Usually expectant American mothers went to a French clinic in Saigon or, in cases where there were known problems, to the hospital at Clark Field in the Philippines. There were no American military facilities for maternity cases in South Vietnam and the doctor at the Naval dispensary recommended that Marilyn go to the Seventh-Day Adventist Hospital, which was on one of the main thoroughfares between our home and Tan Son Nhut.

The Seventh-Day Adventist Church, along with several other Christian faiths, has traditionally been engaged in missionary work abroad. This work usually fell into two categories: teaching and medicine. The hospital was small and crowded, consisting of three stories. The lower floor held a few offices and a waiting room. Above were the wards, a nursery and two tiny private rooms with air conditioning, in each of which were squeezed a bed, table, bureau, and a chair. The room which Marilyn occupied adjoined a large operating room. The nurses were mainly Filipinos. The head of the hospital was a Dr. Ray Smith, on his missionary assignment for the Seventh-Day Adventist Church.

In the room's only window was the air-conditioner, which had only two knobs, one for off and one for on. The on position would produce an icy blast and the off position allowed the room to revert at once to the humid heat of Saigon. The wards on the floor were filled with Vietnamese mothers, having perhaps the only vacation they were ever to have in their lives.

In Korea there had also been a Seventh-Day Adventist Hospital to which Koreans gained admission by professing to be Christians; they were genially referred to by the American medical staff as "rice Christians."

The head of the Naval hospital, Commander Johnson, a good friend of Dr. Smith, and about to return to the United States to a private practice in obstetrics, assisted in the delivery of our daughter. It was found that two pints of a rare type of blood would be needed and our good friend Nan Riordan volunteered. The recovery was uneventful and we were grateful for the excellent care and dedication of these doctors.

With Marilyn and the three children in Baguio, I remained in Saigon rattling around in a large house with a full staff of attentive servants. Beset by loneliness and the press of work, I was seldom in the house except to sleep and occasionally to eat.

Most of my waking hours were spent at the embassy or on field trips; not a few of them were spent in my communications shack, writing cables late at night or reading those that had come in from Headquarters.

Although everyone in the station had worked long, hard hours in the past, it was not until the evacuation of families that nonstop work began. There was really nothing else to do and Lord knows there was enough work to be done. I began locking my office door on Saturday night when I went home, so that on Sunday I would be forced to fish into my pocket for the key, to remind myself it was Sunday, and that another week was finished. Time wore on and the war continued to deteriorate, but the PAT program continued to be the bright hope for the future. Long-laid plans to bring American ground combat forces to South Vietnam came into play, and several U.S. Marine battalions, which had been circling in their transports near Danang, made their appearance on the beach and their presence felt in the Danang area. Meanwhile, U.S. Air Force fighter bombers joined those from the carriers of the Seventh Fleet, which were beginning to pound the southern areas of North Vietnam, as the war expanded.

I knew, from my membership on the Mission Council, that American Infantry divisions were already en route from the jungle training camps in the Hawaiian Islands and I thought soberly of the time when these young men from the Midwest, the Eastern and Western seaboards, and the South would be brought ashore to the environment and terrain of South Vietnam, to find and fight the Vietcong. Although there were already U.S. Marines ashore and engaged in combat in the First Corps area beyond Danang, I personally was spared the experience of vicariously suffering through the period when U.S. Army divisions were first committed into the Vietnam war. I was spared that experience by undergoing one of my own which, given a choice, I would have foregone.

During January 1965, I made a quick trip to Washington, where I visited my own Headquarters, the State Department, the Pentagon, and certain people on McGeorge Bundy's staff in the basement of the White House—the so-called Situation Room.

The main purpose of my trip, besides listening to official Washington, was to explain firsthand, as vividly as I could, the

PAT program, its doctrine, its successes, and its future. From my earlier conversation with General Westmoreland, I had realized that he, on behalf of the U.S. military, would sooner, rather than later, seek control over the entire program, claiming that it was too large for CIA to handle, too "military" in concept for the American civilian AID program to direct, and beyond the ability of the Vietnamese themselves. I hoped, during this visit, to set a backfire to this anticipated threat to the only viable U.S.-supported, armed effort against the Vietcong infrastructure in the Vietnam countryside that had yet been developed. At CIA Headquarters at Langley, the reaction to the PAT program had already been stated by Bill Colby; favorable, full-steam ahead, don't worry about funding. Advance word about the program had reached the State Department and the basement of the White House, where there was considerable interest, curiosity, and enthusiasm. The Pentagon was somewhat more distant and reserved, reflecting, I felt sure, the kind of reporting from MACV that could be expected in the light of Westmoreland's year's-end comments to me.

We in CIA felt at the time that our appraisal of the situation in Vietnam was the right one and that our approach to the Vietcong problem was substantially correct. Conversely, we felt that MACV in appraising the situation in South Vietnam in purely military terms was off on the wrong track. However, the massive nature of MACV's resources and influence left CIA anguished and impotent. Though we never stopped trying, our efforts to change the course of action being taken by MACV were rather like trying to stop the inexorable advance of a glacier.

The total mood about Vietnam in Washington was one of gloom. American troops and airpower were on the way and it was, interestingly enough, assumed that this tragic policy decision would soon put all Vietnamese matters on the right track and bring the war to a prompt conclusion. The anticipation of the arrival of American ground forces and air forces in considerable power provided a kind of upbeat note at the close of my visit to Washington; I flew to San Francisco and took the next flight out to Saigon.

In Saigon the CIA station was functioning at high speed and I dug into the work backlog that had accumulated during my absence of less than a week. One Saturday morning, I caught a ride to Clark Field and on to Baguio to visit my family. They had settled into a routine, with the help of Connie, our Filipino housekeeper, and I went back the next day at peace, except for the return flight. General Joseph Moore, in charge of the Seventh Air Division, based in Saigon, had been at a staff meeting at Clark Field in the Philippines, and I flew back with him in his T-Bird. It was a high-performance aircraft which Joe enjoyed flying himself. As we took off from Clark, he sat in the left-hand seat, handling the throttles and controls during takeoff, while the Air Force captain in the right-hand seat unobtrusively extended his left hand to cover Joe's right hand during adjustments, throttle movements, and takeoff maneuvers, rather apprehensively, I thought.

We were soon airborne and climbing to ten thousand feet over Clark Field when the jet outside my window gave a thunderous clang and stopped dead. Joe got us back to Clark Field, and as we landed, the chief of maintenance pulled up beside us in his jeep. They unbuckled an aluminum panel of the ailing engine, removed it, and about twenty pounds of aluminum and steel litter dropped out onto the concrete parking area. The chief, wearing an embarrassed look, said another T-38 was being wheeled out. We transferred to this aircraft, Joe gave me a thumb's-up gesture, and we were soon on the ground at Tan Son Nhut.

Life and work in Saigon became a blur. One day slid into the next, reports from our field elements were optimistic, yet the military conflict continued to deteriorate. There was literally no time to think—only to work and act. One day, which began the same as any other, this came to an end. During the morning of 30 March 1965, I took a short break to go to a shop on Tu Do Street, called Tanh Ly, to buy some ceramic elephants which Marilyn had wanted and I had long intended to get. From Tanh Ly, I went back to the embassy and up to my office. It was about eleven in the morning when I phoned one of my section chiefs in an embassy annex, located down the side street which ran under my office windows. Paul answered the phone and I stood there talking, my foot on the low windowsill, looking absently down into the street one floor below, paralleling that side of the embassy. Perpendicular to it, going toward the canal leading to Cholon, the Chinese section of Saigon, ran another narrow street. On the right-hand corner was a small Vietnamese restaurant, with the usual outdoor tables where one could go for tea. Many weeks before, after the bombing under the Brinks Hotel, wooden road barricades had been set up around the perimeter of the embassy to prevent automobiles from being parked along the sidewalks by the embassy. Additional Saigon policemen were on duty in front of the embassy, along the streets bordering the embassy and below my office windows.

Gazing out casually, I noticed an old gray Peugeot sedan being pushed up to a position directly beneath my window. The Vietnamese at the wheel got out, the person pushing the car, also a Vietnamese, walked up the side street past the corner restaurant, and the policeman on the sidewalk below walked out to the curb. The driver raised the hood of the car, peered in at the engine, and began to argue with the policeman, who was armed with an M-1 carbine. Suddenly, I saw it. Looking from my window down into the Peugeot, I saw, jammed between the back of the driver's seat and the seat itself, what we in the trade call a time pencil. This is a detonating device, consisting of a brass tube, pencil size, filled with an ignition powder. At one end of the tube is a detonator and at the other end is a knurled ring, which, when ground around, ignites a powder train which circles around down the time pencil to the detonator. The brass cylinder, pierced along its length to allow oxygen for combustion, emitted thin gray smoke as the powder train burned down toward the detonator.

That is what I saw, the time pencil and the gray smoke emerging from the ports. My world turned to glue and slow motion as my mind told me this car was a bomb. With the phone still in my hand and without conscious thought, I began falling away from the window and turned as I fell, but I was only halfway to the floor when the car exploded with 350 pounds of C-4 plastic explosives packed into its frame.

I remember an enormous thud, which has since reminded me of being inside a base drum when it was beaten heavily. My next conscious thought, apparently a few seconds later, was being on my hands and knees next to my desk, facing away from the window. My hands, buried in rubble and glass, were bleeding; I knew there had been a bomb and my first thought was, is there to be another one? My eyes could distinguish nothing and what I could see appeared only as light filtered through a red screen. My face, my throat, and chest were warm and wet. I groped on the floor and found some shreds from the curtains and covered my head and what seemed to be a gaping wound in my throat.

My upper lip was folded down over my lower lip and my left ear was hanging. Other aches and pains didn't manifest themselves until later. Using the curtain, I stuffed it against my throat, struggled to my feet, and stumbled across my office floor which was littered with masonry and debris to the doorless doorway. At that moment, one of my station officers, Herb, came in, grabbed me, and sat me down on the open balcony walkway overlooking the inner courtyard of the embassy.

Unable yet to think clearly, I sat there until Herb helped me up and led me down the stairs to the embassy entrance. Although my eyes were filmed over with blood, I could tell I was being led past a couple of stretchers on which women's forms lay. I later found that one of them was one of my secretaries, Barbara Robbins, who was dead. Outside the embassy, confusion reigned. Sirens and ambulance bells could be heard in every direction. I simply stood there and waited to be told what to do. Again, we all seemed to be waiting for a second bomb. Luckily, there was none. Helpful hands put me into the back of a sedan and I was off. I heard a voice tell the driver to take me to the Navy dispensary, the only U.S. medical facility in town.

In retrospect I think it must have been strange to Vietnamese along the sidewalk as they saw an American sedan draw up to a stoplight and then drive on, the occupant of the back seat sitting quietly erect and drenched with blood. The driver gently but unceremoniously unloaded me in the driveway of the dispensary, where I was to wait for medical attention along with other victims of the bombing. I sat there trying to think of who I was when someone took me by the elbow and steered me into the building. There I was placed on a bed and told to lie still; I would soon be seen by a doctor. I couldn't see but could hear the murmur of urgent voices as people were brought in, placed on beds, cleaned, and made ready for treatment by Navy medical officers.

Lying there waiting, I began to hurt. No sooner had that reaction occurred than an attendant came in and filled me full of Demerol. The world at once became blissful. I then tried to figure out what had happened, but not being able to see was the worst thing, and I lay there helplessly. There were other voices in the room and I recognized one of them as that of my secretary, Rhody, who was apparently being seen by a nurse. I remember the nurse telling her to sit up on the bed so that her dress and slip could be cut off before the doctor examined her, and Rhody replying in effect, "You can't do that, you can't do that. It's a brand-new slip and I just got it from Hong Kong." This was followed by a firm male voice telling her to lift her hips so they could cut the skirt off. Rhody's voice answered obediently, "Yes, sir." Shortly after that I became aware of someone dabbing my eyes with liquids and pads; bright light began to pour in on me accompanied by acute pain. I could discern nothing, but at least now there was a white haze. I lay quietly. Soon a man and a woman were at my bedside and asked if I could see anything. I told them I could see only light and a red mist. They murmured and I felt more liquids going into my eyes and then bandages being placed on them and being taped down. The Demerol squad came around, stabbed me once again in the hip, and I receded into another world.

My next recollection was of waking up. It was apparently still the same day, but I had been moved to another bed in the same room. With both eyes patched over, I could only assume what was happening. Voices came and went with varying degrees of urgency and all I knew was that I hurt. I had been bombed as so many others had been. I was offered food, wanted none, and was periodically stuck with the Demerol needle. Someone came and sewed on my lip and ear and told me that during the evening my throat wounds "and others" would be taken care of. There was no immediate danger. I remember these things though I don't remember saying anything, but do recall an urgent conversation at the foot of my bed to the effect that I should be moved to a private room, that I was a "special case," and should not be left in a ward. I was moved and later wheeled into a treatment room, where they began repairing my throat, through which chunks of metal had passed at the time of the explosion. I listened to the doctors as they hummed and murmured while probing into the open areas of my throat, I being blissfully and painlessly protected by the liberal application of Novocain. They removed the glass and metal and sewed everything up nice and tight.

Several days later when the stitches were removed, one of the doctors told me that when they had examined me, they had found my carotid artery, white and pulsing, exposed for about an inch and a half. He told me the only reason he could figure why I was alive was that when the metal went through my throat, the artery momentarily was not distended by a pulse, but relaxed during the resting phase. Had the artery been distended and nicked by the shrapnel, the doctor cheerily observed, curtains for me. I believe I dozed off as he was talking to me.

Back in my bed the Demerol man came around again and that was it until the next day, when I felt better physically and wanted desperately to let Marilyn know I was all right, having no idea what kind of information had reached her. That night a kindly Navy nurse arranged a telephone patch via the military radio telephone system to Manila and my call was passed on to Baguio, where I was finally able to speak with Marilyn. Still unable to see, I told her I was fine. Strangely, she had been one of the first to hear of the bombing, as she had tuned in to the eleven-thirty news and the events of the previous half hour were already on the air. She immediately went to tell Chris, the wife of one of my officers, George, who lived in the apartment below us and they managed to reach our office staff in Manila, who until then had no idea of what had happened in Saigon. They called back to say that all the lines to Saigon were down and they would let them know when it was possible to get through. Meanwhile, George had managed to call and say that everything was all right and I only had a few scratches.

I remained in the Saigon dispensary about five days. My thoughts were with the CIA station, the embassy, and other victims of the bombing. Rhody had been badly wounded and two of my officers, Don and Bob, were permanently blinded. The Vietcong who had set off the time pencil had been killed by the policemen, who in turn lost their lives in the blast. More than fifteen Vietnamese passersby and customers sitting in the restaurant across the street had been killed by the explosion, which ripped a hole more than four feet deep in the concrete beneath my window.

In the private room in the dispensary to which I was assigned (because of secrets I knew and might reveal under anesthetics) I lay for five days and nights, my eyes patched up except for a daily examination by a Vietnamese lady ophthalmologist. I was not otherwise really hurt or injured and quickly figured out a method of tying towels leading from my bed to the bathroom—I had a private bathroom—so that I could find my way without assistance. Someone had to feed me.

I was hoping that I would be able to remain in Saigon until I had recovered and then return to work. I was suddenly visited by the chief of the medical service and told I would be transferred to Clark Field for an overnight stay en route to Washington to Bethesda Naval Hospital in Maryland for further treatment. Over my protests, he calmly informed me that I had a very bad problem with my left eye and could easily develop a similar problem with my right eye. There was no way to take care of my eyes in Saigon. In a flurry of closing activity—every day I had station officers come to talk to me—I finished off some unraveled edges of station business and turned the station over to my Deputy, Gordon. Next day I was taken to Tan Son Nhut and put on a medical evacuation plane.

The flight went from Tan Son Nhut to Danang, where wounded Marines were put on board, destined for Clark Field. The plane was fitted for litter cases of which I was one and at Danang the additional patients were loaded, including a Marine who had been gut-shot only a few hours before. He was in great pain, and while the flight nurses did their best to ease his pain, his groans showed there was only so much that Demerol could do.

I was put into a private room at the Clark Field hospital and was told my wife and son were driving down from Baguio and would be in to see me that evening. I was in little pain and most of my stitches had been removed but I still looked a pitiful sight to Marilyn and Perry. They remained for only a short time, but came back again the next morning to visit until it was time for us all to be loaded on the evacuation plane for the States. We talked and she took photos; my son, looking at me covered with cuts and stitches all over my head, face, and chest, wondered what was going on.

John McCone had arranged a special medical evacuation flight non-stop for injured CIA station personnel from Clark Field to Davis Monthan Field in California, a flight that was to be the most depressing I've had in all my years of flying. My eyes patched up, I could see nothing, and as the motors roared and we rose into the air, I thought about my friends aboard the aircraft and wondered what would happen to them. We flew on and on over the Pacific. I had begun to appreciate flight nurses by the time we sailed in to land at Davis Monthan Field, remaining only long enough to refuel for the flight to Andrews Air Force Field near Washington, D.C. There the patients were unloaded, some to go to Walter Reed and the others to Bethesda

Naval Hospital. Heavily sedated, I was taken to a single room in the tower of the hospital.

The stay at Bethesda was uneventful and for some reason I felt almost unconcerned about my sight, confident it would return. Bill and Barbara Colby came to see me, as well as Marshall and Lisa Green, with whom we had served in Korea and again in Hong Kong when Marshall had been consul-general. In my patched-up condition I could see no one and could only imagine what they thought of me. Agency people came to visit, along with my good friend George and his daughter Eva. Every day I was loaded onto a Gurney transporter (eye cases are thought to be sensitive to motion and jarring) and taken to the eye clinic.

Every morning the nurse would ask me to get out of bed so they could "clean it." I found out from one of the nurses that I had been peppered through with glass and metal and every night I would shed some of this material, which they would sweep from the sheets the next day.

During the explosion, a piece of metal had penetrated my left chest; the wound had been promptly sewn up. Weeks later at Bethesda, this bit of metal had found its way, under my skin, to my right side, where it was excised by the doctors.

There were three girls from the Saigon office who had been very seriously wounded and were recovering in other rooms in the hospital. As soon as I had walking privileges, I went to visit them, finding them in depressed spirits. The senior nurse on my floor, an attractive blond, came into my room one morning to report excitedly that Cabot Lodge was on his way to visit me. He was escorted to my room attended by perhaps fifteen fluttering nurses. We talked briefly about Vietnam but could only commiserate about the way things were going in southeast Asia. Being a "walking wounded" I was able to accompany Ambassador Lodge on his visit to our three girls in the hospital. After being led back to my room, we had a glass of orange juice and the nurses, still excited by the visit of this truly handsome man, walked him to the elevator.

Being bandaged and unable to see began to get to me. My eyes couldn't see, but my mind could and my brain conjured up visions of past events as vividly as though I were actually witnessing them. To make matters worse, I couldn't turn them off; I couldn't will them to go away. I very often had a nonstop technicolor movie running before my mind's eye, an expression I came to understand.

One morning two of the eye doctors came to my room, removed the eye patches, and gave me a thorough examination. After talking together, they said the eye patches were no longer necessary, my condition had improved greatly, and while I had to remain in the hospital, I could get up and move around on my own whenever I wished. The doctors further informed me that while at the moment there was some vision in my left eye, that eye would almost certainly go blind in the next few months. I would need glasses to give me effective vision in the right eye. I asked when I could go back to Saigon; this question produced a conference, and the result was that they would check to see if there was a qualified ophthalmologist in Saigon or at Clark Field; they would let me know. The next day they told me there was an ophthalmologist at Clark Field and in two weeks I would be released and allowed to return to Saigon, on the understanding that I would see the ophthalmologist at Clark at least once a week. Considering myself fortunate, I put on a dressing robe and went down to see the three girls, still there. They were mending well, their spirits had improved, and they were having minor cosmetic treatment to eliminate facial scars. We talked about Ambassador Lodge's visit; he had clearly excited all three, as he had electrified the entire nursing staff on my floor. The girls themselves were mending nicely, and were to go on a month's sick leave before returning to duty at CIA Headquarters.

Every day from then on an officer from the agency came to brief me on developments concerning the war in Vietnam. When needed, a secretary would appear for stenographic work, and slowly I got back into the routine of working, sitting cross-legged on the hospital bed. During my last few days in the hospital I was allowed to dress and to walk about the hospital grounds. I had frequent telephone conversations with Bill Colby as I made ready to check out and to go back to Vietnam. I had been fitted with eyeglasses by the hospital, and my good eye, the right one, had improved tremendously and was back to normal; the left eye was steadily becoming dimmer and dimmer.

Sharon, a daughter of my first marriage, was working and living not far from Bethesda while her husband was in military service; she had visited me several times during my stay in the hospital. On the day I was turned loose, she picked me up and drove me to Dulles airport where we had coffee until my flight to San Francisco was called. In San Francisco I saw my brother, my mother, and my oldest daughter, Robin, catching up on news and showing them I was still able to maneuver. Eager to get back to Marilyn and the children, I was relieved to settle back in my seat that night on the Pan Am clipper to Manila.

Our station in Manila had a car and driver waiting for me at the airport which took me to Clark, where I checked in at the eye clinic. The ophthalmologist saw me briefly and commented that my eyes seemed not to have changed but asked that I come back in ten days for a thorough examination. Then back to the car for the drive through the mountains to Baguio, to Marilyn and the children.

It was four weeks to the day when I returned to Saigon. While in Baguio I had several telephone conversations with my deputy, Gordon, who arranged to have a T-Bird jet pick me up at Clark Field for my return flight to Saigon.

At thirty thousand feet and five hundred knots an hour, we approached the Vietnam coast in the vicinity of Nha Trang. As we neared Tan Son Nhut, I realized how much I had missed Vietnam and the Vietnamese people, and my work there. They had trusted us and we had come only to wag fingers at them and lecture them and cluck disapprovingly when they acted like Vietnamese. As we flew over the South China Sea, I mused about the characteristics of the Americans. At home we endured political scandal, Joe McCarthy, and Communist influence in high places. Our home-grown faults were enormous, pervasive; only the wealth of our national resources, our population, and our democratic initiatives had saved us from political extinction. However true that might be, as a people we almost never dwelt on our own faults; as soon as we crossed the twelve-mile limit, especially going east to the Orient, our political standards and requirements of conduct soared to heights we had never ourselves attained.

With a moralizing confidence I found to be revoltingly smug, we had criticized the Koreans for being Koreans, the Chinese for being Chinese, and now the Vietnamese for being Vietnamese. The American official posted in Asia very often finds himself, whether he realizes it or not, standing solemnly before the Asians, his finger pointed skyward and the word "repent" on his lips. I thought ruefully of the expression sometimes attributed to the American missionaries in Korea: "They came to do good; they certainly did well." Our efforts in Asia had by and large proved to be grotesque. We had come to help them and instead had given the kindness of the Russian bear. We had embraced them to the point of suffocation, all the while demanding that they act like us. When they stumbled, made mistakes, and otherwise acted in ways of which we disapproved, our forefinger shot heavenward and we would say, "You're not listening." Dear God, would we ever learn?

Once more the coastline of South Vietnam drifted under our wing and we began to lose altitude for the approach to Saigon. The emerald paddies marked off in squares by the earthen dikes, the reddish dirt, the brown thatched roofs of hamlets and villages, all unrolled beneath me as we approached Tan Son Nhut for the customary steep dive which was the landing pattern (don't give anyone time to set you up as a target). We whistled over the runway, touched down lightly, and taxied off to the CIA parking area. There, Gordon and Gil Strickler awaited me.

On the ride back to town, I was filled in about station business and the state of the war. We stopped by my house to drop off my bags on the way to the embassy. Gordon, at my suggestion, had already moved in to share the house with me, the wives being gone. I had asked that all of my household effects be shipped back to Washington, being prepared to live in the large villa on a Spartan basis.

Therefore, I found all of our furniture and effects in the process of being packed and crated. Ba and Duc were there to greet me, grinning broadly, and asking about "Madam." The three of us, Gordon, Strick, and I, sat in the study and talked about station business as we sipped lemonade. Strick pointed out that he had arranged for a display in my home of some sixteen Vietnamese ceramic elephants, as he thought I would like to ship some home. I asked him to pick out any two that he thought we might like. When we later unpacked back in the States, all sixteen elephants emerged.

At the embassy the afternoon was spent in checking in with Ambassador Taylor and others in the embassy and calling on station officers to bring them up-to-date on the wounded remaining hospitalized back in the States.

The month of May 1965 was depressing and discouraging. The station programs upcountry (the PATs, the census grievance, the counter-terror), were all progressing with great success, especially the PAT program, which all other station programs in the countryside were now supporting. In addition to Marines, U.S. Army Infantry divisions had entered South Vietnam, with more to come. Still, the overall situation was deteriorating rapidly. The war was being heightened, tragically, and at the same time Americanized. My Vietnamese friends were disturbed and uneasy, as they saw their own dignity and sense of authority gradually being eroded as the American military establishment began to exercise ever greater authority. In a manner of speaking, General Westmoreland had come to sit at the head of the Vietnam table. His ARVN colleagues sat along the table, mostly below the salt. The loss of fifty thousand American dead, and the Vietnam War itself, had begun.

During May, I made two trips away from Saigon to check on the performance of the PATs. I went to the delta, working out of My Tho from where we had launched several PAT teams during my stay in the hospital. My other trip was to Quang Ngai to inspect the strongly reinforced PAT program. I was overjoyed to find that PAT teams were taking the initiative away from the Vietcong. Nothing ever made me happier. I went to Vung Tau to talk with Major Mai, the moving spirit behind the whole program at that point.

Per instructions I made a weekly visit to Clark to see the ophthalmologist. Finally, about the first of June 1965, he informed me of a continuing deterioration in my left eye and said that, on balance, I would be better off back in the States where the remaining right eye might be better protected. Cable traffic went back and forth while these appraisals were being judged and decisions made. I was then instructed to turn over the station to Gordon, collect my family, and return to Headquarters.

Leaving Vietnam was wrenching. I knew that Westmoreland and MACV had put their sights on the PAT program with an eye to taking it over completely, making it a military endeavor and, in order to produce more forty-man teams, drastically cutting back on the motivational and political training, which was the fundamental reason for the program's success to begin with. Having made my views on this score known to our headquarters, I went back to Baguio. We sailed on the *President Wilson* from Manila on 12 June 1965 for San Francisco.

23 Vietnam Turning Point

Fifty thousand American dead. Several hundred thousand South Vietnamese dead, even more North Vietnamese also dead. How did this whole tragedy come about and how had it ended so fearfully? The well-known American correspondent Marguerite Higgins called it our Vietnam Nightmare; it was exactly that. I call it the only war we chose to fight, but lost. This particular memory of Vietnam is buried deep in the heart of America, deep in our psyche, deep and troubled in our subconscious. It is not an ordinary thing for Americans to lose at anything they set out to win. It is not only our desire to win, it is our confident expectation. In that sense, we are poor losers. But why did we lose? Not only did we lose, but the Vietnamese lost as well and all of this was done with the entire world as witness. Why?

Fundamentally we lost because we were arrogant, prideful, and dumb. If a Vietcong *can* lie for hours under water in a rice paddy, breathing air through a straw, so *can* we. This is what we were told by Robert Kennedy and by the President himself and by those who were at their elbows and before the press. The murder of the Kennedy brothers gives rise to sorrow, but the questions remain. The major decisions leading to the Vietnam tragedy were made by others who followed them, among whom are Robert McNamara, Maxwell Taylor, and General William Westmoreland. These men had no comprehension whatever of the kind of warfare with which they were faced or how to counter it. They were determined to fight the war the way they wished, not the way victory required. The nature of this requirement was not understood.

The war in Vietnam is over and there is no blinking the fact that we and the Vietnamese lost it. For the first time in our nation's history we engaged ourselves massively in an armed conflict, and lost. The Vietnamese lost even more: their sovereignty and their freedom. The Vietcong had soaked ever more extensively throughout the population of rural Vietnam, to the point where only sizable ARVN formations could move through the countryside with any safety. Increasingly, the people and the countryside belonged to the Vietcong, a fact which made it ever more possible for Vietcong main force units, and North Vietnam Army units who had come south, to move at will throughout all the populated areas of South Vietnam.

During 1964 and 1965 the CIA station and our Vietnamese counterparts in the Ministry of Interior and in the provincial and district headquarters had, almost by accident, happened on a formula consisting of a combination of local Vietnamese armed force and civic action, coupled with psychological indoctrination which was increasingly proving itself able to provide local security for villages and hamlets and which made it reasonable for the farmers in the countryside to cooperate willingly with the Vietnamese government grassroots program, working and growing from the family and hamlet level upward through the district level to the province capital. Perhaps the most heartening feature of this program was its indigenous quality; it consisted of Vietnamese who themselves were digging out of the Vietcong infrastructure, while the American side provided massive help with money, weapons, and supplies. It was the Vietnamese themselves who produced these irregular guerrilla teams, who trained and led them. The tremendous boost to Vietnamese morale continued to expand as the program expanded in 1965.

My deputy, Gordon, remained in Saigon, and after my family and I had left Manila for the States he was named station chief, a richly deserved promotion for a very able officer and a fine human being. Gordon continued the PATs program with effectiveness, extending it constantly throughout the year.

At Headquarters, my return coincided with the departure of John McCone as director of the CIA and the arrival on the scene of Admiral William Raborn, newly appointed by President Johnson. New to the intelligence team and new to the Vietnam problem, Admiral Raborn seized on me to establish a new office reporting directly to him, with the resounding title of "Special Assistant for Vietnam Affairs" (SAVA).

My wife and I bought a house not far from the agency at Langley and I set about my duties with some slight apprehen-

Vietnam Turning Point

sion; it had been over ten years since I had been assigned to Washington; these were now wartime years and the official State Department, White House, and Pentagon, with whom I had to establish myself, were, in the main, new to me. Admiral Raborn was a pleasure to work for: courteous, calm, informal, and very sharp. Midsummer 1965 saw the American military buildup in South Vietnam swelling in size from week to week. There was a succession of Vietnam governments, as political instability continued to plague the nation with unsettling effects on the Vietnam war effort, at a time when the Vietcong and North Vietnam Army elements in the south were growing in strength and in the quality of their armaments.

By early 1965 the complete picture of Vietcong insurgency seemed to consist of two distinct efforts. One was the Vietcong military apparatus, which was then being constantly stiffened and strengthened by the arrival of more and more units of the North Vietnamese army. This developing military structure was a well-equipped and experienced army, no longer simply bands of partisans. The second part of the insurgency consisted of the Vietcong infrastructure itself as opposed to the permanent armed units just mentioned. These were the activists, the tax collectors, the terrorists, and assassins, who extended their web of subversion throughout the countryside, family by family, hamlet by hamlet. The population of South Vietnam was inexorably being absorbed by the Vietcong insurgency.

The main American effort seems to have been one of constantly strengthening the Vietnamese armed forces and of course directing them from the national level. Relatively little emphasis had been given to Vietnamese civil agencies at the provincial and district level, where the pacification war was actually being fought.

The situation in the Vietnam countryside had become so serious that several simultaneous efforts had to be devoted to rescuing the people from being swallowed up by the Vietcong. First, the resupply and strengthening, with men or matériel, of the Vietcong insurgency from North Vietnam, entering South Vietnam from the Ho Chi Minh trail, clearly had to be stopped, severely curtailed, or made exceedingly dangerous for the north. Further, it was essential that the armed forces of South Vietnam be given whatever equipment and weapons necessary to assure them a flat and constant superiority over Vietcong main force units and North Vietnamese Army units. Lastly, the time seemed long overdue for the active involvement of the peasantry and others who lived in the countryside, in their own armed protection in a climate of growing mutual confidence between GVN elements active in each district of the country and the rural families among whom they lived.

To summarize, we in the CIA felt that our experiences in Quang Ngai and elsewhere in the north where the roots of Vietcong insurgency were embedded in the rural population constituted a threat and a problem which the armed forces of South Vietnam, and for that matter our own growing military strength, were ill-equipped to handle. We also saw the problem as being essentially civilian in composition and local in character and felt that only by working from the grassroots up would the South Vietnamese be able to win out over the growing Vietcong and the North Vietnamese Army presence in the south. However, the inevitable growing momentum of American military involvement brought about by the arrival of more and more infantry divisions worked against any concept of civilianizing the Vietnam war. Contrarily, it worked in favor of taking the road of imposing inflexible military decisions from above. Thus the war was bound to be Americanized with the Vietnamese feeling less and less involved and responsible in their own country.

The war ground on, many more thousands of American troops were dispatched to Vietnam, but there was no noticeable improvement in the Vietnamese or American position vis-à-vis the Vietcong. Casualties on both sides were mounting, but as 1966 drew to a close, one could detect in Washington, among the policy makers, the beginnings of unease with regard to a massive American military buildup. At the beginning of 1966 there were almost 200,000 American soldiers in Vietnam, plus strong Marine contingents, reinforced U.S. Air Force units, and the U.S. Seventh Fleet, almost daily involved in bombing forays against the north.

One day in January of 1966 Admiral Raborn called me to his office. As his special assistant for Vietnam affairs, he wanted me to go to Saigon, travel around the country as I saw fit, and come back with a firsthand report for his benefit. I spent two days in Honolulu en route, to get the general feeling of the Commander in Chief, Pacific (CINCPAC) staff on the current state of the war and to be brought up-to-date by our own CIA station there. My stop in Honolulu happened to coincide with a planned meeting involving General Westmoreland, General Thieu, and Air Marshal Ky, as well as Ambassador Lodge from Saigon, the CINCPAC commander, and Secretary McNamara, accompanied as usual by a full retinue from the Pentagon. At the last minute, President Johnson decided to attend the meeting, which became something of a summit conference. The purpose of the meeting was to bring everyone up-to-date on the state of the conflict and to consider both Vietnamese and American military force levels for the year ahead. The general problem of pacification and the fight against the Vietcong insurgency came up for thorough discussion at the Honolulu conference. With the exception of the ever-increasing successes of the PAT teams, the population of the Vietnam countryside was rapidly falling under Vietcong control. The one bright spot was the PATs. Although I was in Honolulu and available, and had volunteered to sit in on any meetings involving the PATs, the day they came under discussion on the Camp Smith agenda, it passed without my being asked to attend; I left the next day by plane on my trip to Saigon.

Two days in the station in Saigon brought me up-to-date on current affairs and I then borrowed an aircraft and an escort for a quick swing through the delta, then north up the coast to Danang and back down through the central highlands of Kon Tum and Pleiku. I spent my last evening with Gordon and other station officers and was on my way back to Washington the next day. There I prepared a written report for the director, which we discussed over lunch. Admiral Raborn shared my concern over the upcoming militarization of the PAT program under the control of MACV, but the Washington surge to concentrate more and more authority under our military presence in the country left him powerless; CIA could not prevent the shift which ultimately took place in November of 1966. By that time I was in Bangkok at our embassy, on a new assignment, listening sadly to the stories coming out of Saigon concerning the radical and disastrous reworking of the PAT program.

I realized then and am more convinced now that my fifteen months in Saigon from 1963 until the end of March in 1965 covered the critical decisions regarding the American conduct and participation in the Vietnam War. The succession of coups and constant political turmoil in Vietnam during 1964, following the overthrow and death of Diem in November 1963, had shaken the Vietnamese social and governmental structure so fundamentally and had confused it so thoroughly, the Vietcong efforts were enormously successful in pursuit of their fundamental goal: the overrunning of the bulk of the Vietnam rural population, and the destruction of U.S. morale and determination. In spite of increased armament and American support, ARVN had been stymied by the constantly shifting political alignment and structure in Saigon. These fifteen months saw the arrival of General Westmoreland, a soldier's soldier, who was determined to organize the war into a form militarily familiar to him, and gradually to move to the head of the American/Vietnam table to fight the war American-style. While Westy made all of the expected pronouncements to the effect that the war in South Vietnam was basically a political war and one the Vietnamese must fight themselves, he nevertheless had little patience for what he considered ARVN mistakes, or the fact that the Vietnam government and military had been virtually shattered by the fall of Diem and the coups that followed, and that the Vietnamese simply didn't act like Americans. Honest, courageous, but intellectually uninspired and short on imagination, he instinctively distrusted pacification efforts which he did not control, and also instinctively reached out to control them and make them conform to his military style of operation. The arrival of Maxwell Taylor in the summer of 1964 gave him easy and influential access to the source of all American authority in South Vietnam. At the Washington end of this command line, real authority regarding our role in Vietnam had been concentrated under Secretary of Defense Robert McNamara. McNamara seemed to have two main driving impulses: to support Ambassador Taylor and General Westmoreland's position and doctrine, and to please President Johnson at all costs, never mind dissimulation from time to time.

So much for 1964 and 1965. Certain other events transpired in 1966 and following which should be mentioned here, although I was not present in Saigon. The Honolulu conference of 1966 had really concentrated on the problem of pacification. The conferees had finally become enthusiastic about the success of the PATs and the Vung Tau training camp that produced these teams. But 1966 also saw the transfer of the pacification responsibility from civilian hands to MACV, a goal long sought by General Westmoreland. The same year saw the complete militarization of the PATs. The dispatch of Robert Komer, formerly an assistant to President Johnson for Vietnam matters, to Saigon to join General Westmoreland as a staff member of MACV, brought full American military influence to bear upon the program. The first thing that was done was to rename the program the "Revolutionary Development Program" and after briefly fooling around with a Vietnamese civilian ministry for Revolutionary Development, the entire effort was brought into the Vietnamese Ministry of Defense as the Revolutionary Development Directorate, which in practice functioned under MACV under Robert Komer, who headed a MACV staff section known as CORDS (Civil Operations and Revolutionary Development Support).

I couldn't help but be struck by the informal news that drifted my way from Saigon regarding this successor to the PAT program. Because the PATs had been so successful in the field, it was decided to scale up the rate of production of PAT teams and to increase them from forty to fifty-nine man teams. To do this, the new American Embassy team in Saigon scrutinized the training curriculum at Vung Tau, examined the staff of instructors under Major Mai, and came to the conclusion that the only thing to be done was to shorten the course of instruction and to spread the instructor teams more thinly over the Vietnamese undergoing training.

An important decision was made with regard to training and a tragically wrong one at that. To shorten the curriculum in order to put out more teams in the provinces, the trainee staff at Vung Tau was pressured by CORDs to cut back severely on the motivational and political training which we had earlier devised and which had proved to be the real mainspring behind the success of the PATs. The PATs had been fiercely loyal to their program, their province, and their district. Team members had come sincerely to believe that they must never molest the village women or steal food, but they must be of service and help to their neighbors and within their home districts must comport themselves as models fully devoted in their service to the people.

Under the influence of CORDs, the deletion of major parts of this motivational and doctrinal training rather quickly resulted in the production of Revolutionary Development teams whose performance, when once back in their home districts, began to slump sharply from the high standards of the PATs. While in the past there had been practically no desertions, there was now a rising incidence of desertion among the RD teams. The rapport with the farmers and villagers declined and the intelligence flow from the villagers to the RD teams began to dry up, as evidenced by the increasing incidence of Vietcong ambushes of the RD teams.

What had happened was that once the driving spirit of the PAT training program had been eviscerated; the teams were simply another form of rural militia, poorly motivated and increasingly ineffective. Sadly, I and others associated with the original program noted to ourselves, "There goes the best chance we and the Vietnamese ever had."

I later made a special trip to Saigon to talk with Komer about these disheartening developments. I was unable to get an appointment, and returned to Bangkok really depressed.

To take the ill-fated pacification program to its conclusion, there are a few points yet to be made. Under the direction of Robert Komer and under the aegis of the American military command in Vietnam, the RD effort went rapidly from bad to worse. By 1968, it bore no resemblance to the original PAT program, which it had absorbed early in 1967. It was no longer effective, was riddled with corruption, and was headed for an early grave, although the program dwindled on into the early 1970s when everything came to an end in April 1975.

Bill Colby was sent to Saigon to be Robert Komer's deputy in CORDs, but even this outstanding and imaginative officer found it difficult to regalvanize what had been a successful program. The decision in 1967 to reconstitute the program and place it under MACV control had been lethal. As a subordinate arm of the military effort, the program was doomed.

By 1968, the war against the Vietcong and their North Vietnam Army allies was deteriorating rapidly and spiraling downward. In these tragic months, Secretary of Defense Robert McNamara decided to leave the Vietnam problem to someone else (Clark Clifford) and accepted inconspicuous sanctuary as head of the World Bank. A clear and logical thinker, McNamara had made the fundamental mistake of assuming that the Vietcong and Hanoi behind them were just as rational as he himself was, and that once they saw they could not win would cease their aggression against South Vietnam. To this end, he tried every strategy a rational man could use: he supported the involvement of more than half a million American soldiers, and he vastly expanded the U.S. Air Force and the U.S. Seventh Fleet. Short of nuclear weapons, every form of modern armed assistance was provided to the Vietnamese and used by our own forces. And still the North Vietnamese came, ever stronger and ever more threatening. I rather think that, to this day, Robert McNamara cannot understand why, as rational people, the Vietcong and North Vietnam did not back away from the war. Because he had no appreciation of the irrational side of man, Robert McNamara failed.

Ambassador Maxwell Taylor had already departed the Vietnam scene in 1967, weary and unsure, baffled at not having presided over a victory. In 1968, having fought the good fight, but unsuccessfully, Westmoreland packed up and returned to Washington to assume the duties as chief of staff of the U.S. Army. His successor, General Creighton Abrams, intelligently and with resolution assumed the duties of ministering to the ailing condition of South Vietnam engaged in a truly mortal combat with the enemies from within and from the north. His patient was, however, irretrievably terminal, mainly, I believe, because of faulty decisions and policies of the past. The bravery of our soldiers, sailors, Marines, and airmen was never in doubt; their performance was outstanding. The fact that we had lost the war was clear to me and to many others, many of whom shared my views as to the reasons for the loss.

By the time the final days had arrived in April 1975, we had disengaged from the war not, I believe, only because the American homefront had rejected continuing the fight, but it had rejected the war because we were clearly losing it, without any prospect of winning.

The real losers, of course, are the people of South Vietnam. We failed ourselves and we failed them, and we failed the scores of thousands of Americans who died in the Vietnam venture and the scores of thousands who were disabled by it.

24 Plowing Back

My last years in the CIA, from 1966 until 1973, were spent in winding down from an active and complicated career. After the Vietnam experience there would be no new major assignments, no new great activities—the time of learning the craft of intelligence, for me, was over; it was now time to plow back into the agency some of the experience I had gained over the years and the lessons I had learned.

After being hospitalized for bomb injuries, I went back to Saigon briefly. Because the eye doctors required me to come back to Clark Field in the Philippines once a week, to see the only U.S. ophthalmologist available in the area, it came as no surprise to me when my left eye began to grow dim. The eye doctor recommended that I return to the States for more expert attention to be given to my good eye.

Thus August 1965 saw us once again in Washington where Admiral Raborn, the Director of Central Intelligence, assigned me to his staff as special assistant for Vietnamese affairs, a new function. The purpose of this staff office was to keep the admiral informed of developments in South Vietnam, the significance of these developments, and to inform him further of the likely courses to be expected in the struggle against the Vietcong.

The year that I spent in Washington, until the summer of 1966 coincided with the period of the growing American military buildup in Vietnam, accompanied by constant deterioration of our military and political fortunes in that unhappy country. During that year we saw the buildup of American military forces which would ultimately reach over half a million men and women, increasingly frustrated and baffled by our inability to achieve a clear-cut victory. What was achieved was disillusionment, frustration, and a growing war-weariness, accompanied by seemingly endless casualties, that provided the spawning ground for antiwar movements both in the United States and abroad. Unable to change or reverse the policy of Americanization of the Vietnam war, the CIA was inevitably carried along downhill with American military and civil reputations.

Only in Thailand was the CIA able to maintain an independent southeast Asia role of major influence in shaping Thai policies and doctrines as they dealt with a relatively small terrorist movement in their northeastern provinces. There the armed Communist subversive movement was largely confined to the mountainous provinces of the northeast; the movement itself was small in numbers, consisting mainly of small armed bands hiding out in the rugged, uninhabited uplands of the Phu Phan range from which they would occasionally launch themselves down onto the populated lowlands in search of rice, money, and manpower. The main characteristic of the Communist effort in this area was that it was not growing significantly; the armed bands were not able to move down from their mountain hideouts and lose themselves among the population in the farming areas.

Aided by my able and imaginative deputy, a Marine colonel, Richard Mample, we were able to persuade our Thai counterparts not to militarize their counterinsurgency effort. To be sure, armed force had to be used against the terrorists, but they quickly came to agree that their armed force must have a civilian coloration and leadership, to avoid the very faults and shortcomings that were even then making themselves so painfully and tragically apparent in South Vietnam. Mample and I had gained the confidence of Ambassador Graham Martin, who understood our approach to our Thai colleagues and agreed with it. He and I were in agreement on what had gone wrong in Vietnam and agreed that American policy in dealing with the Thais would be shaped under him in the embassy and not in the American military assistance command, MACTHAI. It was Martin who had personally requested my assignment to his embassy "on loan" from the CIA. We had gotten to know each other exceptionally well; our views of the insurgency in Thailand were in agreement, and our views as to what course the Thai should adopt in dealing with their insurgency corresponded in every significant aspect.

In the late summer of 1967, however, Ambassador Martin was transferred to become our ambassador in Rome. I at once missed his courage and perception in holding the line against the instinctive philosophy of the Pentagon that if weapons and shooting were involved in any southeast Asian situation, as they certainly were in Thailand, that the U.S. Army should run the show. Luckily, the Thais themselves had come to the conclusion that to concentrate American armed aid under the U.S. military would be disastrous; senior Thai military officials assured me that they felt we were jointly proceeding on the correct track and that, even though the Royal Thai government was a military government, they would not subordinate the Thai armed struggle to MACTHAI, and would indeed keep it independent of the Thai military establishment.

Ambassador Martin's post was filled by the assignment of an experienced and able career minister of our Foreign Service, but it was quickly apparent that he was much less stouthearted or determined to resist the constant pressures from the Pentagon that the coordinated American support of the Royal Thai government against the insurgency belonged under American military supervision.

Being somewhat bloodied and wearied by my own experience in Vietnam in a similar situation, I asked for relief and return to my Headquarters early in 1968. On the arrival of my replacement, this time from the State Department, we all flew to Manila to board ship, even as the Vietcong and North Vietnamese army were staging their demoralizing and spectacular Tet offensive in Saigon and in the northern part of South Vietnam.

It was against this depressing and alarming backdrop that we flew over South Vietnam to Manila for the voyage back to the West Coast.

* * *

Back at Headquarters and settled once again in suburban Virginia, my wife, children, and I began once again to get acquainted with life in the United States and to renew old friendships with other agency officers who, themselves, had been long abroad, but had returned to duty at Headquarters. At Headquarters, I was informed that my next assignment was to be director of the Office of Training.

We took a few weeks' leave during the spring of 1969, enjoying the onset of that delightful time in the Virginia countryside. During these congenial and uncomplicated days, Marilyn and I found ourselves talking about early retirement. For years we had been hopscotching through Europe and Asia, acquiring three children along the way, and neither of us wanted to put more strain on the children or, for that matter, on ourselves. We were full of insurgencies of any sort, Asia, and longed for relief.

In those years, and presumably at the present time as well, the Clandestine Service maintained a small number of domestic-operations bases, located in some of the principal cities in the United States. There was such a base in San Francisco, where I had been born and raised. We had enjoyed our brief visits there to and from the Far East, my mother and brother lived there, and we had over the years rather glamorized the idea of living there ourselves. On learning that the incumbent chief of the San Francisco base was on the verge of retirement, I took the matter up with the director and the chief of the Clandestine Service. We all agreed that it would be logical for me to take over the San Francisco base as its chief in something of a tombstone assignment in the summer of 1969, with the idea of retiring there in the summer of 1972. That is the way the plans and intentions fell into place; developments turned out quite differently.

After a leisurely drive in two cars to California, we settled in a rented house in Marin County, put the children in school, and began familiarizing ourselves with California mores, which we found strange indeed.

The way in which the agency functioned in a domestic setting was completely new to me. There were actually several small elements scattered around the city and down the peninsula. There were a number of different entities which had separate and unrelated functions. For example, there was a small administrative office which looked after certain kinds of matériel procurement on the local commercial market, collecting various kinds of technical or electronic gear, which would be used abroad, but which had to be procured without displaying any agency interest. Additionally, there was an office of contacts, an overt CIA office listed in the telephone directory, whose function was to interview American travelers returning from interesting parts of the world, who might be willing to cooperate in interviews conducted by agency personnel. In addition, there was the Office of Security, which also was not part of the Clandestine Service. This group was subordinated directly to the Office of Security at Headquarters and had its own rather sizable office setup in downtown San Francisco. From this office were conducted security investigations and the establishment of security clearances for persons being hired by the agency either at Headquarters in Langley or elsewhere. Traditionally, within the agency, the Office of Security had been the group which developed interrogation techniques for use abroad, and it was by this security office in San Francisco that the questionable interrogation and interviewing techniques employing drugs were carried out.

The Clandestine Service—that is, its San Francisco base, which I headed—was not caught up in what has become a continuing criticism of the CIA within the United States and, in many respects, a grave embarrassment for all concerned. These small offices within the city were quite distinct from each other in location and function and there was little contact between them.

Our Clandestine Service's base in San Francisco was charged largely with examining the local scene or foreigners passing through this gateway city to foreign areas of interest, principally in the Far East or southeast Asia. There were very slim pickings indeed available to the CS base, bearing in mind that the CS was under the strictest of injunctions not to operate or to work on any campus or with any foreign student who might be attending local universities. There were some foreign consulates in San Francisco, but jurisdictional agreements had placed these, insofar as domestic coverage was concerned, under the purview of the local office of the FBI. Only very infrequently did our routine liaison with the local FBI office result in their passing a promising operational lead to us, concerning a foreigner who was returning to his native country and who might have a potential for operational use there.

On the other hand there were, of course, several large corporate institutions based in or near San Francisco with whom I maintained contact, with their full knowledge of my agency status, with the objective of seeing whether or not the corporations' foreign offices could be used by agency officers as "cover." Our use of this kind of cover was diminishing as agency policy gradually turned against its use on security grounds. From the San Francisco base, however, I maintained a loose contact with several corporate officials to see if their changing administrative structure might present an operational opportunity suitable for use by a CS officer. Invariably, this kind of involvement presup-

Plowing Back 291

posed the advance knowledge and blessing of the top leadership of the corporation.

All-in-all, our presence in San Francisco provided our CS officers scant benefit or opportunity. There was very little to do or that we were permitted to do and the handful of officers and secretaries in the base were woefully underworked. In January of 1969, Marilyn and I both found ourselves bored beyond belief, I with the lack of operational challenge and my wife with the hedonistic life-style of California. An agonized phone call from me to the CIA director quickly produced orders taking us back to Washington, where I was quite willing to empty wastebaskets, if only to get away from the general purposelessness of my life in San Francisco.

My first duty assignment in the CIA back in 1951 was as assistant to the chief of Foreign Intelligence staff, the able and respected Eric Timm, now deceased. It was now my turn to become the chief of the FI staff. This was my first regular Headquarters assignment since coming back from Germany in 1951 and I thoroughly enjoyed the two years I served in that capacity. The duties were interesting, the politicking not too onerous, and I took pleasure in seeing so many old friends once again—the big white building in the woods at Langley seemed very much like home.

The Foreign Intelligence staff had a continuing responsibility for monitoring intelligence-collection projects and programs carried out abroad. These operations and collection programs were of course controlled and directed by the area divisions concerned; the FI staff simply read the progress charts on the various projects (or the lack of progress) and played the role of determining which intelligence-collection programs should be continued, changed, or terminated. With the exception of a few individual operations of special sensitivity, this FI staff function was worldwide in scope and gave me a full overview of the Clandestine Service's operations abroad.

The Foreign Intelligence staff was one of three senior staffs primarily concerned with the quality, structure, and composition of the Clandestine Service as a whole. As chief of the FI staff, I was a member of the board which considered CS officers for promotion to the senior grades. Also, senior assignments to some of the more important posts abroad were reviewed by the senior staff at regular meetings conducted for the purpose. This collection of staff chiefs, numbering less than a score, met regularly every week under the chairmanship of the chief of the Clandestine Service or his deputy, voting on those matters which came before it as a form of assistance to the chief of the service in considering the serious decisions he was constantly called on to make or advise the director of Central Intelligence about. This panel of senior officers constituted a body of officers of broad intelligence experience and varied operational background. I would be the last to say that all of these collective decisions or judgments were always correct, but I can say that the conclusions and recommendations offered by this panel of senior staff members were seriously and thoughtfully arrived at and comprised the best consensus obtainable with the Clandestine Service.

In selecting people for senior promotions or for important assignments abroad, each of us relied on our own experiences as intelligence officers and our intuition concerning the person or the assignments under consideration. There were risks in every decision made. There were the rising stars and there were the losers. There were the successful achievements and the marginal ones. We constantly had to review and arrive at conclusions concerning the worth of what was being done abroad, whether or not our work was appropriate to our government's need and even whether or not we might have provoked a particular need without realizing we were doing so. We certainly were not a group of lugubrious pallbearers sitting around the conference table, but neither were we jaunty or casual in our staff deliberations. We knew it was serious business with many moral aspects to consider; we had each of us been there and had faced the problems in the field.

In the spring of 1971 I asked the chief of our service for another assignment abroad, this one to be my "tombstone" assignment, following which I would retire. The usual deliberations took place concerning where I should go and who would replace me. Being at this point something of a "returned empty," I was offered the post as station chief in Canberra, Australia, a post which dealt exclusively with liaison with our Australian colleagues, with whom we had a long history of friendly cooperation. We went "down under" to Australia in May 1971 and I served in Canberra as liaison with Australian opposite numbers until December 1972. It was an enjoyable post, if unexciting, and our Australian counterparts were competent, friendly, and in all respects good comrades.

Headed for retirement in December 1972, we sailed back to the West Coast in time to join Marilyn's family in Florida for the Christmas holidays. It was on 31 January 1973 that, after spending a week clearing up administrative matters at Langley, I served my last day in the CIA.

Epilogue

In recent years I have frequently been asked, and indeed have asked myself, were the years of effort and hard work really worthwhile, was anything accomplished? Particularly have I been asked this question with regard to the Clandestine Service—that part of the CIA dealing with human sources in the positive intelligence and counterespionage fields. There is no question but that electronic, technical, and other forms of intelligence—satellites, satellite cameras, and communications intelligence have surged far ahead of what their capabilities were in the mid-1950s, and it is unnerving to contemplate a world today in which we would be unable to gather and evaluate such intelligence, destructive forces being what they are and the lethal ability of our potential enemies in the world being as ferocious as it is. It seems that the world becomes ever more dangerous to the survival and flourishing of democracy as we know it, so that to be uninformed of the capabilities and intentions of the enemies of democracy seems, in this day and age, foolhardy and unacceptable.

There will be more technical and scientific means developed for the collection of visual or audible intelligence, and of course we should keep driving ahead in the development of such techniques lest we be left behind. At the same time, it would appear to be dangerous in the extreme for the United States to let its Clandestine Service wither by design or inadvertence. Only human beings can provide the needed intelligence to determine an enemy's plans, capabilities, and actions. Machines or devices cannot do this.

Achieving scientific or strategic intelligence through human sources is the most difficult achievement in the entire craft of intelligence. But there is no substitute for it. There seems to be an attitude permeating the upper reaches of the American intelligence community today to the effect that technical means of collection can do all that is needed, and that collection of intelligence by human resources is not only expensive and difficult, but unrewarding. An attitude such as this only reflects a basic innocence about the structure and flow of intelligence needed by our country, and must not dominate the intelligence picture. If the Clandestine Service is hectored and cut up along the lines of what seems to be present U.S. government policy, the nation as a whole will pay the price. Those who feel there are simple, quick, or principally technical means of collecting intelligence are without question wrong; if they are allowed to prevail, the nation and our children will pay the cost.

There are those who claim that a secret intelligence organization, employing secret methods and cloaking itself in secrecy, is a contradiction to the existence of a democratic and free society. There have been excesses and abuses of intelligence functions in the past, but the marvelous fact remains that these abuses have been identified and corrected. Our efforts should be constant in maintaining a strong and effective Clandestine Service and equally strong in establishing internal controls and philosophies which will bring the possibility of abuse to an acceptable minimum. The future of our nation depends on our having an effective Clandestine Service and in solving this problem of potential excess, at the same time.

Glossary

Agent — In intelligence parlance, an agent is a person who secretly performs tasks of interest or value to an intelligence service.
ARVN — Army of the Republic of Vietnam.
Base — In CIA usage, a base is an intelligence unit established in a foreign country, subordinate to a station. For instance, the CIA base in Munich, Germany, is subordinate to the CIA station in Bonn.
Bug — A listening device (microphone, radio pickup) surreptitiously installed so as to overhear secretly conversations or other audible signals.
CE — Counterespionage. Efforts made by one intelligence service to contain or frustrate the espionage efforts of a hostile intelligence service.
CHEKA — Russian acronym for "extraordinary commission," the first Soviet secret police established by Felix Derzhinsky.
CI — Counterintelligence, essentially the same as CE.
Comint — Communications intelligence. Intelligence gained by solving the encrypted communications of an adversary.
Control sign — An aberration of spelling or text used by an agent in communicating with his superiors by radio or writing when he (the agent) has fallen under hostile intelligence control.
Danger sign — Same as control sign.
DCI — The Director of Central Intelligence.
DDP — In CIA terms, Deputy Director for Plans, now DDO, Deputy Director for Operations. The directorate for espionage and counterespionage.

Deaddrop	A place where money or messages can be left to be picked up by another intelligence agent, e.g., a hollowed-out tree stump, a hole in a brick wall.
Disinformation	In intelligence parlance, information conveyed to deceive or confuse a hostile intelligence service.
Double agent	An intelligence agent who, for whatever reason, while appearing to work for his original intelligence service, is actually working for a hostile intelligence service. Such an intelligence agent has been "doubled."
Elint	Electronics intelligence. Information (intelligence) gained by monitoring electronic transmissions, such as radar.
Fabrication	Intelligence that has been made up to confuse a hostile intelligence service. See disinformation.
FI	The Foreign Intelligence staff of the DDO.
GPU	The historical successor to the CHEKA, succeeded by the NKVD, the MGB, and currently the KGB.
GRU	The Soviet military intelligence establishment, as distinguished from the much larger and more powerful civilian intelligence establishment, the KGB.
GUM	The large and well-known department store in Moscow directly across Red Square from the Kremlin.
GVN	Government of Vietnam, the Saigon government.
KGB	The Soviet Committee for State Security. The Soviet secret police and intelligence service, the present version of the original CHEKA.
Legend	The fictitious or notional background stories or life histories of an intelligence agent living and working abroad, meant to conceal his intelligence origins.
Letterdrop	Usually a person, but perhaps a post office box to which intelligence communications may be sent for later retrieval by another person in an intelligence network. Also maildrop, an accommodation address.

MACTHAI	Military Assistance Command, Thailand. The senior American military office in Bangkok during American military support of the Thai government.
MACV	Military Assistance Command, Vietnam. The American military headquarters element in Saigon during the war.
Make	In intelligence jargon, when a person under surveillance identifies his followers he "makes" them. An identified surveillant is "made."
OSO	The Office of Special Operations, an earlier designation for the DDP.
OSS	Office of Strategic Services. The American civilian espionage organization during World War II.
Penetration	An intelligence agent who has gained access to the organization and work of another intelligence service, unknown by the latter.
Resident	The Soviet chief of a residentura. The equivalent of a CIA station chief.
Residentura	A Soviet secret intelligence unit stationed abroad. The equivalent of a CIA station.
ROK	Republic of Korea, the government of South Korea.
Safehouse	A house, apartment, or other dwelling in which intelligence activities can be carried on safely and secretly.
SW	Secret writing. Writing modified, usually by chemical means, to remain invisible.
Tail	A person who surreptitiously follows another person.
Tap	A metal-to-metal connection made to overhear conversations on a telephone line.
WT	Wireless telegraph. A WT agent is one who communicates by radio.

Index

Abrams, General Creighton, 285
Adenauer, Konrad, 39
Agency for International Development (AID)
  Mission, 216, 221
Allied Control Commission, 8-10
American House, Moscow, 23, 24
Astoria Hotel, Leningrad, 29, 30
Atomic bomb, xi, 3-4
Australia, 259, 292-293
Austria, 5
  displaced persons in, 8, 12
  four-power meetings in Trieste, 86
  Gehlen organization in, 41
  Hungarian refugees and, 127-138
  Red Cross, 129
  Russians and
    occupation by, 148-149
    peace treaty between, 86-88
    repatriation program of, 10-14
  Salzburg, 11-12
    Schloss Fuschl, 89-92
  State Police (Staatspolizei), 128, 134
    cooperation with CIA, 144-145
  World Youth Festival of 1959 in, 147-150
  See also Vienna.
"Averell Harriman Memorial Highway," 198
AVO (Hungarian Secret Police), 121, 130-131, 139

Ba (cook), 214, 274
Baltic countries, 14, 15, 56-57
Bandera, Stefan, 80
Bedell-Smith, General Walter, 75
Berger, Sam, 184, 187-188
Berlin; Germany, 78
Bob (CIA agent), 269

Bogolyepov, Igor, 15-16, 17, 30
Bohlen, Charles, 71-72, 132
Boris (KBG agent), 105-108
Bundesnachrichtendienst, 39, 40
Bundy, McGeorge, 263
Burgess, Guy, 80-81
Burobin (Bureau for Foreigners), 35
Byelorussia, 56

Cambodia, 256
Central Intelligence Agency. See CIA.
Central Intelligence Group (CIG), 6
Central Intelligence Organization (CIO)
  (Vietnamese), 216, 239-240
Chang Myon. See Korea, Chang Myon
  (John Chang).
CHEKA, 25
China, Communist, 192-194
Choe (Korean driver), 160
Christian, John, 20
CIA
  attitude of foreigners toward, 232-233
  Austrian State Police and, 128, 134, 144-145
  Clandestine Service, 71, 73, 84, 118, 289-292, 294-295
  the "Count" and, 43, 45, 47-48, 51
  "cover" for, 153
  creation of, 4
  critics of, x
  danger and control indicators, 56
  double agents, 79, 93, 94, 114, 117
  East European (EE) Division, 84-103
    Austrian surveillance teams and, 88-89
    post-treaty intelligence, 88-89, 92-94
    Soviet-Austrian peace treaty and, 86-88

Soviet-neutral power meeting and, 89-92
electronic surveillance, 112-117
　hesitancy about using, 112-113
　in Schloss Fuschl, 90-92
　of Sokolnikov, 112, 114-117
　in Vienna phone booth, 92-93
espionage in Soviet Union
　early failures of, 55-57, 84
　in the Far East, 58-61
　"forced entry" missions, 61
　during post-World War II era, 17, 18-19
　via third-country nationals, 79
　in the U.S. Embassy in Moscow, 71-72
face-to-face encounters with KGB, 94-103
Foreign Intelligence (FI) Staff, 54
Gehlen organization and, 38
headquarters, 53-61
Hong Kong and
　Chinese intelligence and, 193-194
　problems in, 194-195
Hungarian intelligence gathering, 117-126
KGB and, x-xi
Khrushchev's de-Stalinization speech and, 118-119
Korea and
　coup d'etat and, 172-184
　reopening of "overt" station, 152-153
　resignation of Syngman Rhee and, 170, 171
　Syngman Rhee incident, 151-152
Korean War and, 151-152
line of command of, x
L-pills, 73-74
Office of Special Operations (OSO), 54, 55
Pelican Team, 48-51
photographs
　of KGB agents, 107-108
　from satellites, 194
　of Viennese realtor, 112
prelude to, 3-14
purge of, by Schlesinger, ix
reconnaissance aircraft of, 58
safehouses
　for defectors, 62-63
　in Hawaii, 60
　in Munich, 48-51
　in Vienna, 67
　in Washington, D.C., 63
Soviet cipher lead and, 42-52
Soviet defections and, 62-70, 145-146
　act of, 62-63
　aid to, 65
　erroneously reported, 127-128
　Ivan, 65-70

Khoklov, 80
　motives for, 63
　in 1955, 84
　as one-time sources, 83
　Petrov, 81
　pressures on, 64-65
　Rasterovorov, 63-65
　schools of thought on, 64, 94-95
　Stashinsky, 80
　value of, 84-85
Soviet Russia (SR) Division, 54-61, 66, 76-83
　accomplishments of, 84-85
　DP intelligence teams and, 55-57, 73
　face-to-face encounters and, 94-103, 146
　Far East branch of, 58-61
　Philby spy case and, 80-82
　reorganization of, 83
　termination of agent status, 79-80
　triple agents, 79
United States Ambassadors and, 142-143
Vietnam and
　bombing of Saigon office, 266-273
　Colby in, 196-198
　counterinsurgency, 228-230, 234-236
　Diem coup and, 195-196
　Lodge's attitude toward, 210-211, 212
　Montagnards and, 218
　PAT teams and, 264
　stations in, 216, 219, 220, 228
　Swifts and Nasties and, 218-219
　Vietcong success in the countryside and, 227
　Vietcong strategy and, 220-221, 224-227
　view of the problem, 280
Watergate and, x
work of, ix-x, 82
CINCPAC, 280-281
Clark, Dr., 48-51
Clifford, Clark, 284
Colby, Barbara, 271
Colby, William
　de Silva's sounds and, 271, 272
　as Far East Division Chief, 196-198, 203, 204, 206, 208
　Lodge meeting and, 210-211
　PAT teams and, 260, 264, 284
　trips to Saigon, 208, 222, 230
Cold war era, 23-37, 71
Coloredo-Wels, Graf Friedrich, 42-51
Columbia University, 5-7
"Count," the, 42-51
Counterinsurgency
　Captain Mai and, 228-230, 234-241

Index

counter-terror, 245-246, 256-257, 259
  Kennedy and, 224-225
  key to, 234-236
  See also Vietnam, People's Action Teams (PAT).
Czechoslovakia, 6-7

Dave (acting CIA station chief), 210-211, 214
Dave (Marine Sergeant), 203
Davies, Joseph, 16
defections. *See* CIA, Soviet defections.
de Silva, Catherine, 262
de Silva, Jayne, 4, 36, 85, 104
  divorce and remarriage of, 139
de Silva, Marilyn
  birth of Catherine, 262
  birth of Peer, Jr., 145
  evacuation to the Philippines, 255, 262, 264-265
  in Hong Kong, 191, 192, 198, 202
  in Korea, 154, 160-164, 173
  marriage of, 139-140
  Peer's wounds and, 269, 270, 273
  pregnancy of, 198, 212, 262
  retirement and, 288-289
  Saigon move of, 212-214
  terrorism in Vietnam and, 252, 254
  vacation in Hawaii, 188
  in Vienna, 145-146, 150
de Silva, Michael, 76, 104
de Silva, Peer
  affair with Mielikki, 19-21, 28, 36, 76
  Army course on Russia and, 5-8
  Bankok assignment, 281, 284, 287-288
  at CIA headquarters, 53-61
    testing of, 53-54
  Clandestine Service and, 289-292, 294-295
  at Command and General Staff School, 75
  the "Count" and, 42-52
    shooting incident and, 47, 51-52
  defectors and, 62-70
  denied Soviet reentry visa, 35-36
  dismissal of worthless agent and, 57, 68-69
  Displaced Persons and, 10-14
  domestic difficulties of, 36, 85
    agreement to separate, 104
    divorce, 139
  end of CIA career, 286-293
  friendly foreign intelligence and, 144-145
  Gehlen organization and, 38-41
  Hong Kong assignment, 190-202
    assassination of JFK and, 200-210
    China hands and, 191-192
  with Colby in Vietnam, 196-198
  ending of, 201-202, 212-213
  intelligence inside China and, 193-194
  life in, 198-202
  problems in, 194-195
  residence in, 191
  rules of intelligence in, 192-193
  travel to, 189-191
  injury to, 266-273, 286
  joining the CIA as a civilian, 76
  KGB knowledge of, 94-103, 143-144
  Korean assignment, 147-148, 151-189
    Chang Myon and, 157-161, 165-166, 170-171, 173
    coup d'etat and, 172-184
    election riots and, 161-164
    embassy compound and, 154
    ending of, 188-189
    first impression of, 153-154
    Harriman visit and, 186-188
    informant and, 173, 188-189
    Mike Kim and, 166-170
    Pak Chung Gyu and, 174-183
    Pak Chung Hee and, 181-185
    reception by Koreans, 154-155
    "special connections" of, 156
    travel to, 150-152
    See also Korea.
  Korean War period and, 75
  liason visits abroad of, 76-79
  Manhattan Engineer District and, xi, 3-5
  marriage to second wife, 139-140.
    See also de Silva, Marilyn.
  in Moscow, 15-36
  Radiation Laboratory at Berkeley and, 145
  resignation from the army, 75-76
  San Francisco assignment, 289-291
  Soviet Russia (SR) Division, 54-61, 66
    accomplishments of, 84-85
    amphibious teams and, 56-57
    as chief of operations, 76-83
    Far Eastern branch of, 58-61
    parachute teams and, 56-57
    Philby spy case and, 80-82
  as Special Assistant for Vietnam Affairs (SAVA), 278-281, 286
  "tombstone" assignment, 289, 292-293
  "tradecraft" and, 144
  U.S. Ambassadors and, 141-143
    See also specific Ambassadors.
  Vienna assignment, 82-150
    CIA-KGB encounters and, 94-103, 146
    electronic surveillance and, 89-92, 112-117

ending of, 146-150
Hungarian refugees and, 127, 130-139, 146
Hungarian revolt and, 118-126
KGB pressure on Jews and, 104-111
post-treaty intelligence and, 88-89, 92-94
Schloss Fuschl and, 89-92
Soviet-Austrian peace treaty and, 86-89
travel to, 85-86, 140
World Youth Festival and, 147-150
See also Vienna.
Vietnam assignment, 203-288
birth of Catherine and, 262
bomb attsvk and, 266-273
Colby and, 196-198, 203, 206
counterinsurgency and, 234-236
counter-terrorism and, 245-246, 256-257, 259, 264, 278
ending of, 275-276
evacuation of families and, 254-255, 262-263
Johnson and, 206-208
life in, 214-215
Lodge and, 210-211, 212, 231
McCone and, 203-204
McNamara and, 209-210
Mai and, 228-230, 234-241, 258-259
terrorism and, 252-255
thought about, 281-283
travel to, 208-209, 214, 273-274
Washington trips of, 203-208, 263-264
work load in, 266-273
See also Vietnam.
de Silva, Peer, Jr. "Perry," 145, 150, 202, 252, 253, 270
de Silva, Robin, 4, 104, 273
de Silva, Sharon, 4, 104, 272-273
Diem, Ngo Dinh, 196, 205-206, 208-209, 215, 282
Displaced persons (DPs), 7-8
Baltic, 14, 56-57
intelligence teams of, 55-57, 73, 84
in the Soviet Far East, 59-61
Soviet repatriation of, 8, 10-12, 14
attitude toward, 12, 14
used as instructors, 7, 15
families of, 17-18, 30
letters from, 17-18, 19, 24, 28, 31
Don (CIA agent), 269
double agents, 79
listening devices and, 93, 94, 114, 117
Dowling, Walter, 154-155
drugs
L-pills, 73-74
narcohypnosis and, 48-50
Soviet mind-altering, 74
Duc (houseboy), 214-215, 274

Dulles, Allen, 72, 73
as CIA director, 75-76, 204
KGB agents in M16 and, 81
Dunn, Colonel Michael, 231
Dzerzhinski, Feliks, 25

East Germany, 37-41, 53
Ed (CIA agent), 59, 61
Eisenhower, Dwight D., 132
Korean visit of, 185-186
England
conflict with Holland, 78-79
Hong Kong and
intelligence in, 192-193
Kuomintang agents in, 194-195
M16, 78-82
Penkovskiy and, 142

FBI, 290
Fedeev, Alexander, 28
Felipe, Consolacion, 255
Fitzgerald, Desmond, 196, 223
Fomin, Nokolai Petrovich (Boris), 105-108
Formosa, 194-195
Froschl, Willy, 46-47

Galkin, Major Ivan, 43-46
Garson, Greer, 202
Gehlen, General Reinhard, 37-43
Gehlen organization, 37-43
background of, 37
CIA and, 38
functions of, 40-41
Soviet cipher lead and, 42-43
George (CIA agent), 57-58, 203, 269, 271
defector and, 66
Penkovskiy and, 142
Gero, Erno, 120, 130
Germany, 5
alliance with Russia, 14
displaced persons in, 7-8
Dutch intelligence during World War II and, 78-79
East, 37-41, 53
Gehlen organization and, 37-41
Nazis, 39
partition of, 38
West, 38, 41
Gougelman, Tucker, 219, 223
Graves Registration and Repatriation Team, 8
Great Britain. *See* England.
Green, Marshall and Lisa, 192, 271
Grishin, Valya, 96-103
Groves, General Leslie, 3, 4, 5
GRU (Soviet military intelligence), 88, 92, 99

Index 303

Gulf of Tonkin incident, 255-256

Harkins, General Paul, 210, 219, 221, 231
Harriman, W. Averell, 205
  "Harriman Highway," 198
  Laos and, 186-188
Heinz (Gehlen's aide), 42
Helms, Richard, 146-147
Helsinki, Finland, 18-22
  diplomatic mail and, 20, 24, 26
  released U.S. prisoner escorted to, 26-28
  Soviet reentry visa and, 35-36
Henry (CIA agent), 43-51
Herb (CIA agent), 267
Herfurt, Jack, 222
Hermitage, Leningrad, 29-30
Higgins, Marguerite, 277
Hilsman, Roger, 205, 206
Ho Chi Minh trail. *See* Vietcong, Ho Chi Minh trail.
Holland, 78-79
Hong Kong, 190-202
  Chinese defectors to, 195
  Communist Chinese influence in, 192-193, 199-200
  Kuomintang agents in, 194-195
  residents of, 198-199
  rules of intelligence in, 192-193
  typhoon Wanda and, 193
  water shortage in, 199-200
Hope, Bob, 254
Huh Chung, 170, 185
Hungary, 100, 118-126
  refugees from, 127-139
    aid for, 130
    AVO and KGB agents in, 139
    Duna girls, 130-131
    intelligence from, 127, 130-131, 136, 146
    Nixon and, 131-136
    World Youth Festival of 1959 and, 149
  revolt in, 102, 121-126
    AVO and, 121, 137-138
    flashpoint of, 121, 137-138
    Hungarian Army and, 122, 125
    intelligence during, 118-126
    Kadar and, 136-137
    low profile of Soviets and, 120, 121
    Nagy and, 125, 136-137
    police and, 121-122
    Soviet attack, 125-126
    State Railway System, 122
  unrest in, 119-120

Intourist, 29
Irving (embassy clerk), 108-111
Ivan (Soviet defector), 65-70, 71
Jack (polygraph operator), 48-51, 144

Japan, 151, 153
  Korean influence of, 154
  rule over Korea of, 156, 159, 172
Jarai tribe, 218
Jerry (CIA agent), 96, 100, 101, 190
Jews, KGB pressure on, 104-111
Johnson, Commander, 262
Johnson, Lyndon B., 278, 281
  election of, 257
  evacuation of dependents and, 255
  Lodge and, 206-207, 220, 231
  meets with de Silva, 206-208
  orders de Silva to Saigon, 203-204
Johnson, Ural Alexis, 221
journalists
  aid to CIA by, 114-115
  Hungarian revolt and, 119, 120, 121
  Duna girls and, 130-131
  erroneous defection reports and, 127-128

Kadar, János, 136-137
Kaiser Wilhelm Institute, 5
Kaysen, Karl, 208
Ken (interpreter), 162, 166
Kennan, George, 71-74
Kennedy, John F., 204, 205, 277
  anti-Diem attitude of, 208, 209, 215
  assassination of, 200, 204
  counterinsurgency and, 224-225
  Laos and, 186, 188
Kennedy, Robert, 225, 277
  anti-Diem attitude of, 209
Keyes, General, 9, 10, 11
KGB, x-xi
  agents in MI6, 80-82
  bugging of telephone used by, 92-94
  defections of agents, 62-70
  Department 13, 80
  Department V, 80
  DP parachute teams and, 56
  executions by, 80
  face-to-face encounters with, 94-103, 146
  Greek ambassador incident and, 35
  in Hungary, 130-131
  as refugees, 139
  Korean War intelligence and, 82
  Ninth Sector, 80
  in post-treaty Austria, 88-89, 92
  predecessors to, 25
  pressure on Jews in embassy, 104-111
Khanh, General Nguyen, 216, 256
Khoklov, Nikolai, 80
Khrushchev, Nikita, 118-119
Killen, James, 221
Kim Chong Pil, Colonel, 177-180, 182, 183
Kim Chong Yol, "Mike," 166-170
King, Robert, 132-136

Index

Kireyev, Colonel, 10-14
Kirkpatrick, Lyman, 222-223
KMT (Kuomintang agents), 194-195
Komer, Robert, 283, 284
Korea, 151-189
  Chang Myon (John Chang)
    elected prime minister, 170-171
    leadership of, 184
    meetings with de Silva, 157-161
    warned of coup against, 173, 188
    warns of impending violence, 165-166
  Democratic Party, 157
  economic growth of, 184-185
  Eisenhower visit to, 185-186
  election of March 1960 and, 159, 161
    aftermath of, 161-171
  governmental corruption in, 156, 159, 165, 171
  hostility toward government of, 156
  Japanese rule over, 156, 159, 172
  Liberal Party, 156-161
    downfall of, 164-171
    reaction to riots, 164-165
    rigged election of, 159, 161-162, 164
    ruling clique of, 156, 157, 159, 164
  names in, 178-179
  Pak Chung Hee, General
    brother of, 180, 183
    Communism and, 177, 180
    coup staged by, 172-184
    de Silva and, 181
    Korean values of, 172, 177
    leadership of, 184-185
    Pathet Lao and, 187, 188
    U.S. acceptance of, 184
  political crisis in, 161
  political system in, 156-157
  Rhee, Syngman
    CIA incident and, 151-152
    declining mental condition of, 156, 157, 159
    downfall of, 164-171
    election riots and, 164
    Japanese rule over Korea and, 156, 159
    Liberal Party of, 156-171
    U.S. policy on Korea and, 155-156
  reopening of "overt" station in, 152-153
  ROK Army, 71
    coup d'etat and, 172-184
    murder of demonstrated by, 163
    unintentional corruption of, 172
  traditions and customs of, 172, 177, 179
  weather in, 161
Korean Central Intelligence Agency (KCIA), 178
Korean War, 75, 155
  CIA and, 151-152

KGB agents in M16 and, 82
Kostikov, Lieutenant, 67-68
Ky, Marshall Nguyen Cao, 281

Laos
  General Phoumi and, 186-188
  Ho Chi Minh trail in, 217, 256, 258
  Pathet Lao, 186-187, 198
Litvinov, Maxim, 15
Lodge, Emily, 231
Lodge, Henry Cabot, 281
  attitude toward CIA assistance, 210-211, 212
  Diem overthrow and, 205, 208-209, 215
  firing of Richardson and, 195, 196, 204, 208-209
  haunted house of, 211
  Johnson's and, 206-207, 220, 231
  leaves Vietnam, 220, 221
  McCone and, 210-211, 230
  as terrorist target, 253-254
  visits de Silva in hospital, 271, 272
London *Times*, 82
L-pills, 73-74
Luman, Joe, 240

M16, 78-82
Macao, 192
McConaughy, Walter P., 155, 160, 167-170, 173, 176, 186
McCone, John, 212, 270, 278
  cable to de Silva from, 201
  Johnson and, 203-204, 206-208
  Lodge meeting and, 210-211
  trips to Saigon, 208-209, 230
Maclean, Donald, 80-82
McNamara, Robert S., 260, 281
  failure in Vietnam and, 277, 284-285
  MACV briefing and, 209-210
  role of, 282
  as terrorist target, 250-251
  visits to Vietnam, 230, 250-251
MACTHAI, 287, 288
Magruder, General Carter, 167-170
  Korean coup d'etat and, 180, 182, 183, 184
Magruder, General John, 4, 6
Mai, Major, 228-230, 234-241, 258-259, 275
Mample, Richard, 287
Manfull, Melvin, 221-222
Manhattan Engineer District, xi, 3-4
Martin, Graham, 287
Masaryk, Jan, 6-7
Masaryk, Thomas, 7
Matthews, H. Freeman "Doc," 141, 146
Max (CIA agent), 38-39, 42-45

Index

MGB (Ministry for State Security), 25, 25, 29, 80
Michel, Monsieur, 109-111
Mielikki (Finnish girl), 19-21, 28, 36, 76
Mindszenty, Cardinal, 136
mokrie dela, 80
Molotov, Vyacheslav, 15, 34
Montagnard tribes, 217-218
Moore, General Joseph, 265
Moscow, Russia, 15-36
  American Negro incident in, 31-32
  atmosphere of, 24-26
  Lenin's tomb, 24-25
  May Day 1949 in, 32-35
  newsmen in, 23
  political terror in, 25-26
  surveillance in, 23, 24, 31
  Greek ambassador incident, 35
  U.S. Embassy in, 5
  Ambassador and, 71-74
  American House and, 23, 24
  CIA agent in, 71-72
  location of, 24
  NKVD espionage in, 16
Munich, Germany, 44, 48-51
Murphy, James, 4, 6

Nagy, Imri, 125
  murder of, 136-137
narcohypnosis, 48-50
Nazi party, 39
Nelson, Steve, 145
Netherlands, 78-79
Nguyen, Comrade, 244-245
Nhu, Madame (dragon lady), 205
Nhu, Ngo Dinh, 196, 205-206, 208, 215
Nixon, Richard M., 131-136
NKVD (Soviet secret police), 15, 16, 25
Nnong tribe, 218
Nolting, Frederick, 195
Norwood (communications officer), 113-117

O'Brien, Colonel, 34
O'Daniel, Colonel Michael "Iron Mike," 33
Office of Strategic Services (OSS), 3
Operation Northpole, 78
Orient Express, 8-9

Pak Chan Il, 167-169
Pak Chung Gyu, Captain, 174-183, 188
Pak Chung Hee, General. *See* Korea, Pak Chung Hee, General.
Pammer, Dr. Max, 134
Pathet Lao, 186-187, 198
Pelican Team, 48-51
Penkovskiy, Oleg, 66, 141, 142
People's Action Teams (PAT). *See* Vietnam, People's Action Teams (PAT).

Peter (CIA agent), 59, 61
Petofi Circle, 119
Petrov, Vladimir, 81
Phat, Comrade, 244-245
Philby, Harold A. R. (Kim), 81-82
Phoumi Nosavan, General, 186-188
Pius XII, Pope, 72, 73
Pold (Austrian waiter), 9-10

Quat, Phan Huy, 216

Raborn, Admiral William, 278, 280-281, 286
Radek, Karl, 15
Rade tribe, 218
Radiation Laboratory, Berkeley, 145
Radio Free Europe, 137
Rajk, Laszlo, 119
Rakosi, Matyás, 119, 120, 130
Rastovorov, Yuri, 63-65
Rebet, Lev, 80
Rhee, Francesca, 170
Rhee, Syngman. *See* Korea, Rhee Sungman.
Rhody (CIA secretary), 232, 267-268, 269
Richardson, John, 195, 196, 204, 205, 208-209, 210, 211
Riordan, John, 252
Riordan, Nan, 252, 262
Robbins, Barbara, 267
Rusk, Dean, 205
Russian Institute at Columbia University, 5-7
Russians, 13, 14
  customs inspection of, 28-29
  defection of, 63
  as Displaced Persons, 8, 10-12, 14
  drunken soldier incident, 26-27
  May Day 1949 celebration, 32-35
  Moscow purge incident, 25-26
  prisoner transport train, 27
  See also Soviet Union.

Sam (embassy officer), 104-108
Schlesinger, James, ix
Shchukin, Aleksandr (M. Michel), 109-111
Smith, Dr. Ray, 262
Sokolnikov (KGB agent)
  electronic surveillance of, 112, 114-117
  face-to-face encounters and, 95-97, 102, 144
Song, General "Tiger," 187
Soviet Union
  alliance with Nazi Germany, 14
  assembling foreign scientists, 5
  atomic bomb airfield and, 58-61
  Austrian peace treaty and, 86-88
  ciphers of, 42-52

cold war and, 23-36
constant troop movement of, 53, 58
customs inspection, 28-29
defections to, 81
DP intelligence teams within, 55-57
Gehlen organization and, 37-41
Hungarian revolt and, 102, 119-126
  attack during, 125-126
  Kadar and, 136-137
  Nagy and, 136-137
intelligence gathering, 12
  bomb project and, 4
  officers of, 63-64
  Radiation Laboratory and, 145
  See also KGB.
Leningrad, 29-30
mind control research in, 74
neutral power meeting with, 89-92
Providence Bay, 58-61
reentry visa for, 35-36
repatriation program of, 8, 10-12, 14
  attitude of DPs toward, 12, 14
Sakhalin Island, 58
telephone books in, 17, 29, 30
Twentieth Party Congress speech, 118-119
U.S. intelligence in postwar, 5, 31
World War II and, 37
World Youth Festival of 1959, 147-150
See also Moscow.
Spanish Civil War, 15
Stalin, Joseph, 15, 34
  death of, 77
  Khrushchev's de-Stalinization speech, 118-119
Stashinsky, Bogdan, 80
State Department, 74, 82
  chain of command and, 142-143
  CIA and, 71-72, 85
  Diem cable from, 205, 215
  evacuation of dependents and, 255
  face-to-face encounters and, 94-95, 146
  Korean coup d'etat and, 180
  PAT teams and, 263-264
  Soviet-neutral power meeting and, 89, 91
  surveillance of Sokolnikov and, 117
Steiger, Baron, 15-16
Strategic Services Unit (SSU), 3-6
Strickler, Colonel Gilbert, 223, 274
Sullivan, William, 221
Switzerland, 77-78
  Soviet attack in Hungary and, 128-129

Taiwan, 194-195
tanks, intelligence and, 66-67
Taylor, General Maxwell, 220, 255, 260, 271
  failure in Vietnam and, 277, 285

Mission Council of, 221-222, 240
orders to Westmoreland, 222, 282
PAT teams and, 239-242
as Vietnam Ambassador, 220, 221, 231
"termination with extreme prejudice," 79-80
Thailand, 281, 284
terrorist movement in, 287-288
Thieu, General Nguyen Van, 281
Thompson, H. Llewellyn, 87, 146
  CIA-KGB encounters and, 94-95
  in Moscow, 140-141
  Nixon's Vienna visit and, 131-133, 136
  Penkovskiy and, 141, 142
Timm, Eric, 54-55, 291
Tom (CIA agent), 228-230
"tradecraft," 144
Trich Tri Quang, 232-233, 256
triple agents, 79
Turkey, 77

Ukrainia, 55-56
United States
  Ambassadors of, 141-143
    CIA subordinate to, 143, 153
    differences with CIA and, 142-143
    foreign perception of CIA and, 232
  attitudes toward foreigners, 273-274
  citizens of, as targets of Vietcong, 250-255, 266-268
  diplomatic ciphers of, 108-111
  Gulf of Tonkin incident, 255-256
  Korean policy of, 155, 160
    critics of, 184-185
    response to coup d'etat, 177, 183-184
  Laotian policy of, 187
  presidential election of 1964, 203, 204, 220, 257
  Vietnam policy of
    buildup of troops, 280, 285, 286
    counterinsurgency, 224-225
    described, 223-224
    Diem overthrow and, 205, 208-209, 215
    failure of, 277-278, 282, 284-287
    gloom concerning, 264
    Honolulu conference, 280-283
    leaders of, 220, 277
    Taylor and, 222, 277, 285
    World War II influence on, 222-225
United States Army
  Korean War period and, 75-76
  Manhattan project and, 3
  Reserve Corps and, 75, 76
  Russian training program of
    at Columbia, 5-7
    in Germany, 7, 11, 15, 16
  Special Forces, 218, 224-225
  Tripler General Hospital, 169, 170

Index 307

United States Congress, 178
United States Information Service (USIS), 221
United States Navy, 58-61

Vic (CIA agent), 131
Vien Hoa Dao, 234, 235, 236, 238, 240-241
Vienna, Austria, 9-11, 84-103
  Allied Control Commission in, 9, 10
  Bristol Hotel, 9-10, 85, 86
  defections in, 65-66
  Hungarian invasion by Russia and, 125-126
  KGB pressure on embassy in, 104-111
  post-treaty intelligence in, 88-89, 92-94
  repatriation program in, 10
  Soviet cipher lead and, 42-43, 45, 48, 51, 52
  surveillance of Sokolnikov in, 112, 114-117
  World Youth Festival of 1959 and, 148-150
Vietcong
  battalion-sized ARVN units and, 257
  Ho Chi Minh trail and, 279
  CIDG and, 197-198
  CIO and, 217
  in Laos, 217, 256, 258
  intelligence and, 226
  NVA and, 258, 278-280
  PAT teams and, 235-246, 256-257
  post-Diem pressure by, 215-216
  recruitment practices, 229
  rural population and, 220-221, 224, 226-227, 235-246, 247
  strategies of, 220-221, 225-226, 278
  techniques of, 224
  terrorism of, 220-221, 224, 226-227, 229, 247-276
    directed toward Americans, 250-255, 266-268
  turning point in war and, 277-285
Vietnam, 203-288
  Agency for International Development (AID) Mission, 216, 221, 244, 264
  An Quang, 232-233
  ARVN, 210, 215
    size of, 224
    U.S. advisers to, 197, 224-225
    U.S. influence on, 225-226, 275
    vietcong and, 221, 226, 236, 245, 257-258
  attitude toward Montagnards, 218
  Cao Dai, 256-257
  Central Intelligence Organization, 216, 239-240
  CIA stations in, 216, 219, 220, 228
  CIDG and, 197-198
  Communism and, 235
  CORDS and, 283-284
  counterinsurgency, 224-225
    key to, 228-230, 234-246
  counter-terrorism, 245-246, 256-257, 259
  death benefits in, 236-237
  death of Diem, 196, 205-206, 208-209
    aftermath of, 215-216, 282
    U.S. role in, 215
  description of war in, 223-224
  desertion from military, 238, 284
  evacuation of families from, 254-255, 262-263
  failure in, 221, 277-278
  fall of, 219, 222, 285
  Gulf of Tonkin incident 255-256
  GVN, 226, 227, 228, 236
  interrogation in, 217
  Khanh coup and, 216
  MACV, 218, 219, 222, 223, 236, 251-252
    briefing of, 209-210
    Westmoreland and, 221, 222, 242, 275
    See also People's Action Teams (PAT).
  Ministry of Interior, 243-244, 258, 260, 278
  National Interrogation Center, 216-217
  National Police, 216-217, 234
  North Vietnamese Army and, 258, 278-280
  Peoples Action Teams (PAT), 234-246
    activities of, 235-238, 278
    checking on, 239
    continued success of, 258-261, 275-276, 281
    counter-terror of, 245-246, 256-257, 259
    death benefits to, 236-237
    effectiveness of, 238, 239, 244-245, 256, 257
    MACV staff and, 242-244, 257, 258, 260-261, 264, 275, 281, 283-284
    manpower for, 242, 261
    militarization of, 281, 283
    naming of, 234
    successor to, 283
    Taylor and, 239-242
    training of, 238-241
    Vietnamese control of, 258, 259-260, 264, 278
    Westmoreland and, 241-242, 260-261, 264, 275-276
  political instability in, 215-216, 232-233, 256, 279, 281-282
  Popular Force, 236, 248, 249
  rural population of, 226
  RVNAF, 224
  structure of society in, 260

terrorism in, 220-221, 224, 226-227, 229, 247-276
Tet offensive, 288
toll of, 275, 277
turning point in war, 277-285
U.S. leadership in 1964 and, 220
Vietnamese authority in, 258, 259-260, 264, 275, 278
Voznetsensky, Nikolai, 32

Watergate, x
West Germany, 38, 41
Westmoreland, General William C.
arrival in Vietnam of, 219-220
in command of MACV, 221, 222, 275, 281
failure in Vietnam and, 277, 282
orders from Taylor, 222
PAT teams and, 241-242, 260-261, 264, 275-276
World War II, xi, 3
displaced persons and, 7-8
Dutch intelligence service during, 78-79
Gehlen organization and, 37, 38, 40
postwar optimism, 6
World Youth Festival of 1959, 147-150

Yugoslavia, 136-137

Zorthian, Barry, 221